Black Religion / Womanist Thought / Social Justice
Series Editors Dwight N. Hopkins and Linda E. Thomas
Published by Palgrave Macmillan

Black Theology and Pedagogy
By Noel Leo Erskine

The Origins of Black Humanism in America: Reverend Ethelred Brown and the Unitarian Church
By Juan M. Floyd-Thomas

Black Religion and the Imagination of Matter in the Atlantic World
By James A. Noel

Bible Witness in Black Churches
By Garth Kasimu Baker-Fletcher

Enslaved Women and the Art of Resistance in Antebellum America
By Renee K. Harrison

Ethical Complications of Lynching: Ida B. Wells's Interrogation of American Terror
By Angela D. Sims

Representations of Homosexuality: Black Liberation Theology and Cultural Criticism
By Roger A. Sneed

The Tragic Vision of African American Religion
By Matthew V. Johnson

Beyond Slavery: Overcoming Its Religious and Sexual Legacies
Edited by Bernadette J. Brooten with the editorial assistance of Jacqueline L. Hazelton

Gifts of Virtue, Alice Walker, and Womanist Ethics
By Melanie Harris

Racism and the Image of God
By Karen Teel

Self, Culture, and Others in Womanist Practical Theology
By Phillis Isabella Sheppard

Sherman's March and the Emergence of the Independent Black Church Movement
By Love Henry Whelchel

Black Men Worshipping: Intersecting Anxieties of Race, Gender, and Christian Embodiment
By Stacy C. Boyd

Womanism against Socially-Constructed Matriarchal Images: A Theoretical Model towards a Therapeutic Goal
By MarKeva Gwendolyn Hill

Indigenous Black Theology: Toward an African-Centered Theology of the African-American Religious
By Jawanza Eric Clark

Black Bodies and the Black Church: A Blues Slant
By Kelly Brown Douglas

A Theological Account of Nat Turner: Christianity, Violence, and Theology
By Karl Lampley

African American Female Mysticism: Nineteenth-Century Religious Activism
By Joy R. Bostic

A Queering of Black Theology: James Baldwin's Blues Project and Gospel Prose
By EL Kornegay Jr.

Formation of the African Methodist Episcopal Church in the Nineteenth Century: Rhetoric of Identification
A. Nevell Owens

Toward a Womanist Ethic of Incarnation: Black Bodies, the Black Church, and the Council of Chalcedon
Eboni Marshall Turman

Religio-Political Narratives: From Martin Luther King Jr. to Jeremiah Wright
Angela D. Sims, F. Douglas Powe Jr., and Johnny Bernard Hill

Churches, Blackness, and Contested Multiculturalism Europe, Africa, and North America
Edited by R. Drew Smith, William Ackah, and Anthony G. Reddie

Womanist and Black Feminist Responses to Tyler Perry's Productions
LeRhonda S. Manigault-Bryant, Tamura A. Lomax, Carol B. Duncan

James Baldwin's Understanding of God: Overwhelming Desire and Joy
Josiah Ulysses Young III

A Womanist Pastoral Theology against Intimate and Cultural Violence: A Narrative Approach to Self-Recovery
Stephanie M. Crumpton

Kairos, Crisis, and Global Apartheid: The Challenge to Prophetic Resistance
Allan Aubrey Boesak

Religious Resistance to Neoliberalism: Womanist and Black Feminist Perspectives
Keri Day

Religious Resistance to Neoliberalism

Womanist and Black Feminist Perspectives

Keri Day

First published 2016 by
PALGRAVE MACMILLAN

The author has asserted their right to be identified as the author of this work in accordance with the Copyright, Designs and Patents Act 1988.

Palgrave Macmillan in the UK is an imprint of Macmillan Publishers Limited, registered in England, company number 785998, of Houndmills, Basingstoke, Hampshire, RG21 6XS.

Palgrave Macmillan in the US is a division of Nature America, Inc., One New York Plaza, Suite 4500, New York, NY 10004-1562.

Palgrave Macmillan is the global academic imprint of the above companies and has companies and representatives throughout the world.

Hardback ISBN: 978–1–137–56942–4
E-PUB ISBN: 978–1–137–56944–8
E-PDF ISBN: 978–1–137–56943–1
DOI: 10.1057/9781137569431

Distribution in the UK, Europe and the rest of the world is by Palgrave Macmillan®, a division of Macmillan Publishers Limited, registered in England, company number 785998, of Houndmills, Basingstoke, Hampshire RG21 6XS.

Library of Congress Cataloging-in-Publication Data

Day, Keri.
    Religious resistance to neoliberalism : womanist and black feminist perspectives / Keri Day.
        pages cm.—(Black religion/womanist thought/social justice)
    Includes bibliographical references and index.
    ISBN 978–1–137–56942–4—
    ISBN 1–137–56942–5
        1. Womanist theology. 2. Black theology. 3. Feminist theology.
    4. Neoliberalism—Religious aspects. 5. Christianity. 6. Judaism.
    I. Title.
BT83.9.D39 2015
230.082—dc23   2015021050

A catalogue record for the book is available from the British Library.

To my mother, Connie,
who has never been afraid to practice religious defiance
And to my Godmother, Mildred Haygood,
who continues to teach me the power of hope.

Contents

Acknowledgments

This project would not have been possible without a number of important people, conversations, and experiences. I want to first note three critical conversations I had with three scholar/activists after I published and lectured from my first academic text, *Unfinished Business: Black Women, The Black Church, and the Struggle to Thrive in America.* Dr. Stephanie Crumpton, Rev. Osagyefo Sekou, and Dr. Marla Frederick raised important questions about the *gap* in my first text surrounding neoliberal cultural forms of alienation and women of color's agency in resisting such dehumanizing cultural forms. While I did well in investigating the structural-material modes of inequity and inequality poor black women experience within a neoliberal capitalist context, Stephanie and Sekou wondered whether I might extend my argument to render visible the various ways in which poor women of color challenge and protest neoliberal values and practices. I understood their question to be about detailing how poor women of color operate as *agents and subjects* within neoliberal matrices even though they endure the brunt of market exploitation. Sekou made it a point to lift up the importance of describing social movements among women of color within neoliberal patterns of globalization and the difference these movements make for how we think about the social transformation of neoliberal cultures. Similarly, Marla encouraged me to attend to the inequitable gendered circumstances poor women of color suffer within globalizing processes such as human trafficking in order to clarify how they experience and resist economic and cultural exploitation. These three scholar/activists helped water the initial seed of this text. For this "holy trinity," I am grateful.

While writing this text, I also benefited from specific womanist scholars who helped me think about other important aspects of neoliberalism. Dr. Melanie Harris challenged me to rewrite the text in light of ecological concerns, as ecological justice is not peripheral but central to neoliberal capitalist exploitation. I appreciate her taking serious time out of her schedule to read parts of my manuscript in order to help me think and write more clearly with this in mind. I also want to thank Dr. Andrea White who had long conversations with me about realized eschatologies in light of my project and how I might articulate my commitment to this point of view.

Similar to Andrea, I want to thank Dr. Christophe Ringer for our many conversations about neoliberal capitalism and eschatology as well as his critical feedback on parts of my manuscript surrounding the myth of progress in chapter 1. While we had points of disagreement, I was stretched by his generous reading of apocalyptic eschatology, which compelled me to consider a more complex relationship between realized and apocalyptic eschatolgies. Thanks, my brother. I also am extremely appreciative of black religious scholar Dr. Preston Williams who I personally met while delivering a set of lectures at Princeton Theological Seminary in the summer of 2013. After my final lecture on King's notion of beloved community, Preston approached me and told me that while he thought my lectures were excellent (I certainly felt honored!), I was totally wrong about seeing Royce and King as similar in their deployment of this term. This began a long Socratic conversation between me and him about how King's project of beloved community radically differs from Josiah Royce's articulation of this concept. This helped me tremendously as I theorized my own idea of beloved communities in the final chapter.

I also want to thank my institution, Brite Divinity School, who offered both funding and a pre-tenure sabbatical to begin thinking about the ideas and arguments that show up in this text. Some of these ideas were discussed and debated in two advanced graduate seminars I taught during the 2014–2015 academic year ("African American Political Theologies" and "Christian Ethics and Economy"). Graduate students in these two classes pushed me to critically re-think some of my intellectual questions surrounding neoliberalism and its relationship to race, gender, and late capitalism. I want to offer a special word of gratitiude to David Gouwens, my colleague at Brite who recently retired. David has been a top Kierkegaardian scholar in the fields of theology and religion and I appreciate his nuanced critique of my second chapter in which I employ Kierkegaard's social writings. I am grateful to be at an institution that empowers scholars to delve deeper into their research and teaching.

I also want to extend an important note of gratitude to Afro-Caribbean scholar and art activist Alanna Lockward and Cameroonian intellectual and art activist Bonaventure Soh Bejeng Ndikung, two amazing minds I met while in Berlin in July 2014. I was moved by their intellectual work surrounding the arts and African diasporic liberation. Both of them employ the arts (as form-ideas) in articulating rich visions of justice and flourishing for two-thirds world subjects. I enjoyed engaging Bonaventure, Founder and Director of SAVVY Contemporary Center in Berlin, in order to learn and write about the important transcultural artistic work the center is doing in contesting neoliberal cultural life. Their intellectual/artistic endeavors influenced me deeply and shaped how I wrote about beloved communities in the final chapter.

This manuscript was written in different parts of the world over a three-year period in various coffee shops. From Dallas to New York, from Paris to Berlin, I labored over these ideas with a vanilla latte in hand. However, I must say that Avoca Coffee House in Fort Worth, Texas, was my writing sanctuary. I would walk in and immediately be greeted by the baristas. They knew my name. They asked me what I was working on. It was like coming home and their great coffee gave me the energy to write during the afternoons. Thanks so much to my Avoca friends.

I remain grateful for Rev. Dr. Frederick Haynes III, who is my pastor and friend. His support is steadfast. He beautifully models the importance of religious leaders challenging forms of capitalist oppression through radical activism. It is wonderful to worship with a church community that is dreaming about new possible worlds where racist, capitalist domination does not have the "last say." I also appreciate my "community of pastor friends" who have listened to me and taught me much about religious leadership in relation to activism: Rev. Dr. Irie Session, Rev. Dr. Ralph Douglas West, Sr., and Rev. Alex Byrd. You three are wonderful gifts to my vocational life.

Most importantly, I want to thank my family and friends. My parents remain critical to my success as a researcher and writer, and I appreciate that they understand that my love still remains despite my few calls during intense seasons of writing! My mother, Connie Woods, would often ask me what I was writing about only to forget and ask me the next day (this went on for three years). But thanks Mom, as it forced me to become more clear each day as I recited my ideas to you! My close friends have been invaluable, as they offered meals, conversation, and sometimes a listening ear through the frustration and joy associated with completing this project. Dr. Tamura Lomax, Rev. Cece Jones-Davis, and Dr. Shively Jackson Smith, your friendships enable me to thrive. I am indeed blessed to have a supportive and loving community.

Introduction

Neoliberalism and the Religious Imagination

The Kenyan Afro-futuristic film *Pumzi* provides a vivid, compelling account of how unregulated global markets might devastate all forms of life on Earth. Written and directed by Wanuri Kahiu, this film opens on an apocalyptic note, specifying a new era known as "post-Earth" in which there are no visible signs of life. It is 35 years after World War III, what countries once referred to as "The Water War." Various old newspaper clippings move across the screen, which give us some indication that most life forms are now extinct. One newspaper clipping reads, "People Journeying a Whole Day in Search of Water." Newspaper images show devastation created by nuclear radioactive waste as well as the Greenhouse Effect. There is no living human, animal, or plant left within the natural environment of the Earth. One can infer in this film that World War III was caused by the increased scarcity of water (among other things that depend upon water, such as food crops) due to humanity's competitive, destructive environmental and economic practices, destroying most of the world's population. At this point, the viewer encounters the only known small community surviving within a technological bubble in East Africa. They are known as the Maitu community ("Maitu" means mother in Kikuyu language). The rest of the world is pure desert, showing no signs of life. As the movie unfolds, even the rationing of water among members in the Maitu community is indicative of the catastrophe that was engendered due to economically competitive and ecologically unfriendly practices among humans. Global economic institutions and their objectifying practices toward human bodies and nonhuman bodies are certainly rendered culpable in this movie.

It is against this backdrop that we are taken into the Maitu community. We encounter the protagonist and heroine, an African girl named Asha, who is a community member and works at the Virtual Natural History Museum within this community. We first view Asha having a dream about a large, lush green tree. She is reaching out toward this green tree with anticipation and hope. As we watch the film, one begins to see that the green tree is a metaphor that represents potential life as well as a new possible future for humanity and all of Creation. Asha does not get to enjoy her dream for long. She awakens to an alarm on her computer (programmed by the "Council of Authorities"), instructing her to take her "dream suppressant." The Council of Authorities is able to detect dreams (visions of new futures) and orders members to take pills that will suppress their visions, longings, and yearnings for a potential future or new world. One senses that the Council of Authorities does not allow community members to creatively imagine possibilities beyond the status quo.

One afternoon, Asha is sent a package containing a soil sample from an anonymous source, which generates a new set of possibilities in her mind about a future world. She looks up this soil sample to catalogue it in the Virtual Natural History Museum when she realizes that this soil sample is fertile with high water content. The soil shows signs of life. She initially contacts the authorities about this fertile soil sample, but the authorities command her to dispose of the soil and take her suppressants. Disobeying this order, Asha places a seed in this new soil and waters it. Immediately, the seed begins to blossom and grow. She informs the authorities of this new exciting discovery and asks for an "exit visa" to search for life outside their community. Her visa is denied. She is also immediately arrested for disobeying the earlier orders to throw away the new soil. They decide that Asha will no longer work for the Virtual Natural History Museum but will be confined to cleaning bathrooms. However, Asha courageously resists. With the aid of another friend in the community, she escapes through a garbage outlet in order to find life on the outside. She also takes the seed that began to grow in the small fertile soil sample.

Asha journeys through vast spaces of desert. Each step she takes expresses hope in a possible new future that Western economic practices of greed and profit destroyed 35 years ago in World War III. It seems as if Asha is journeying toward nothing but more vast areas of lifeless desert until she finally spots the luscious green tree that she saw in her dream. However, when she walks closer to the tree, she realizes that the tree is barren, without leaves of any color. Instead of giving in to despair, Asha decides she has only one option left. She takes the growing seed she has carried with her in the fertile soil sample and plants it in the soil surrounding the barren tree. She pours the rest of the water she has on this seed and even wipes the sweat from her body to use as additional liquid to water the seed. She then uses her body to provide shade for the seed as the intense heat of the sun beats down upon the earth. Lying there in the desert, she waits for the seed to grow. She hopes for a possible future filled with new life. The movie ends with the camera zooming further and further away from Asha's body until she is only a speck in the world. Suddenly, a green tree is seen sprouting, which multiplies into green trees all around the world, representing new life and new possible futures. New life begins again because of Asha's courage and resistance. This new world will be oriented toward loving and sharing with and for each other (and all of Creation) instead of hyper-competitive, fear-based, and profit-driven modes of being that characterize global markets of a bygone era.

Contrasted to Western heroism, the film *Pumzi* highlights the heroic efforts of a young African woman named Asha, the Mother of a new civilization, which would be marked by compassion, care, and peace. One might infer that this film is asserting the importance of a trans-African feminist epistemology. Unfortunately, women of color bear the brunt of economic, social, and cultural injustices around the world. Women of color disproportionately endure material and symbolic oppressions that make it difficult for them to survive and thrive. However, in this film, it is an African woman who restores humanity. An African woman becomes the savior of the world. She offers a new view of what is possible. *Pumzi* provides a profound black feminist/womanist metaphor of transformation and change in response to neoliberal danger and violence.

It is Asha who provides the mother seed of life from which all life begins again. It is her truth and knowledge that create a new future built on radical love and self-giving. It is this African girl's courage that generates a politics of hope. This movie is deeply subversive as it privileges an African girl as the key to new futures. Although impoverished African women are objectified and treated as dispensable within current global economic processes to meet profit goals, these women's epistemologies and practices of courage, trust, love, and hope are articulated as central to how we might think about new worlds oriented toward love and flourishing. It is also important to remember that Asha did not challenge the Council of Authorities by herself as people helped her (the anonymous person who sent the fertile soil sample to her and the young woman who helped her escape from the Maitu community). Transformation of our world is a collective, communal endeavor rather than simply an individual pursuit.

Asha's sense of hope invites us to dream dangerously within our present neoliberal global economic context about preferable futures. A politics of hope is necessary to address the destructive consequences associated with contemporary forms of market economies. In this text, I am interested in interrogating how neoliberal economies and their contradictions distort human meaning and inhibit human flourishing. Neoliberal global economy is riddled with contradictions. These contradictions include how neoliberal economies promote "progress" through contending that markets have produced unprecedented wealth around the globe while simultaneously eclipsing hope itself through untold forms of disparities and inequities; how the neoliberal economy seems to connect people across time, space, and place from many different continents while simultaneously generating chronic forms of alienation and social disintegration that weaken what it means to be human; how neoliberal capitalism argues that blind trust in markets will help form virtuous individuals while simultaneously producing individual subjects who are trained to get ahead through duplicitous socio-economic practices that sponsor social distrust. Neoliberalism is not only an economic program in the sense that it promotes the proliferation of unregulated (or under-regulated) free markets but also a cultural project in that it distorts what it means to be responsible moral agents in our globalizing world today.

The deleterious effects of neoliberal economy are as much a theological and religious question concerning how we speak about love of neighbor, care of environment, social trust among human beings as it is a material question about transforming structures and systems to reflect economic parity and justice. This book then offers religious critiques of neoliberalism. As I will discuss, neoliberalism is the driving rationality of contemporary global capitalism. Neoliberalism is a market rationale that orders people to live by the generalized principle of competition in *all* social spheres of life, making the individual herself or himself an enterprise (and reducing social relations to monetary relations). Neoliberalism raises religious questions about human meaning and flourishing.

This text argues that engaging U.S. black feminist and womanist religio-cultural perspectives with Jewish and Christian discourses exposes and deconstructs alienating modes generated and exacerbated by neoliberal economy (alienating modes such as social distrust, absence of care and compassion, and rabid individualism). For this text, black feminist and womanist discourses interrogate how poor women of the African and Carribean diasporas are disenfranchised within the matrices of global markets. I take my cue from Joy James and Tracey Sharpley-Whiting's *The Black Feminist Reader* and Alice Walker's *In Search of Our Mother's Gardens: Womanist Prose* that poor women of the African and Caribbean diasporas share unique and interconnecting experiences and circumstances within the nexus of white racist hetero-patriarchal capitalism. I am interested in exploring these interconnections, as global markets are ravaging poor women of color around the world.

On a methodological level, black feminist and womanist religious perspectives function as an "ideology critique," which explores the roots and possibilities of crises associated with modern neoliberal capitalism and its cultural forms of alienation. Black feminist and womanist religious perspectives also foreground the importance of literature, history, critical social theory, and feminist political philosophy in articulating religious critiques and responses to neoliberalism and its forms of fragmentation within society. Black feminist and womanist religious perspectives offer a politics of hope that defiantly resists and protests neoliberal values (profit maximization to exclusion of social care, endless acquisition of things, and the objectification of the environment), as these values impede the fashioning of compassionate and just communities. These perspectives demonstrate that a politics of hope can also creatively imagine a future of care and love in response to the demonic circuits of neoliberal economy.

Critiquing Neoliberalism: The Art of the Possible

There is a dearth of religious and theological literature that challenges the existential forms of alienation neoliberalism produces. Over the last several decades, most theological and religious scholarship has focused on critiques of free-market economy rather than neoliberalism. These critiques of free-market economy have focused on both the absence of the state in regulating "free markets" as well as social pathologies (competition, lack of care, etc.) that result from market individualism.[1] However, neoliberalism is a much broader rubric than market economy as this rabidly individualistic, *state-regulating* ideology operates not only within capitalist societies but also within totalitarian and socialist arrangements. Capitalist *and* socialist societies (and even mixed economies) are employing global markets in ways that foster alienation and commodification among human beings, producing neoliberal policies and forms of ideological regulation (which will be discussed later in this chapter). Within neoliberalism (unlike present religious critiques of free-market societies), the argument is not that the state needs to regulate markets more but that the state must cease to be complicit in the (re)production of alienating, individualistic, and hyper-competitive modes of being associated with neoliberalism. One cannot simply equate neoliberalism with "free-market societies," as contemporary capitalist logic is integrated into diverse socio-economic arrangements. This text addresses this complexity by exploring neoliberalism from a religious perspective. But what exactly is neoliberalism?

The historical emergence of neoliberalism in the 1970s is tied to a revival of classical economic liberalism, which emphasized the virtues of a "self-regulating" free-market economy (virtues such as economic freedom, unfettered market enterprise, and international free trade). For classical economic liberalism (i.e., Adam Smith and David Ricardo), "big government" or state regulation of markets always results in market failures. Because free markets contain their own self-correcting mechanisms whenever economic crisis emerges, classical liberals argue that markets should be left alone to naturally return the economy to equilibrium in employment, prices, and so forth during a recession.

However, with the Great Depression in the 1930s within the United States and around the world, these assumptions of classical liberalism fell apart.[2] Economists such as John Maynard Keynes contended that governments should play a policy role during times of economic recession and crisis through government spending on jobs and welfare programs. This Keynesian economic rationality undergirded Franklin D. Roosevelt's New Deal social programs as well as Lyndon B. Johnson's Great Society social policies. From 1930 to 1970, "regulated capitalism" generated a number of safety nets (Medicare, Medicaid, food programs, etc.) for vulnerable groups affected by market shifts.[3]

However, severe global economic crisis in the 1970s such as unprecedented price increases in oil as well as unemployment and inflation led a new group of economists to reject Keynesian economic logic in favor of a revival of old classical economic liberalism.[4] They were termed "neoliberal" economists. In the 1980s, these new neoliberal economists (i.e., Friedrich Von Hayek and Milton Friedman) succeeded in shifting the tide of economic logic and policy toward *laissez-faire* economics, which included free trade and commerce with limited government regulation and oversight. A central part of neoliberal economic thinking was the dismantling of welfare states around the globe in order to sponsor unregulated free-market activity and economic growth.

The "Washington Consensus" associated with Washington, DC-based economic institutions such as the International Monetary Fund (IMF) and World Bank established policy prescriptions based on free-market approaches (government deregulation, relaxed taxation, a reduction of public expenditure on welfare programs, free trade, etc.) for crisis-ridden countries in the Global South such as Chile, Argentina, and post-apartheid South Africa.[5] Also known as "structural adjustment programs," these policy prescriptions were mandatory if these crisis-ridden countries desired to obtain loans from the IMF or World Bank. However, these structural adjustment policies often had disastrous effects within these countries' economies. For instance, the gap between the rich and poor in "developing" countries widened with the dismantling of welfare provisions. Poor women were also disproportionately impacted by exploitative processes associated with neoliberal market practices around the world (i.e., sweatshops). As a result, neoliberalism came under an increasing backlash as a set of failed economic policies oriented toward "economic growth." This brief history of neoliberalism demonstrates the precarious situation that vulnerable populations experienced around the globe.

While this brief history provides a general picture of how and why neoliberal economics emerged (or was "revived"), there is no single definition of neoliberalism among thinkers who critique neoliberalism. To the neo-Marxist, neoliberalism has meant a free-market system that has privileged economic redistribution to the wealthy, a social policy system characterized by structural adjustment policies created by the IMF and World Bank that have disproportionately hurt poor women and their children in Two-Thirds World countries. For Foucaultian scholars, this term is understood as a *cultural* project, premised on the shift toward "governmentalities that merge market and state imperatives in order to produce self-regulating 'good subjects' who embody ideals of individual responsibility."[6] For political theorists, neoliberalism has created a new model of statecraft in which the privatization of goods and services, the destruction of the welfare state, and the increasing shift toward a prison industrial complex and militarism (national security) have shaped economic policy and cultural practices around the world.[7] While views of neoliberalism are somewhat different across disciplines, I find it helpful to acknowledge that neoliberalism may be seen as an economic, political, and cultural project that has gained currency within our global order, (re)producing and exacerbating the impoverished position of the poor around the world.

It is also important to acknowledge that neoliberalism is a contested analytic category. Some maintain that the category is not useful at all. Black cultural theorist Stuart Hall notes that intellectual critics tend to contest the term, arguing that this term attempts to describe and explain too many processes under a single category.[8] Some contend that the term neoliberalism ends up being reductive, "sacrificing attention to internal complexities and geo-historical specificity."[9] Because neoliberalism has many variants within different nations and economies, one might properly refer to this contemporary capitalist logic as "neoliberalisms" (or something else altogether). How neoliberal logic articulates itself in American and British market economies is different from how neoliberalism forms and functions in China's state capitalism or Latin America's "monetarist" experiments.[10] However, I would argue that there are enough similarities among nations to give this ideology a *provisional* conceptual identity, being neoliberalism.[11] Moreover, giving neoliberalism a conceptual identity allows one to articulate strategies of resistance to the content and practices of this term. Neoliberalism is not just an intellectual question but is a political question of profound importance. "Developing" nations around the world remain captives of structural adjustment programs that force them to set up market forces in their countries to promote free trade and foreign investment, rules that only further contribute to the impoverishment of a wide majority of "Third-World" citizens.[12] In light of critiques of neoliberalism, I employ it as a term that has multiple variations and articulations around the world, as neoliberalism reveals diverse, complex, and messy cultural and economic processes.

While neoliberalism may have diverse articulations and manifestations, it nevertheless ideologically functions as a form of rationality. I draw primarily on a Foucaultian understanding of neoliberalism as a type of rationality and governmentality that reshapes and transforms the human subject within our modern global context. Neoliberalism is not merely a set of economic policies or a partisan political or cultural ideology but a *rationality* that structures and governs human conduct and behavior within societies that employ markets. Neoliberalism is a market rationale that orders people to live by the generalized principle of competition in *all* social spheres of life, making the individual herself or himself an enterprise.[13] It demands that individuals relate to each other in instrumental ways. It produces human subjectivities that see social relations (such as friendship, care, love) as market relations wherein persons are nothing more than material means toward the ends of another person's goals (individual financial success, social status, etc.). This neoliberal subject reflects social pathologies. Neoliberalism is not just about the destruction of corporate regulations and personal liberties, but it is also about the production of certain alienated ways of living and particular kinds of "market" subjectivities.[14]

Neoliberalism then provides the normativity of our very existence as it tends to totalize in the sense of "creating a world in its own image and through its power to integrate all dimensions of human existence."[15] To misrecognize neoliberalism simply as a set of market policies or a new economic regime is to miss the ways in which neoliberalism serves as a normative rationality, offering answers to existential questions within contemporary capitalist contexts (such as free-market societies, state capitalism, and mixed economies). It aims to create a different community of persons.

Through the state, neoliberalism as a normative rationality is made complete through its power to govern individuals. When I speak of neoliberal rationality as a kind of governmentality, I am not merely referring to government as political institutions. Instead, I am referring to Foucault's notion of government as an activity. Government is understood in the broadest sense as techniques and norms used to conduct and regulate people's behavior in ways that compel individuals to claim such behavior as self-regulation.[16] Because individual rights are the bedrock of democratic societies, neoliberal governmentality shapes human subjectivities in ways that cause individuals to feel as if their market values and choices are due to their own freedom or self-governing.

Moreover, neoliberalism as a governmentality is important in understanding that neoliberal economics is not a "retreat from the state" (as in the state is excluded from market activity). Unlike neoliberal thinkers such as Friedman, I argue that neoliberalism is not merely a revival or exacerbation of classical economic liberalism, which was about delineating the *limits* of the state.[17] Neoliberalism is not concerned solely with the limits of the state. Rather, neoliberalism promotes this question: How is the market to be made *the principle* of moral formation among human beings? Ironically, neoliberalism seeks to fully encroach upon our economic and cultural ways of life. Neoliberalism is backed by the state as the state aids in creating a normative way of life grounded in the principle of hyper-competition and the commodification of all spheres of life. The state does not govern against individual liberty but *through* liberty so that individuals will experience themselves as morally conforming to neoliberal values due to their own desires and choices.[18] Hence, in critiquing neoliberalism, one cannot just fight partisan economic theories or immoral conduct associated with global capitalism but must dismantle the normative rationality of hyper-competition and governmentality that undergirds neoliberal activity within global capitalist contexts.

As one can see, the "innocence" of the state (contrasted to the market) becomes questionable when turning to how the state employs neoliberal rationality. Arguments provided by political liberals emphasize the importance of the state in "correcting" market excess. However, neoliberal norms are employed *through* the state in legitimating market values and practices around the world. Even when the state offers forms of social assistance (welfare, medical care, education, etc.), it still operates with neoliberal norms based on individualism and profit. Consequently, neoliberalism is a normative framework that not only grounds the state's practices but also reshapes and governs human subjectivities in the name of "individual freedom." State or government intervention is not the primary solution to instabilities created by markets. The solution is more complex than this and involves attacking the entire normative neoliberal rationality underwriting the state's activities.

When discussing neoliberal rationality and governmentality, gender analysis also needs more attention. What brings gender to the center of this neoliberal project is the ways in which its policies and values have led to the instability of caring relations around the world. Monopolies generated by multinational and transnational corporations have led to the squeezing out of local competition in various industries, which has contributed both to the unavailability of jobs or jobs that offer little security. Jobs that offer small security in healthcare, childcare, paid family leave, and so forth disproportionately affect women. Welfare states are dismantled within many countries as these nations struggle to legitimate themselves to the corporate financiers as countries worthy of investment and economic development. Poor women who are the primary caretakers of children primarily feel this dismantling of welfare benefits, as these benefits balance the economic disequilibrium often caused by market competition. Many poor women in "developing nations" try to craft modes of survival through sex tourism or dehumanizing domestic work. Hence, the sexual commodification and exacerbation of gender-stratified labor markets are the result of neoliberal practices that shape economic logic and production. Neoliberalism can then be understood precisely as a shift both in gender relations *and caring relations* over the last several decades.

Because neoliberalism is central to any analysis on gender relations within present economies around the world, this organizing category can provide important insights into the cultural, social, and religious contexts out of which contemporary womanist and feminist movements speak and struggle for social justice. For instance, feminist scholar Kate Bedford suggests that the promotion of "complementary love" within heterosexual familial arrangements was a central part of the World Bank's push to embed markets within national cultures in more sustainable ways.[19] This idea of complementary love was supported by religious voices and organizations in order to promote a certain hetero-normative agenda, which has profound implications both for women and same-gender loving persons. Consequently, it is important to understand the religious arguments that ground this idea of complementary love and how this idea is then used as a neoliberal policy tool to advance unregulated global free markets. Religious institutions, particularly fundamentalist in character, support hetero-patriarchal practices that place women at a severe disadvantage in labor markets, providing no safety nets (welfare and living wage) for these women whose lives are deeply affected by the decisions of powerful elite European men.

Neoliberalism has also partnered with churches in the United States and on other continents such as Africa, to nurture its narrative of moral renewal among individuals, intentionally directing attention away from deeper systemic inequities within global economy. Religious conservatism colors neoliberalism in a "religious shade" in order to secure and buttress neoliberal's normative commitments and ethical values such as hard work, personal responsibility, and self-improvement. These religiously conservative groups offer a religious template of personal responsibility that aligns with neo-liberalism's larger cultural project of producing and regulating "good subjects" who are industrious and therefore economically successful. For example, poverty becomes a religious issue as one's impoverishment not only refers to their indolence and lack of work but also reveals their failure as a religious subject to receive favor with God through material wealth and well-being. As a result, the poor are not seen as "good subjects" and are disciplined, punished, and regulated by the state through social policies, policies that are legitimated through religious ideology about the poor.

Neoliberalism engenders contradictions as well. While neoliberal projects create alienated subjects and further impoverish vulnerable populations (disproportionately women of color) by polarizing resources and wealth, it simultaneously generates a set of human rights responses seen in many social movements that have emerged in relation to the gross inequalities associated with global free markets. This paradox is worth exploring. For instance, while female sex workers are often trapped in the commodifying markets of global capitalism, these women audaciously violate the neoliberal ideals of middle class femininity and white Victorian sexuality associated with global market systems. While neoliberalism is the grounding upon which economic and cultural hegemony is practiced, it is also the conditions under which poor women have responded through their religious modes of collective organizing and forms of moral protest around the world. In particular, one may be able to see the "Janus-faced" nature of religion in relation to neoliberalism: religious ideas and practices both fuel neoliberal logics and subvert these logics.

I suggest throughout this text that neoliberal values and practices affect our moral and religious imaginations. Our religious and moral imaginations are imprisoned to the fundamental market rationality of atomic individualism, which makes questions of caring relations seem idealistic and even naïve. We are often unable to imagine deeper modes of social connectedness or cooperation, as the grid of social intelligence that neoliberalism offers us is based on the pessimistic premise of radical individual self-interest. Within the logic of fragmented individualism that neoliberal markets articulate, certain cooperative visions, which people depend upon for their survival, are stretched and manipulated into new configurations. Negative cooperative configurations of greed and deception become normative within financial institutions, undermining the belief in the possibility of positive cooperative visions within societies. Many people no longer believe that we can cultivate economic and cultural practices oriented toward flourishing for all. This deeply affects the moral and religious life out of which we articulate our deepest sense of human meaning and hope.

Religious perspectives are deeply resourceful in articulating morally imaginative possibilities. The religious imaginations of Jewish,

Christian, and black religious perspectives have been central to morally envisioning better social worlds. A significant aspect among such traditions has been the "art of the possible." From the prophetic traditions of the Hebrew Bible and Christian gospels to the imaginative orientations of black feminist/womanist religio-cultural discourses, one is able to see what has been possible in past communities gripped by oppression, marginalization, and helplessness. The "thinning out" of caring and loving relations within this neoliberal moment is triggering a re-envisioning of what is morally possible in order to flourish and thrive together as human beings. Radically re-imagining what kind of human beings we desire to be in our hyper-competitive, self-centered, materialistic economy remains central.

We must ask what human and social values will underwrite our economic lives together in this neoliberal moment. As discussed earlier, because economic efficiency is seen as the end goal of market exchanges, societies are unable to see the importance of promoting a richer texture of imaginative social values out of which economic efficiency is ethically sustainable. The argument is not that markets and economic efficiency are intrinsically evil. Instead, my contention is that the market principle of competition must not *be the organizing principle* of all of social life, as it impedes visions of human flourishing.

For this text, I am interested in asking what new critiques of neoliberalism black feminist and womanist religio-cultural perspectives might generate when engaging Jewish and Christian discourses. It seems that black feminist and womanist religio-cultural perspectives foreground three emphases when religiously critiquing neoliberalism and its forms of alienation (emphases that Christian and Jewish discourses may not privilege when discussing neoliberalism). First, although neoliberalism affects all individuals across race/gender/class categories, black feminist and womanist discourses privilege how neoliberalism disproportionately affects marginalized women of color. Black feminist and womanist discourses have highlighted the material and cultural experiences of poor women of color around the world as these women disproportionately experience the fallout of neoliberal capitalism. Neoliberalism's dark side is more adequately captured through the deep inequities and heartbreaking melancholy "expendable" populations often endure such as brown and black women.

Second, black feminist and womanist religio-cultural perspectives recover the idea of "the erotic" as a life-giving force that can challenge neoliberal forms of human disconnection and alienation. This directly contests the ways in which the erotic has been deeply prob-lematized as sinful and profane within much of traditional Jewish and Christian thought. Black feminist and womanist discourses argue that the erotic remains central to experiencing personal *and* political forms of connection and friendship within our neoliberal moment.

Finally, black feminist and womanist perspectives ground a pragmatic politics of hope not in abstract theorization about love but through articulating love as *a concrete revolutionary practice that shows up in the ordinary and mundane lives of poor women.* Specifically, black feminist and womanist discourses turn to how social movements among women of color offer a "prophetic politics of the ordinary" that "enflesh" love or beloved communities. We do not need to turn to "supernatural events" (i.e., supersessionist logic seen within much of Jewish and Christian religious thought) in inaugurat-ing new ways of being marked by social concern and care. Rather, resistance to neoliberalism is always and already found in the daily, ordinary acts of courage and love that vulnerable populations (such as poor women of color) embody with and for each other. Moreover, black feminist and womanist religious projects turn to literature as well as the empirical and social sciences in grounding possibilities toward loving, compassionate, and just communities.

The Flow of the Argument

This text employs an interdisciplinary method, drawing upon Jewish and Christian theologies, history, critical social theory, black feminist and womanist religio-cultural perspectives, feminist political philoso-phy, and neoliberal economic studies. This text uses an interdisciplin-ary approach in advancing its primary argument that an engagement among Jewish, Christian, and black feminist and womanist religio-cultural perspectives can generate more robust religious critiques of neoliberalism. Moreover, such religious perspectives provide rich moral imaginations about a pragmatic politics of hope, which is needed to combat the loss of meaning, despair, and helplessness asso-ciated with neoliberalism. In this text, each chapter represents one condition under which a politics of hope can be fashioned in response to the deleterious effects of neoliberalism. I suggest that six theoreti-cal, theologically constructive arguments are necessary in offering religious critiques of neoliberal economy, as neoliberalism raises theo-logical and religious questions about human meaning and hope.

These six arguments include deconstructing the myth of progress; resisting the "acquiring mode"; recovering the erotic as a life force in response to the radical disconnection of neoliberal culture; articulating love as a concrete revolutionary political practice; emphasizing a pragmatic politics of hope that is rooted in mundane and ordinary lives rather than in supersessionist logic (i.e., apocalyptic thought); and "radicalizing" hope in which one is able to creatively and *practically* imagine a future of care and love in response to the demonic circuits of neoliberal economy. I engage Jewish critical theorist Walter Benjamin; Slovenian philosopher Slavoj Zizek; Danish theologian Søren Kierkegaard; womanist postmodern religious scholars such as Karen Baker-Fletcher, Melanie Harris, and Monica Coleman; as well as black feminist theorists and novelists such as Audre Lorde, Jennifer Nash, Alice Walker, and Toni Morrison because these thinkers can be read as forms of *prophecy*, exposing the crisis-ridden character of neoliberal logics that fuel capitalist markets. I substantively engage these six theoretical arguments with womanist and black feminist religious perspectives as these perspectives not only privilege women of color who are disproportionately impacted by the neoliberal patterns and processes but also employ literature, history, critical social theory, and feminist political philosophy in offering religious criticisms of culture and economy.

Chapter 1 argues that the inner logic of global capitalism must be disrupted, which is the myth of progress. Drawing upon Jewish social theorist Walter Benjamin, Slovenian philosopher Slavoj Zizek, and postmodern womanist theologian Karen Baker-Fletcher, I offer a religious critique of this myth by naming our current global market model as catastrophic rather than democratizing and progressive for the world. There is minimal literature on theological/religious critiques of the "myth of progress" that undergirds contemporary capitalist logic. Through a religious critique of progress, one is able to see global capitalism as "crisis-ridden" for vulnerable populations (such as poor women of the African and Caribbean diasporas), which may also help one envision the conditions toward the possibility of a new socio-economic order governed by ideas of love, solidarity, and hope. I ground possibilities of a new socio-economic order in a *realized eschatology* rather than an apocalyptic eschatology marked by Benjamin and Zizek's religious thought.

Chapter 2 contends that the transformation of the "self" within global neoliberal capitalism is a necessary precondition for prophetic social action. In order to investigate the individual within global capitalism, one must turn to the primary mode of being within global capitalist processes, what I refer to as the "acquiring mode." The acquiring mode is a capitalist way of being that defines human meaning based on the material things one can acquire. This mode then shapes the consciousness of the human subject within capitalist societies. In *Two Ages*, Danish theologian Søren Kierkegaard's discourse on "money as abstraction" explores how religious inwardness forms morally virtuous selves in response to the acquiring mode in our social and political spheres of society. I critique and expand Kierkegaard's idea of religious inwardness through engaging womanist religious discourse, as his idea of religious inwardness does not fully integrate considerations of structural inequalities and interreligious concerns, which can impede religious inwardness itself. The quest for religious inwardness or wholeness of self is simultaneously the grounding for prophetic action and witness against the reduction of social values to monetary meaning. The "self" needs to undergo radical transformation within the context of market consciousness in order to see oneself and others rightly.

Drawing upon black feminists such as Audre Lorde, Toni Morrison, and Alice Walker, chapter 3 argues that the power of the erotic must be recovered within our neoliberal society. Neoliberalism numbs individuals' longings, yearnings, and desires for each other. Traditional notions of the erotic tend to equate this term with the pornographic. Lorde, Morrison, and Walker challenge this traditional understanding of the erotic. Instead, the erotic is about deep feelings, sensation, and connection with and for each other that wake us up to love, freedom, and pleasure. The erotic is about self-expression and connection rather than repression and disconnection. Black feminist religious and cultural thought has provided rich counter-discourses on the power of the erotic in our neoliberal capitalist structures. I turn to two novels, Toni Morrison's *Sula* and Alice Walker's *By the Light of My Father's Smile*, in order to demonstrate how the power of the erotic can shape communities that are pulled toward each other through connection, desire, and freedom rather than pushed away from each other through fear, apathy, and disconnection.

Chapter 4 explores the radical potential of affect, being love. Employing Zizek as well as black feminists such as bell hooks and Jennifer Nash, I argue that love is not merely an ideal sentiment but a concrete revolutionary practice. Love is a movement. It *is movement* toward each other.[20] Concepts of neighbor-love within Jewish, Christian, and black feminist traditions foreground the importance of an *affective politics*, as love is profoundly political and deeply revolutionary. Within black feminist and womanist religious traditions, love has been a practice of self as well as a strategy for constructing compassionate political communities. I argue that "assemblage" theory rather than theories of intersectionality is better poised to speak of love in political terms as an affective politics, which challenges neoliberal forms of projective disgust based on fear and hatred of difference.

Chapter 5 explores a pragmatic politics of hope. This politics of hope is not seen through super-ordinary interventions into our neoliberal moment (i.e., supersessionist logic seen within much of Jewish and Christian religious thought). Instead, this pragmatic politics emerges at the *site of mundane and ordinary lived experience*. Religious studies scholar Vincent Lloyd helps one understand the importance of the mundane and ordinary in relation to any politics of hope. I turn to a feminist social movement, Madres de Desaparecisdos (Mothers of the Disappeared), as this movement embodies a pragmatic politics of hope at the site of ordinary lived experience, being motherhood.

Chapter 6 suggests that radicalizing hope and love leads to a new collective community out of which new alternatives are "enfleshed," opening up possibilities beyond neoliberal forms of rationality and governance. Radicalizing hope leads to beloved communities. This chapter suggests some *practical* implications of beloved communities when imagining a future of care and love in response to the demonic circuits of neoliberal economy.

The pages that follow seek to tell a story about how a politics of hope and love is profoundly subversive in a political and economic climate that attempts to render us cynical and apathetic about our ability to be different from the calculating, radically self-interested individual that neoliberal capitalism presumes as given. The religious perspectives represented in this book offer new ways of conceptualizing projects that are deeply subversive and dangerous to the status quo of neoliberal economy. We must strengthen our moral imaginations in relation to neoliberal values associated with capitalist production and Jewish, Christian, and black feminist and womanist religio-cultural perspectives allow one to do this. We can dream of another possible world, filled with political possibilities and a deep sense of social connectedness. We can dream dangerously.

1

The Myth of Progress

Free-market ideology is lauded around the world, as it is equated with the linear movement toward progress. However, some economists such as Amartya Sen and Joseph Stiglitz offer stinging indictments of how global financial institutions hinder economic and human development through unregulated or under-regulated "free" market models. Similarly, feminist political philosophers, such as Martha Nussbaum, also expose the exacerbation of inequities, especially among poor women and children, due to unfettered market forces. There has been minimal literature on religious critiques of neoliberal economy, and particularly, its "myth of progress." There needs to be an intervention here.

This chapter interrogates the neoliberal myth of progress by framing a religious critique of this myth around notions of crisis, redemption, and hope. I argue that postmodern womanist religious ideas of hope critique and expand Jewish and Christian sources when discussing the neoliberal myth of progress. Postmodern womanist religious thought grounds its critique of progress in the social conditions of poor women of color, who are disproportionately affected by neoliberal economy. Including an empirical analysis of poor women of color's social conditions within markets is important to refuting the myth of progress, as some economists simply interpret the economic and cultural fallout of globalizing processes (extreme poverty and inequality) as "unintended consequences" and therefore ethically neutral. This religious critique not only names impoverished social and political conditions associated with global markets as inequalities but also attempts to envision the conditions toward the possibility of a new socio-economic order, governed by ideas of love, solidarity, and hope through a *realized eschatology*. Drawing upon Walter

Benjamin, Slavoj Zizek, and Karen Baker-Fletcher, I offer a religious critique of progress that names our current global market model as catastrophic rather than democratizing and progressive for the world. This critique also invites one to envision a new socio-economic way of being beyond current neoliberal models, to participate in "writing a future of hope" through a realized eschatology.

The Angel of History: A Religious Critique of Progress

Because unregulated (and under-regulated) markets are fundamentally seen as progressive, we are unable to see the barbarity associated with our market models around the world. If competition and commodification constitute the inner logic of neoliberal capitalism, the myth of progress is neoliberalism's *legitimation*. Through a religious critique, I am interested in disrupting the legitimizing, justifying power of the myth of progress in order to render visible what lies behind neoliberal globalization: gross commodification and excessive competition that ruptures and deteriorates possibilities of individual fulfillment and human flourishing.

Specifically, critical social theorist Walter Benjamin's work is helpful because he offers a religious critique of capitalism, challenging the Western idea of "History" and its capitalist machinery as movement away from barbarism to liberation, from poverty to well-being for all. I recognize that I am employing a male theoretical voice for a black feminist/womanist project. However, I find Benjamin's critique of capitalism and political economy to be a valuable theoretical resource for understanding religious criticisms on the legitimatizing power of "progress" associated with neoliberalism. Benjamin's critique is one of the most fully articulated efforts to not only theologically assess the modern myth of progress associated with global market hegemony but also affirm the necessity of privileging oppressed communities' historical narratives as a way of envisioning worlds beyond inhumane neoliberal capitalist production. While one cannot refer to Benjamin's work as feminist or womanist (he certainly uses a plethora of masculine images in how he nuances his concepts), his critique of history specifically might be construed as in keeping with a radical black feminist or womanist commitment in the sense that his perspective sees the meaning of world histories in non-linear terms. He challenges the modern metanarrative of history and its singular meaning of progress, inviting a postmodern re-thinking of history itself in relationship to oppressed communities. I find that his project resonates with my black feminist and womanist aims in theologically critiquing neoliberal ideologies and structures. In *Unfinished Business*, I briefly introduce Benjamin's religious critique of capitalism but do not offer a sustained treatment of his critique in relation to womanist religious thought, of which I now turn to provide.

Benjamin uses an image to describe the problem of singularly interpreting "History" and its capitalist processes as progress. He purchased a painting by Paul Klee in 1921 entitled, *Angelus Novus*. For Benjamin, he interprets this painting as tragically depicting the enigmatic and paradoxical character of Western history, capitalism, and the claim to progress. He writes about the painting:

> A Klee painting named "Angelus Novus" shows an angel looking as though he is about to move away from something he is fixedly contemplating. His eyes are staring, his mouth is open, his wings are spread. This is how he pictures the angel of history. His face is turned toward the past. Where we perceive a chain of events, he sees one single catastrophe which keeps piling wreckage upon wreckage and hurls it in front of his feet. The angel would like to stay, awaken the dead, and make whole what has been smashed. But a storm is blowing from Paradise; it has got caught in his wings with such violence that the angel can no longer close them. This storm irresistibly propels him into the future to which his back is turned, while the pile of debris before him grows skyward. This storm is what we call progress.[1]

In Klee's painting, the angel is depicted with his "eyes wide open." It is "scared of what it sees in its inverted view," according to Benjamin. The back of the angel "faces toward the future, although it is powerless against the storm of progress."[2] This angel does not perceive history as following any rational course nor does it see it as "progress." Instead, history is "frozen for an instant by the Angel's petrified look of horror."[3] For Benjamin, history and its capitalist patterns are not a chain of democratizing events, but a single catastrophe.

Benjamin understood well the contradictions of progress the West proclaimed at the beginning of the twentieth century. The idea of Western modernity claimed a linear movement of world history toward civility, a world free of prejudice, poverty, corruption, and political vice. However, for Benjamin, modernity's claim to happiness was belied by the horrors of destruction that found ultimate expression in the 1930s and 1940s with the rise of the Third Reich in Germany and World War I. Being a Jew, Benjamin witnessed the carnage, suffering, and exploitation that was unleashed by the same set of historical conditions that also gave rise to the presumed modern idea of progress and civility. Alongside discourses on democracy and hope emerged the dark forces of authoritarianism and maddening violence in Germany. The "angel frozen in time" who is "paralyzed by the storm we call progress" that Benjamin alludes to is referring to these contradictory horrors the angel is witnessing in the 1940s. The storm is the violent force of Benjamin's present period that is called progress in theory but is experienced as maddening, irrational, and violent.[4]

Benjamin's angel of history provides an interesting counterargument to the neoliberal economic idea of "creative destruction" in which poverty, job losses, ruined companies, vanishing industries, and more are a part of economic growth and renewal. In *Capitalism, Socialism, and Democracy*, Austrian economist Joseph Schumpeter contends that there is a paradox to capitalist progress which inevitably involves acknowledging the fact that some people's lives will be worse off (in the short-term or perhaps forever) in order to create new industries and economic opportunities that generate greater profit and economic wealth.[5] For Schumpeter, capitalism naturally destroys previous economic orders (old companies, industries, etc.) in order to reconfigure old orders into new economic orders marked by the emergence of new companies and industries that are more efficient and profitable, expanding economic wealth and growth. Although Schumpeter thought that creative destruction paradoxically leads to the failure of capitalism itself,[6] neoliberal economists, such as Milton Friedman and Friedrich Hayek, argue that creative destruction ultimately enables economic growth and sustainability within free-market capitalism.[7] By attempting to "soften" such creative destruction through government regulation, neoliberal economists insist that capitalism will be robbed of its efficacy in producing unprecedented wealth and economic growth. Hence, the "march toward progress" involves a "creative" destructive force, which is not a negative reality as this creative destruction enables global capitalism to become more efficient (more profitable).

Benjamin's depiction of the angel of history categorically rejects this neoliberal idea that the destructive forces of capitalism are ultimately "creative goods." Benjamin asserts that the effects of capitalism have been catastrophic not simply creative within human history.

This angel of history attempts to render visible the human carnage and large-scale devastation that has resulted from Western systems (such as neoliberal market economies), which necessities a different kind of future hope that is not grounded in the unfulfilled neoliberal promise of progress. In fact, one might suggest that this idea of creative destruction is a secular eschatology of sorts in which history moves toward the promise of material wealth and abundance for all. Benjamin uses the "angel of history" as an image to disrupt this false promise and secular *telos*.

To be sure, Benjamin's "angel of history" has been subject to multiple interpretations. One might argue that Benjamin presents the angel of history as on our side within the historical project of liberation, although the angel is unable to intervene (it does not have the power to do so). However, he does describe the angel of history in Klee's painting as longing "to remain in the present for a while, actualizing historical redemption by awakening death and reconstructing the destroyed past."[8] For Benjamin, the angel of history provides possibilities of hope and redemption within history. If Benjamin's angel of history offers a theological notion of hope and redemption within the context of capitalist crisis, what might this redemption entail?

Benjamin situates his idea of history and redemptive hope within the tradition of Jewish Messianic thought. In particular, the angel of history shows Benjamin's understanding of the dialectical relation between the Christian baroque ideal and Jewish mysticism.[9] Christian Baroque was an artistic style that was associated with European art and architecture during the seventeenth and eighteenth centuries, particularly in Italy where Roman Catholicism was dominant. The Roman Catholic Church was a highly influential patron of this form of art as its Counter Reformation (a movement to combat the spread of Protestantism) employed emotional, realistic, and dramatic art as a means of propagating Catholic faith. In particular, the Christian baroque style often dramatized classical doctrines of the human fall and redemption through paintings, architecture, and other artistic expressions. It depicted the tragic view of life through human sin and God's providential act in human history. Christian religion during this time determined many aspects of baroque art. The Christian baroque perspective reflected the classical Christian view that history is in a process of continuous decay. This decay is the wreckage, "the pile of bodies," and general catastrophe that the angel is not able to turn away from, that the angel can directly intervene into and alter.

Within Catholic baroque, angels are often depicted as messengers and agents of God that can act in history, responding to catastrophe.[10]

Yet, Benjamin seems to use Jewish mysticism as a way to temper the intervening capacity of angels within the Christian baroque ideal. According to the *kabbalah*, Jewish mysticism expresses the belief that it is not the angel's responsibility to intervene and make whole the catastrophe of history, but it is the Messiah's responsibility.[11] Benjamin stipulates that historical materialism (society's movement through economic modes of production due to class struggle in efforts to realize a socialist or free, collective way of life, sharing basic necessities for surviving and thriving) cannot be successful without the Messiah.[12] This is where Benjamin makes the leap to messianic belief. The past is so horrific that even the ideal historical materialist cannot redeem the past. Human beings cannot redeem the past on their own. For Benjamin, the only way redemption can come is from the Messiah. In fact, *Thesis on the Philosophy of History* is clearly one of his last works, and the final paragraph about the Jewish quest for the Messiah provides a traumatic culmination to Benjamin's work, with its themes of destruction, Jewish heritage, and the fight between good and evil. The Messiah sets in motion the Messianic Age, which is the age of universal peace and justice.[13] While this brief account is in no way exhaustive of Benjamin's thought on Jewish Messianic thought, this brief account offers a glimpse into how he understands the ways in which redemption or the Messianic Age is actualized: through divine forces outside of the human historical process.

While redemption largely was found in the "Messianic return" for Benjamin, he does provide a space wherein humans participate in the redemption of history. Benjamin asserts, "like every generation that preceded us, we have been endowed with a weak messianic power, a power to which the past has claim. That claim cannot be settled cheaply."[14] This "weak messianic power" is the ability we have to make the ground ready for redemption. It is "weak" in the sense that it cannot proclaim the end of history. Only the arrival of the Messiah can do that.[15] Yet, similar to the Messiah, this power has the ability to "arrest the flow of time" in the form of an interruption.[16] In this interruption, the history of the oppressed is redeemed "from the ideological forces that have distorted it."[17] This interruption is about disrupting the flow of meaning related to "history," by turning to the past dreams and longings of oppressed ancestors who yearned to actualize their visions of justice and peace.

For him, progress is not achieved by moving forward in history; rather redemption lies in turning to the past in order to see what the past speaks about, what horrors from the past need to be made right. As seen in the painting, the angel of history's face is "turned towards the past" for Benjamin. This is critically important because the past can only be redeemed by turning back to see what the hopes, dreams and promises of the ancestors were. Oppressed communities from the past cannot "turn to their liberated grandchildren" for a future of hope. They must turn backward and critically remember the dreams and hopes "lodged in the hearts and minds of their oppressed ancestors."[18] Benjamin calls the hopes of past ancestors "dream images." It is about the redemption of dream images and these are the seeds of protest, the grounding of projects toward a liberating future. This space for human action in redemption is critical because we must fan "the spark of hope in the past,"[19] remembering these dream images in order to resurrect murdered possibilities. The past is the true abode of future possibilities.

Benjamin's notion of redemption through redeeming and retrieving past hopes aims at a primary task: to disclose and "unearth the hidden utopian emancipatory potential which was betrayed in the actuality of a past revolution and in its final outcome."[20] This hidden potential from the past in the form of hopes and revolutionary dreams do not die as the bearers of those dreams do. Instead, these radical-emancipatory potentials continue to "insist" as types of "historical specters, which haunt the revolutionary memory, demanding their enactment, such that the later proletarian revolution should also redeem (or put to rest) these ghosts of the past."[21] These alternate versions of the past persisting in a spectral form constitute the "openness" of the historical process.[22]

These hidden, emancipatory potentials or past revolutionary hopes are "what-if" histories. Slovenian philosopher and cultural theorist Slavoj Zizek asserts, "The first thing to note is that the what if histories are part of a more general ideological trend, of a perception of life that explodes the form of the linear, centered narrative and renders it as a multi-form flow."[23] What-if histories point to the problem of history itself, that the idea of objective history is often the narrative of the victors, of the imperial conquerors. Consequently, we seem to be haunted by the "chanciness" of alternate versions of history and reality.[24] Rather than closed and fixed, history and the future remain an "open situation" and this view expresses the notion "that other possible outcomes are not simply cancelled but continue to haunt us as specters of what might have been, conferring on our 'true' reality the status of extreme fragility and contingency."[25] These histories speak of injustices that cry out for redemption, injustices we may forget. These "what-if" histories remind us how bad things are and prompt us to repair past abuses, atrocities, and infractions. They urgently *compel us to act to realize a different future sitting inside of the present.*

These "what-if" histories signal a postmodern commitment to the legitimacy of oppressed communities' alternative histories, which are often rendered inaudible and invisible. In fact, one might infer from the idea of what-if histories that "the actual history that we live is itself a kind of realized alternative history, the reality we have to live in because, in the past, we failed to seize the moment and act."[26] For example, the overturning and ending of formal segregation in the United States, at one point, was only the "stuff of hope" as oppressed black communities stared down the failures of the Emancipation Proclamation to liberate them. The dream of ending formal segregation in this country was a what-if history that had not yet been lived into, a history that continued to "insist" upon being actualized, haunting the American democratic imaginary. With the prophetic sacrifices of many Civil Rights leaders, oppressed black communities were able to "hope against all hope" in realizing the formal dismantling of early Jim Crow laws. However, a new form of legal segregation based on race continues to persist, a kind of racial apartheid that can be seen through mass incarceration in this country. Coined by legal theorist Michelle Alexander, the "New Jim Crow" disproportionately imprisons young black men and women, signaling a prison industrial complex that continues to disenfranchise poor black men and women in relation to employment, housing, and more based on race. Structural racism persists.

The history we live in now (characterized by the New Jim Crow) is because we have failed to seize the moment and act on past revolutionary visions of racial justice and equality. These past revolutionary hopes are now "what if" histories that continue to await actualization. The persistence of structural racism demands that people seize the moment and act in order to call forth a repressed past, a what if history, into the present for realization, the realization of racial justice that is unfinished business. This example affirms the oddity of "history" as an open situation, an opportunity and invitation to call forth what has been envisioned from the past, what we have been unable to live into. We live in a history that is still being written from the present.

This kind of thinking is what one might call "thinking backwards." In thinking backwards, we "have to leap back in time, before the fateful decisions were made or before the accidents occurred that generated the state which now seems normal to us, and the way to do so, to render palpable this open moment of decision, is to imagine how, at that point, history might have taken a different turn."[27] However, in talking about historical repetition or thinking backwards, I do not mean that we can simply make the one right choice by returning to the past. Rather, it's about being able to *discern the possibility of different choices* as well as which choices could go fatefully wrong.[28] Thinking backwards expresses one truth: our "understanding of actual history always implies a (hidden or not) reference to alternative histories – what really happened is perceived against the background of what might have happened, and this alternate possibility is offered as a possible path we should follow today."[29] Thinking backwards to what-if histories is part of the "redemptive" process. We "redeem the past" by rehearsing and repeating past revolutionary efforts, being different possible choices, until we finally actualize the missed potential.[30]

Benjamin's theological idea of redemption offers a Janus-faced notion of redemption and hope. Such redemption is entirely dependent upon an apocalyptic view of the coming Messiah but also wholly dependent upon human efforts oriented toward remembering and repeating past hopes and revolutionary dreams, *until they are actualized*. Such an apocalyptic idea of redemption focuses on the importance of Divine agency *and* human intervention within and beyond human histories to effect hope and the final act of universal peace and justice. It is not humans that can singularly cause redemption within human history but God who comes to offer the final act of redeeming hope beyond the histories of the world. Such a view of redemption accords a primary role to Divine agency in actualizing the fulfillment of human meaning and hope within the world.

Although such a theological view frames redemption in Divine terms, it also makes room for human agency. Benjamin's view holds human agency in tension with the Divine role in the narrative of redemptive history. We are called to "fan into flame" past revolutionary efforts. Within this theological view, human moral action is about oppressed communities turning their gaze back to the failed dreams of their ancestors, which *makes ready the grounding of redemption*. This grounding of redemption through human revolutionary action to actualize the oppressed past is about hope being a real possibility against death-dealing forces of hegemonic oppression. Hope is not immortal. It is vulnerable and often can be easily exterminated. Writing in the middle of the Holocaust as a Jew, Benjamin knew that the "killing of hopes is the most common of human pastimes."[31] Hope that resides in the past is often murdered with the bearers of such hopes and dreams. However, remembering and repeating past hopes, having faith in their realization, points to the possibility of them being resurrected and redeemed. Hope can be revived. Hence, human efforts in making the ground ready for redemption in the face of diabolic forces of oppression is critical to the larger narrative of Divine redemption in history. In particular, oppressed communities must gaze backward and return to the egalitarian visions of love and justice lodged in the hearts and minds of those who have come before them.

However, critical questions certainly linger for me in relation to Benjamin's work. For instance, I am somewhat uneasy with how Benjamin situates human agency in relation to Divine agency. The Messiah is the primary agent in his idea of the "Messianic Age," being the final point of universal peace and justice. This account of how peace and justice come about may not allow enough room for humans to work creatively toward peace and justice. Although communities help to make the "ground ready" for redemption through a "weak Messianic power" that we possess (which signals a different concept of moral agency), the final act is nevertheless in the hands of a Divine agent who breaks into historical time suddenly. One may be drawn to how human communities can "make the ground ready" but also may wonder what is lost in human action being constricted only to this kind of role within the arc of redemptive history.

At a more fundamental level, one might also question if history can be redeemed or be redemptive. Could it be that human history is creative but not redemptive? The historical process discloses many ambiguities and complexities on the "redeemability" of history in relation to human oppression. If redemption of history promises and guarantees both the meaning of life and its fulfillment, it may be that human beings cannot redeem history as such but rather act creatively within history toward ultimate meaning, transcendence, and hope. Certainly oppressed communities have acted creatively at particular periods in history to reclaim agency, meaning, and hope.

Redeeming the past does not need to be equated with "redeeming history" as such. Can we redeem the past (revolutionary efforts from the past), a past that should not necessarily be equated with a linear narrative of History but rather narratives of past-oppressed ancestors who never experienced the actualization of their longings for justice and peace? Could "redeeming the past" say something about remembering "dead" voices and their yearnings from the past that can take new life among the living? The best way to honor and remember ancestors from the past and their struggles is perhaps to help them speak to the living. We must pursue dialogue with the dead, helping their voices to be heard again. Past voices need their due justice, an opportunity to breathe new life into the present from the past.[32] So in redeeming the past, it does not need to mean reconstructing the original meaning of the past or restoration to some previously utopian state. Rather, redeeming the past has to do with being "firmly convinced that even the dead will not be safe from the enemy if he is victorious."[33] Both the past and dead are never safe if the oppressor's victories allow him to determine the past or what the past means.

Consequently, when I speak of redeeming the past, I refer to *recasting our relationship to the past in order to reconstitute the meanings of the past.* The histories of oppressed communities challenge the dominant histories and their concomitant meanings, which are often in service to the powerful. We must be able to re-imagine the meanings of the past (especially by turning to the histories of the vanquished) and employ these meanings toward emancipatory projects. Remembering or redeeming what if histories are essential to ensuring that narratives of oppression are not denied but acknowledged, opening the way up for honest exchange over what human flourishing might entail for all. My way of understanding redemption is unlike Benjamin's idea of redemption, as his idea envisions some eschatological condition of final freedom. To the contrary, my idea of redemption might be understood as an *ongoing practice of reclaiming* a suffering or wounding experience of oppression in order to participate in meaning making, which offers alternate interpretations of the past in order to fight domination and hegemony. This idiom of redemption, I think, also avoids the damage that has often been wrought by redemptive language within Jewish and Christian theologies in which redemption often involved the sanctioning of divine violence against "pagans" and racialized others (Canaanites, Native Americans, Africans, etc.) in order to liberate another group or bring about "universal salvation."

While I offer a more postmodern idea of redemption, Benjamin's "retrieval" of a Jewish Messianic tradition is *defiant* (although it is cryptic and somewhat absolutizing). His retrieval of this tradition allows us to leap outside of the taken-for-granted ways in which we think and live, inviting us to re-imagine how we perhaps understand the past, redemption, the dead, power, religion, and more. His thought also helps us creatively imagine and foster new forms of communion between the past, present, and future. Moreover, Benjamin asserts that we have a "weak Messianic power." We can remember the dead and share kinship and solidarity with them. The greatest danger is that the memory of oppression from previous generations will be suppressed and forgotten. In "re-awakening" the past (or reclaiming "what-if" histories), we rescue the cause of the dead from the obscurity of forgotten histories, which are often rendered invisible by victorious oppressors. While I disagree with Benjamin placing primary emphasis on Divine agency in transforming society, I acknowledge that he does reserve a small space wherein one might articulate a hope actualized from within human histories, a hope that is the stuff of human yearnings and action.

Although I have presented some objections to Benjamin in efforts to render distinctive what I mean by "redeeming the past," I think it is important to remember that Benjamin's idea of the redemption of history, particularly in the "apocalyptic key" that he writes, is less about a biblical fundamentalist view of the return of Christ and more about writing a future of hope that detects both forthcoming horrors and potential hope. It is about the discernment of inevitable catastrophe in historical and capitalist processes as well as the emergence of a new social order through radical intervention. This "apocalyptic point" can be seen in the ecological breakdown we are experiencing, in the digital control over our lives, in the radical commodification even of the human subject, in the all-out exploitation of people of color in relation to the prison industrial complex, and in the almost inevitable movement toward nuclear war. To use Zizek's language, "apocalypse at the gates" is about the impending doom that characterizes our technocratic, greedy, profit-driven way of life around the globe within the context of neoliberal capitalist processes.

Womanist Religious Critiques of Progress

Benjamin's angel of history and Zizek's "what-if" histories resonate with postmodern womanist religious projects on neoliberal economy. Womanist literature highlights how marginalized women of color question and challenge the neoliberal promise of progress through the devastating realities they experience. These women are able to uncover "the pile of bodies" the angel points to in the Klee painting (the bodies of their sister-friends, mothers, aunts, cousins, and others who endure the sex trade and other forms of violent gender labor due to neoliberalism). Poor women of color around the world question the idea that we are pulled forward by happiness and global peace within our world economy as they endure many maddening patterns of neoliberalism. Instead, they are pushed from behind and forced to face the horrors and atrocities that they continue to experience from the past and into the present within capitalist processes. "Paradise" (the utopian idea of progress and social harmony) then is not the actual reality they experience; instead, they experience "wreckage upon wreckage," and this chokes and strangles any hope they might project into the future. However, because competition and profit are seen as the end goals of global markets, the economic abuses that poor women of color experience are not seen as catastrophic but as "unintended consequences" within the best economic model available to human societies.

Womanist religious thought would challenge Benjamin and Zizek to consider how women of color's experiences of exploitation substantiate the charge that the neoliberal promise of progress remains unfulfilled. In fact, neither of these scholars (Benjamin or Zizek) integrates race or gender analyses into their intellectual discourses on capitalist hegemony. Womanist perspectives on neoliberal economy privilege the empirical experiences of poor women among the African and Caribbean diasporas in order to deconstruct the myth of progress. Any religious critique of neoliberalism and its secular myth of progress must be grounded in a social analysis of poor women of color's diverse experiences, as they disproportionately bear the brunt of neoliberal cruelties. For black feminist and womanist religious thought, deconstructing this myth can be done through turning to the contradictions poor women of color endure around the world. This critique is rooted in uncovering the material deprivation and exploitation these women experience in order to disrupt this linear narrative. Neoliberalism exacerbates forms of violence against women, particularly women in poor countries. The narrative of progress is "unrobed" and left naked before breeding discontents endured by poor women of color.

The global sex industry is a major site that exposes neoliberalism's adverse and maddening impact on poor women of color. The explosion of the global sex industry has been largely in response to the effects of neoliberal globalization on developing countries. With poor countries trapped in debt, there have been diminishing prospects of employment for men and women, a lack of opportunity in traditional businesses, cuts in social services programs that have especially helped women and children, and a decrease in government revenues as many national governments attempt to pay back the astronomical debt they now possess due to unfair IMF and World Bank loans. Consequently, it has become important for people within these countries to think more creatively of ways to make profit and generate a living. Unfortunately, such conditions have deeply affected women in these countries. Human trafficking of women and children into the sex industry is an increasingly popular way to make a profit.[34] A considerable amount of research indicates that debt has had a disastrous effect on government programs (such as healthcare and education) for women and children in developing nations. Austerity and structural adjustment programs that the IMF and World Bank often mandate to developing countries who borrow money also produce unemployment in these countries, adversely affecting women and children. In response to these deleterious economic conditions, women turn to informal domestic work, sex work, and subsistence food production.[35]

Examining the economy of desire, pleasure and profit allow one to see how neoliberalism is intimately connected to corporate economics and policies around the world that partner with "shadow economies" in commodifying poor women of color's sexual and affective labor. The global sex industry is not a "shadow economy" separate and oppositional to governments. Rather, governments within poor countries depend upon the global sex industry to generate revenue to pay down debt and maintain national infrastructure, which provides greater wealth to global networks of finance and capital in "developed" worlds. As a result, many forms of gender violence associated with the global sex industry is directly supported and reinforced by nation-states and global markets. This direct connection between the global sex industry and neoliberal economy belies the narrative of progress that underlines free-market theories that support globalization. The narrative of progress remains unfulfilled for the majority of the world's population. This is neoliberalism's blind spot: it is ravaging entire communities around the globe and poor women are especially affected due to the cutting of social service programs that have helped them survive in the past.

In discussing the global sex industry, an important conceptual distinction within sex trade involves the difference between the coerced human trafficking of women's bodies and voluntary forms of sex tourism in which women choose to sell their bodies in exchange for other things such as visas and marriage. This distinction is important because it highlights that although sex workers' sexual and affective labor is objectified and exploited, some of these women do retain social agency. All sex workers should not be reduced simply to victims without any sense of social agency. As Anne McClintock notes, "Depicting sex workers as slaves only travesties the myriad, different experiences of sex workers around the world. At the same time, it theoretically confuses social agency and identity with social *context*."[36] Many women who choose sex work are women with capabilities of making their own labor choices. This is clearly seen through sex tourism around the world in which poor women consciously choose to sell their bodies in order to "buy" their way into Western countries through marriage. While this distinction is important in foregrounding these women's sense of agency, these labor choices are nevertheless within the exploitative circuits of global capitalism that limit opportunities and choices for these women. These women remain locked in an economic system that disables them from making other kinds of choices due to the dearth of opportunities present. Most importantly, households and even communities within poor countries become dependent on these women's labor choice to sell their bodies as poverty and unemployment persists.

Not only are households and communities becoming dependent on women's bodies for their survival but governments are also becoming dependent on the commodification, selling, and purchasing of women's bodies and labor for male pleasure. Pleasure and profit are intricately bound together by the purchasing, objectification, and consumption of women of color's sexual labor. In response to decreasing revenue, governments within the Global South have turned to tourism as a strategy for development. In many countries, the entertainment industry includes sex tourism and its "shadow economy." In fact, both have grown alongside each other. Sex tourism has become one major strategy in cultivating economic development within poor nations desperate for employment, revenue, and hard currency. The sex trade is then crucial to expanding the entertainment industry and tourism in many poor nations, which in turn leads to greater government revenue. These links are *structural* in that the commodification and selling of women's bodies are not merely discrete actions or symptomatic of an illegal economy. Sex tourism is built into the economic and social institutions of these societies, which profits from the objectification and consumption of women's bodies.[37]

One can easily turn to how the commodification of women of color's sexual and affective labor plays out as some poor women sell sex for visas. For these women, they are engaging in a familiar strategy within the context of global capitalism: they are attempting to capitalize on the same global conditions that exploit them. They capitalize on sex tourism by using their sexual labor to "buy" visas to the United States and Europe, hoping for a way out of poverty through marriage. To be clear, sex work is exploitative and often involves the forced involvement of women and girls around the world. However, as discussed, it is important not to depict all sex workers as slaves and victims. There are different experiences among sex workers around the world. And some of these women are consciously and willingly making their own labor choices, opting to perform sex work in order to survive. For some women, they articulate a sense of social agency within the sex work they do, while other women may not feel any sense of agency at all. Yet, it is reasonable to argue that most of these women remain caught in a web of global economic relations that never offer them what they ultimately want (well-being and thriving), which reinforces the exploitative nature of sex work despite some of these women's sense of personal agency in relation to their labor choices.

Sociologist Saskia Sassen writes about Dominican sex workers in the town of Sosua as one example of how women of color's sexual and affective labor is commodified within neoliberal economy. Sosua is a small town in the Dominican Republic that has built a strong entertainment industry and tourist context through sex work. Consequently, these women in Sosua sell sex for visas, which is really about getting out of their poverty-stricken country through marriage. Some might argue that these women are exercising agency in relation to their labor choice as most of these women do not have pimps and retain all of their earnings. But how Dominican women's bodies in Sosua are displayed and commodified, particularly online, is deeply problematic. Online travel services provide names of "tour guides" that give information and allow consumers to share information about trips. One sex tourist who had visited Sosua stated that he was impressed with the availability of "dirt cheap colored girls" there.[38] Another sex tourist stated that he felt like he was in heaven as there were a plethora of colored girls for everyone's taste.[39] In fact, a number of articles and ads in European magazines portray these women as sexually voracious. These women are reduced to *things* that can be consumed, according to one's taste or preference. Cultural anthropologist Denise Brennan even reports that a café owner in Sosua stated that Dominican women have become known as prostitutes worldwide and that they are this country's "biggest export."[40]

These women however use the capitalist system to reach for what they ultimately desire: a visa to escape poverty and live better. They often perform sex work by pretending to be "in love" with the tourist they meet, in hopes that this relationship will bloom and lead to them securing a visa. Securing a visa to Europe or the United States allows these women to dream of a better life marked by abundance, wealth, and more opportunities for themselves and their children. This is what Brennan refers to as "transnational courting." These women hope to secure a visa through selling their body and pretending to offer their love to the men they engage. Sex work and the selling of their bodies are seen as a stepping-stone to migration to other countries and a way out of permanent cycles of deprivation. Carla, a first time sex worker in Sosua, asserted that women from their country are drawn to this town because they not only dream of an airline ticket but also ultimately dream of a visa, which they can only obtain through marriage.[41]

Female sex workers of Sosua sell their bodies for purchase because they imagine that "foreign men will provide them with material comfort and better treatment."[42] They hope that European or American men can "rescue" them from cycles of poverty and the complete absence of opportunities. They believe that they can trade love and romance for financial security and economic well-being. Love for them becomes something to be bought and sold. The idea of "love" then takes on a different meaning within the context of neoliberal globalization and its deleterious effects on countries like the Dominican Republic. These women's poor environment causes them to capitalize off of the very commodified practices that seek to exploit them within neoliberal economy.

Yet, these women's migration stories, should they get a visa and marry the men they meet, often end disastrously. The case of a Dominican sex worker, Nanci is traumatic and heart wrenching. She tells a story of falling in love with a German man close to her age that would come to Sosua yearly. He spoke Spanish and treated her little son very well. He helped her get a tourist visa so she could visit him in Germany. While in Germany, she met his parents and friends. After marrying and living in Germany for a year, Nanci and Frank moved back to Sosua and had a little girl. However, over a short time period, Frank abandoned Nanci and ran off with another Dominican sex worker. Nanci saw less of Frank over time and he stopped sending financial support. After a few years, Frank left Sosua with another Dominican sex worker and moved back to Germany. Nanci experienced a reversal of fortune. She now has two children and is living in even worse conditions. She gambled and loss in the sex trade.[43]

Nanci's case demonstrates that these sex workers continue to operate within the context of exploitative neoliberal capitalist relations, despite their feelings of personal agency. These women are driven by the dream of what visa and marriage can buy. Yet, these dreams are really fantasies as very few of them actually make it out of their impoverished environments. Many of these women express their transnational relationships in terms of an economic strategy but this strategy rarely works for them. They attempt to fashion strategies to gain control over their economic lives. Globalization has so deeply altered the lives of poor women of color around the world that many of them simply feel out of control, unable to survive. They are not exempt from a desire to gain control over their economic destinies within the unpredictable context of global markets that keep them mired in poverty. These women attempt to use commodified processes for their advantage. But this rarely works. Their sexual and affective labor remain commodities to be bought, sold, exploited, and consumed for the benefit of wealthy men around the world. As a result, even love, a non-economic gift, is redefined within the neoliberal context of market exchange.

Governments and local economies in the Global South who financially benefit from the migration and trafficking of these women often indirectly promote sex work. Businesses, underground traffickers, and even governments around the world end up making money off the backs of these women.[44] Through their earnings, these women "infuse cash into the economies of deeply indebted countries."[45] As a result, the inequitable effects of globalization and the debt trap that poor countries experience motivate governments to profit from underground economies or "shadow economies" such as sex tourism.

Neoliberal globalization has also produced labor dynamics in the Global North that feed into the commodification of women of color's bodies and lives. Human trafficking is not a problem in the South; it is also an exploitative problem that the Global North deals with. For example, the city of Atlanta (Georgia) in the United States is one of the top cities for the human trafficking of girls around the world.

While Atlanta has been known for the Civil Rights Movement and the upward mobility of African-American communities, it is now a top destination for the human trafficking of girls and child exploitation. In Atlanta, some 1,000 girls and women were forced to prostitute themselves. These women and girls were of ages between 13 and 25. Moreover, an internal police email stated that many of these women were Korean.[46] Human trafficking is often seen as something done within "Third World" countries. However, sex work is a central activity in one of America's most well known cities and disproportionately includes women of color.

In addition, the Global North commodifies and exploits women of color's domestic labor. Global cities in the North have led to a demand for informal domestic workers such as nannies and maids. These women are often immigrant women of color who become the nannies of a highly paid professional class of workers located in urban cities such as New York, Paris, London, and Berlin. These low-wage workers maintain the lifestyles of these professionals. Such low-wage workers are rendered invisible within the context of global economy. Moreover, their labor is commoditized. They are not treated like human beings or subjects but as things to be employed and used within this informal sector. While the work of being a nanny or maid may not be overtly "sexual" work (but sometimes it is), it still involves the objectification and commodification of these women's labor. These women are treated as human objects to be sold and bought within the informal domestic market.

Sociologist Joy Zarembka tells the story of Ruth Gnizako, a 52-year-old West African woman, who was approached by a wealthy leader at the World Bank to serve as a nanny and housekeeper back in the United States. When she arrived in Maryland (where the family lived), she was required to work around the clock, even sleeping with the parents' set of newborn twins. She was allowed no time off or vacation days. When the family left out each day, she was required to wait outside in the hallway of the apartment building until someone returned. In addition, the wife and husband repeatedly beat and abused Ruth and denied her the right to return to West Africa.[47]

The neighbors would hear Ruth screaming and call the police. When the police showed up, Ruth was unable to communicate in English, as her first language was French. She would try to re-enact the beatings but her employers said she was crazy. As a result, she was locked up in a mental institution for a few weeks and by the time the French authorities were contacted to help translate, she was sedated by drugs, unable to communicate the details of her abuse. Frustrated, the mental hospital would ask the employers to retrieve Ruth and the violent cycle would begin again. Only after a few more beatings, did neighbors step in, help rescue Ruth and talk to the police authorities about the abuse. However, because Ruth could not appeal or participate in the US Justice Department, she was simply deported and did not receive a penny of compensation for her domestic work.[48]

In part, this problem of abuse in global cities in relation to informal domestic work that immigrant women often see as their best opportunities is exacerbated by the commodification of informal domestic work. In terms of hiring maids, the customer (highly paid professional) hires the service, not the maid, and speaks directly with the team leader, who is usually authorized to speak to the customer about the service that will be rendered. The customer and actual domestic worker (maid) do not necessarily need to interact. All issues are taken care of through the company and all problems that arise are directed to the local franchise owner. And these women's concerns for wage and working conditions are ignored, as her experience is not valued. She is simply part of an economic transaction or financial exchange. What the customer buys is a service and the maid becomes nothing more than a cog in the machine of domestic work. She is dehumanized. Moreover, her suffering and underpaid labor is reinforced by the middle class professional's need to consume and be pleasured.[49]

The maid or housecleaner is a woman of color and often an immigrant. What is often implicitly assumed is that a woman with dark skin and broken English is a person of inferior status or *something* to be talked at instead of *someone to be engaged*. Unfortunately, highly paid professionals are reproducing exploitative global inequalities in their households that adversely affect poor women of color. This growing servant economy is driven by the need to consume and purchase the labor of women of color who are then treated as objects instead of subjects. Even with nannies, these women (again mostly immigrant women) are treated as something that simply cleans instead of someone who should be treated with respect and dignity as she works. For instance, nannies constantly complain about children who never think about cleaning up behind themselves because a nanny is present (which fosters irresponsibility in the child one might argue). Even worse, nannies complain about parents who do not hold their children accountable to any standard of conduct when dealing with the nanny, which makes nannies feel powerless and worthless within the context of their employed site.

The global sex industry and the informal domestic economy belie global capitalism's assertion of movement toward progress for poor people around the world. Clearly, poor women of color in the Global South and North continue to be ravaged by global economic processes. Poor women of color constantly confront the commodification of their labor within the context of neoliberal globalization and the patterns of inequities that are produced. They are not seen as subjects that can give, share, and receive love and respect. They are seen as objects to be instrumentally used within the context of global economy. In short, neoliberal economy's promise of progress remains unfulfilled for the vast majority of poor women of color throughout the world. As a result, the assumption that any fallout from neoliberal global practices is part of "unintended consequences" of markets falls apart. Neoliberal forms are ravaging the majority of the world's citizens, which disclose the savagery associated with neoliberalism.

Although poor women of color are adversely affected by global market economy, oppressed women of color question and resist neoliberal forces by turning to the past dreams and hopes of those women (and men) who have come before them, who have been denied justice and care. They use the unrealized hopes of their past ancestors as the basis for their longings to actualize justice, care, and love in the present and future. Similar to the angel of history who sees catastrophe in our present capitalist times, these women are fully aware that the neoliberal myth of progress is untrue. Yet, they hope against hope. A number of womanist projects foreground many marginalized women of color who lead social movements, acknowledging that these women's articulations of hope are grounded in both a Divine promise of a radical new community and human agency that partners with the Divine in actualizing such hopes. I will turn in chapter 5 to the ways in which social movements among marginalized women of color resist neoliberalism through a politics of hope.

Although Benjamin's "angel of history" provides religious resources for womanist critiques of the neoliberal myth of progress, womanist projects also critique and enlarge the moral vision and imagination associated with Benjamin's concept of redemption and hope within market societies. For instance, Benjamin is wary of transforming "the political" when speaking of redemption, as the realm of God's ultimate act of redemption is *beyond* human history and its temporal institutions (political, social, and economic). Consequently, Benjamin's moral vision and imagination associated with human history (and therefore market societies) is circumscribed. For womanist projects, moral vision and imagination are enlarged to consider the ways in which women of color articulate redemption *within* the parameters of human history itself. For womanist projects (i.e., works of Katie Cannon, Emilie Townes, Jacqueline Grant, Kelly Brown Douglas, Monica Coleman, etc.), human efforts in making the ground ready for redemption in the face of diabolic forces of oppression is critical to how hope is actualized. Hope is not just beyond history but a "now" hope that envisions the transformation of temporal institutions in efforts to inaugurate justice, care, love, and cooperation. While Benjamin tends to see redemption as a radical break with history, womanist thinkers emphasize a moral vision and imagination that can be actualized and achieved *within history* through human co-partnering with the Divine. The point here is that actualizing hope within and beyond human histories is not mutually exclusive for many womanist religious projects. They can be complexly held together in fostering rich imaginations about hope.

Many postmodern womanist religious projects reflect a *realized eschatology* rather than a strict apocalyptic eschatology.[50] Realized eschatology does not necessarily see redemption as being contingent on some final act that comes outside of history (Jesus coming, Messiah's return, etc.). Rather, realized eschatology points to the possibilities for rebirth, renewal, and "becoming" in the present as the seeds of hope have already been planted in the past that await to be actualized. For instance, within womanist and postcolonial Christian theologies, Jesus' ministry is seen as paradigmatic of how redemption and hope can be actualized in the present. We do not need to wait for some final culminating act outside of history to experience redemptive hope. This realized eschatology provides rich, fertile ways of re-thinking moral imagination in the present in relation to neoliberal economy. Womanist commitments to a moral imagination critiques Benjamin by contending that hopeful transformation can occur within human history, which compels one to consider what kind of moral imagination and action is required in the present.

Womanist postmodern theologian Karen Baker-Fletcher captures this eschatological vision that seeks the moral transformation of hearts and oppressive structures in the present. She states, " For womanists, eschatology does not have to do with the 'last things' or 'end time' in any far-off, abstract, otherworldly sense. Rather, eschatological hope and envisionment have to do with the daily, moment-by-moment business of living."[51] For Fletcher, the "Reign of God" stands at the center

of personal and social salvation. She employs a liberationist herme-
neutic in how she reads the Christian gospels and other scriptures,
arguing that these scriptures point to the actualization of God's reign
of love on earth (within individuals, communities, and societies).
Baker-Fletcher echoes much of black religious and cultural thought
when employing a Social Gospel vision of the kin-dom of God being
"at hand." While Christian reformers Walter Rauschenbusch and
Washington Gladden are known for this nineteenth-century message,
African-Americans were certainly responsible for the birth and shaping of the Social Gospel movement as this movement's realized eschatology could be found in black religious writings, songs, prayers, and
more. Black female religious and social leaders, such as Anna Julia
Cooper and Ida B. Wells, grounded their ideas of social transformation in an interpretation of salvation that comes to morally transform
not just individuals but social instituions. This argument of social
transformation is rooted in a realized eschatology that interprets
Jesus' life and ministry (as well as other non-Christian religious narratives) as an example of *why* social transformation must remain a
possibility: because it inaugurates love, peace, justice, and reconciliation into the present world.

Baker-Fletcher also gestures toward the dangers of fixating on otherworldly eschatological visions. Such otherworldly visions have been
used as tools by the powerful to maintain control. Such otherworldly
visions reinforce the internalization of oppression among marginalized persons. In Alice Walker's novel *The Color Purple,* we meet
Celie, an abused young black woman who lives in the rural South. At
the beginning of Celie's marriage to Mr.__, she internalized the patriarchal abuse she endures, even accepting herself as ugly and unworthy
of love. Walker demonstrates the dangers associated with the otherworldly ideas Celie possessed, which prevented her from exercising
her own agency against her abusive husband. In the novel, we hear
Sophia say to Celie, "You ought to bash Mr.__head open...Think
about heaven later." Over the course of the novel, we witness Celie
shift her religious perspective to a God or Divine force that seeks the
moral transformation and wholeness of individuals, societies, and all
of creation. Celie moves away from traditional ideas of the afterlife,
which kept her from developing the courage to resist her oppression
in the present. She decides to embrace a religious perspective that sees
the transformation of the present order as a possibility.

Making hope a present possibility is critically important within
our global neoliberal moment. As a human community, we can

discern and reclaim past hopes and dreams for more just and loving futures within political economy. Yet, unlike some womanists (Baker-Fletcher), I do not want to *completely exclude* the real benefits of apocalyptic traditions, which radically disrupt the idea that "some kind of hierarchal order is our fate, such that any attempt to challenge it and create an alternative egalitarian order will necessarily end in destructive horror" or abject failure.[52] To be clear, I am not supporting the revival of specific fundamentalist aspects associated with apocalyptic thought such as the return of Jesus Christ within Evangelical Christianity, for instance. Instead, I am intrigued by the ways in which apocalyptic language frames the present order as catastrophic and ridden with crisis, which must give way to a new social order, a different, more egalitarian way of being. The language of apocalypticism seeks to write a future of hope that is different from what we have seen in the present but which the past speaks about. As a result, while a realized eschatology grounds my idea of hope and transformation, the language of apocalypticism nevertheless can function as a form of *defiance* to the status quo and hegemonic power of neoliberal economy. There is certainly a tension between realized and apocalyptic eschatologies that remain fruitful to theorizing hope.

As stated, womanist ideas of hope critique and expand Benjamin's notions of redemption because much of womanist thought argues that God's ongoing redemptive plan is actualized in the present. A number of womanist perspectives maintain the need for a realized eschatology, particularly among marginalized people such as poor women of color.[53] For womanist projects, moral vision and imagination are enlarged to consider the ways in which women of color articulate redemption *within* the parameters of human history itself. As a result, the political (and its temporal institutions) become a site where moral and social transformation is both possible and necessary. Marginalized women of color desperately need to envision new ways of being that can be actualized in the present.

Womanist religious critiques of the myth of progress associated with neoliberalism certainly push Benjamin and Zizek's work in fruitful directions. Womanist religious thought not only provides social analysis as a method in substantiating the argument against the neoliberal promise of progress but also offers a realized eschatology that underwrites moral, social, political, and structural transformation in the present in response to neoliberal forms of life.

The Impossible Possibility: Hope

We are not yet saved. Although scholars, economists, policymakers, and religious leaders announce ways to manage and address the deleterious consequences of global market forces, we remain mired in a declining global order, marked by increasing disparities in income, education, employment, healthcare, and more. We continue to witness the horrors of the global poor living on less than one dollar a day. We also see women being disproportionately represented among the global poor. And the poorest group in the world, children, remain hunger stricken, without basic resources to fulfill their human potentiality. Yet, nations spend money to fight wars for national interests grounded in the rush to grab more money, land, gas, and oil. Corporations then capitalize upon such conditions and further exacerbate and strengthen these disastrous consequences associated with global market forces. This pace of living is not sustainable. It not only is built upon gross imbalances of power but also normalizes patterns of inequity and inequality. A new future within the context of global economy must be imagined. Hope must be revived.

When speaking about writing a future of hope, I mean that there must be a way of "X-raying the present to see what seed of potential shows up, a seed of a potential future that is already in the past and present."[54] A different future is always the future of a particular past and present. We only have a few ways to fashion the future, which is partly conditioned by what has come before us. The future is simply not an "add on" to the present. It must be detectable from within the present. But seeing the potential future in the present is not like seeing a pregnant woman who will give birth.[55] Any potential future is conditioned not only by what is seen in the present but also by what is unseen in the present. There can be many different futures that are seen as impossible or failed, unfamiliar, and even outlandish to the present. A truly genuine new future is not merely a "present extension of the present nor an absolute break from it."[56] If it were either, it would not be recognizable as a truly genuine new future. A new future is not simply a smooth continuity or a radical rupture. It is something new, something different.

When turning to the financial crisis and even economic collapse around parts of the world, what is required is not just a moralizing critique of neoliberal capitalism but an affirmation of something different and new, the contours of new socio-economic arrangements that resonate with a greater egalitarianism. We need to dream dangerously of new alternatives to the existing order. What does it mean to recapture visions of a social order governed by an egalitarian spirit? How do we remain faithful to the egalitarian spirit kept alive over thousands of years through religions of marginalized people and other subversive ideologies critiquing hegemonic systems? How can we reject all traditional hierarchal and community ties that sponsor oppression while simultaneously asserting that a different collective way of being is possible, that just and loving communities can be realized? We might offer *the conditions for the possibility* of a different future. One thing is certain: we are not yet saved. Dreaming dangerously in relation to global political economy is about having the moral courage to imagine and craft new alternatives to the present socio-economic system we find ourselves in. We need alternatives that challenge and disrupt the logic of global neoliberal markets. We need radical interventions into capitalist logic and its alienating ways of being.

In relation to creatively imagining a new socio-economic order, consider two "thought experiments" on ideas of production and love within our economy. Part of imagining new economic alternatives to our global order may be creatively redefining the meaning of "production" in relation to human well-being. Within much of contemporary economic scholarship, production is understood narrowly in an economic sense. However, as Marx reminds us, production means realizing one's essential powers of creativity to transform reality. Production is about the development of human energy and possibility. It is the absolute working out of creative human potentialities. Hence, "production" fulfills any self-fulfilling activity, which includes playing the saxophone, writing a book of poetry, learning a new language, and more. Production is free, self-realizing activity that transforms the world. Production is about meaningful activity that includes friendship, art, creativity, sex, rebellion, laughter, tears, dancing, and much more. From a theological perspective, production is dislodged from its merely economic meaning. Production as meaningful activity can even include spiritual activity. Spiritual activities such as feeding the hungry, clothing the naked, giving to needy, and welcoming immigrants then re-conceptualizes how we view ourselves as productive agents within society. Such spiritual activities redefine how we think about the "Producing Subject." This more expanded concept of production may even make room for fuller human meaning such as compassion, shared wealth, and responsible giving within our economic order.

Another example of imagining new alternatives may also be re-thinking the meaning and practice of love as a profoundly political act. The meaning and practice of love has been lost in our highly com-modified, capitalist culture. The meaning of love has been reduced to a mere feeling or sentiment, something we "fall into." What would it mean to conceptualize love as the practice of compassion, respect, and reciprocity? How would this challenge the notion of love as an impossible ideal? How might this notion of love influence and inform social structures and economic arrangements?

If love is a practice of compassion and respect toward one's neighbor (as well as to all of creation), love is then deeply political, sponsoring an egalitarianism that can serve as a foundation for a new social order. Within some strands of Christian apocalyptic thought, the embodi-ment of love in society is called apocalyptic millenarianism, being "the urge to realize an egalitarian social order of solidarity."[57] Love then as a political practice becomes a universal link, which connects people to each other and allows people to suspend their particular hierarchal affiliations and ties.[58] The real practice of love becomes an option to combat forces of lovelessness and radical human alienation that characterizes global economy and cultures of commodification. Love may be a religious concept but it is important to remember that politics is often grounded in religious views of reality. Every religious view is an ideology of a new collective space (i.e., communities of believers in early Christianity or the *umma* in Islam).[59] I return to love throughout this text.

The point of these two thought experiments is to remember the sig-nificance of moral courage in envisioning a different socio-economic order. We must expand our moral imaginations about the present by turning to the past. These thought experiments invite human com-munities to dream dangerously beyond the limiting strictures of neo-liberal logic and practices. These two thought experiments also draw us into the implications of writing a future of hope. It is about coura-geously envisioning a politics of hope that has always been lodged in the hearts and minds of past ancestors and freedom fighters for a new order. It is about radical interventions into the present order.

The ahistorical assumption of capitalist history as simply progress is an ideological fiction. Catastrophe is inevitable in every capitalist moment that does not question itself. Capitalist systems are gener-ally touted as spreading wealth around the world, being advantageous to the poor as well as the rich. Free-market practices and Western culture are seen as economic saviors to extremely "under-developed nations" who are poverty stricken. The innate goodness and efficacy of global economy are myths and fall apart when turning to global disparities in economics and cultural capital. Capitalism should not be seen as a linear movement through time, which positions the present as "Progress." If neoliberal economy is to be understood singularly as progress then it cannot be understood in terms of its savage inequalities.

Considering neoliberal capitalism as catastrophic, in part, uproots and shocks are understandings of capitalism as a progressive chain of economic events throughout history. It can awaken us to the existential despair and chronic social disappointment that capitalism has engendered for people around the world who are trapped in systems of poverty such as women of color. Neoliberal global economy continues to fuel alienation and displacement for people who are vulnerable and marginalized. The acknowledgment of capitalism as catastrophic awakens one to the "dark side" of market exploitation.

2

Resisting the Acquiring Mode

In the previous chapter, I deconstructed the neoliberal myth of progress that undergirds global capitalism by framing my religious critique around notions of crisis, redemption, and hope. This narrative of progress asserts a false hope, which is grounded in the promise of material abundance and well-being for all. However, this promise has fallen short. Critical theorists and womanists such as Benjamin, Zizek, and Baker-Fletcher remind one that if voices desire to disrupt structural inequities sponsored by global economy, such voices must unsettle what legitimates contemporary capitalist rationality: the myth of progress and the promise of material abundance in the future.

This chapter contends that the transformation of the "self" within neoliberal societies is a necessary precondition for prophetic social action. In much of theological discourse, social transformation is often articulated in binary ways as either individual or community, personal or structural. I seek to move beyond this false division by asking how individual transformation gives way to broader societal change (and vice versa). In order to investigate the individual within neoliberal societies, one must deconstruct what I refer to as the "acquiring mode." The acquiring mode is a neoliberal way of being that defines human meaning based on the material things one can acquire. This mode then shapes the consciousness of the human subject within diverse market societies.

I think Kierkegaard's two discussions on "money as abstraction" and "religious inwardness" can respond to the existential emptiness individuals often experience within a society that is defined by market values of atomic individualism and the selfish pursuit of material things. These two discussions provide religious resources toward a prophetic critique of the acquiring mode associated with neoliberal economies around the world. The quest for religious inwardness or wholeness of self is simultaneously the grounding for prophetic action and witness against the reduction of social values to monetary meaning. The "self" needs to undergo radical transformation away from neoliberal consciousness in order to see oneself and others rightly. Kierkegaard's discourse on how religious inwardness forms morally virtuous selves can offer religious resources in critiquing the acquiring mode within our social and political spheres of society.

In this chapter, I do not offer a reading of Kierkegaard simply to ascertain whether he is womanist or feminist. He clearly did not understand himself as a womanist or feminist. Rather, I am interested in how his two ideas of "money as abstraction" and "religious inwardness" both affirm and open up avenues of thought for womanist religious critiques of neoliberal societies. Kierkegaard offers a religious critique of capital, a critique that remains important to moving beyond equating human meaning to the acquiring of material things. I think that womanist perspectives on neoliberal economy might benefit from Kierkegaard's focus on religious inwardness because it challenges the acquiring mode of society by foregrounding the *telos* toward which our actions are directed and find ultimate meaning: in the love of God/Divine, self, and neighbor. Conversely, womanist religious thought critiques and expands, in interreligious postmodern directions, Kierkegaard's concepts of God and religious inwardness as the grounding of social action.

Counting and Counting: The Acquiring Mode

Within market contexts, the human subject often becomes a commodity through unrestrained competitive impulses, which cause us to define ideas of trust and love according to market practices. Rabid individualism and unrestrained consumerism turn social relationships into mere commercial ones. This commodification of the human subject within neoliberal economies fosters economic exploitation, particularly among those who are most vulnerable. It dehumanizes social bonds and privileges economic profit-maximization as a primary social value. In fact, such capitalist values are even reified by disadvantaged, poor communities as values to be pursued and achieved.

Human meaning is then colonized and commodified within market systems. Human meaning becomes commodified in which human beings see themselves as objects to be bought and sold on the "social status market." This social status market refers to the ways in which human beings derive worth by being able to compete as the most salable commodity among other human "commodities" or personalities. For instance, people within particular industries like law, advertising, finance, writing, and more are constantly forced to measure their worth by how "salable" they are. To be seen as successful, they must overly focus on their ability to "beat out" their competition. They must transform themselves into the preferred commodity or preferred personality in order to land the position or job. As a potential employee, each candidate's sense of human meaning is objectified in the sense that they are only seen as a company instrument that feeds into the bottom line, being organizational profit.

Clearly, this produces a crisis of human meaning itself as one's meaning can only find expression in a "success" that orients itself toward the dehumanizing aspects of neoliberal market logic. This commodification of the human subject becomes a vicious cycle as people perpetuate such practices in order to survive and achieve "success." In fact, this mode of living is worshiped and even lauded as essentially "American" and morally correct (Christian prosperity gospel ideas of wealth as connected to God's favor). In part, this colonization and commodification of human meaning results in the "acquiring mode," which diminishes our ability to share, give, and love within communities.

The acquiring mode of living has several characteristics. It is first an attitude that is devoted to neoliberal values, and its object of worship is material things. This attitude encourages the mode of having as the goal of life. Critical social theorist Eric Fromm reflects on the "having mode." He writes,

> In the having mode, there is no alive relationship between me and what I have. It and I have become things, and I have *it*, because I have the force to make it mine. But there is also a reverse relationship; *it has me*, because my sense of identity, i.e., of sanity, rests upon my having *it* (and as many things as possible). The having mode of existence is not established by an alive, productive process between subject and object; it makes *things* of both object and subject. The relationship is one of deadness, not aliveness.[1]

Late capitalist processes turn both material objects and human subjects into mere things or commodities to be consumed, used, and disposed. For instance, Fromm mentions how the capitalist mode of having objectifies the relationship between private property and the owner.[2] The owner possesses private property but, in many ways, is possessed by such property as it offers a sense of identity and status to the owner. Her property constitutes her sense of self and identity in a capitalist culture that treats property as a symbol of status, influence, and power. Moreover, such property is not oriented toward a shared sense of community in a culture that solely privileges individual ownership and usage. The ownership of private property is not oriented toward the inclusion of others. Hence, this example of private property in capitalist culture is grounded in the having mode of existence in which both the property and owner are treated as objects with no real productive relation.[3]

This idea of ownership even extends further within cultural life. As Fromm suggests, one may *own* one's friends, mates, and even God (presumably one's projected imaginings of God).[4] For example, it is "my mate" or "my partner" who must behave or be what I desire. If this partner deviates from my prescribed rules, I am disturbed because I am fundamentally related to my partner through my power to control them, to make them permanently mine.[5] I do not *share* life or love with my partner. Rather, my mate is a thing, an object under my controlling gaze. Such patriarchal notions of ownership complicate discourses on the humanizing of relationships. My mate is then very similar to the piece of private property in that "it" is something to be possessed and dominated. But the "owning of my mate" also constitutes my sense of self and identity so that I also become objectified and transformed into a mere object as well to be controlled by my partner. We are both subject to each other's objectifying power instead of drawn into a relationship of mutual care, love, and trust. This type of objectifying relationship is life denying. It does not constitute what is "alive" or life giving.[6]

Material objects and objectifying relationships are life denying in the sense that they have no capacity to give, share, love, or create. Human beings or humans "becoming" are constituted by dynamic processes that are evolving, ever changing, and alive. To be human is to be present to one's human capacities to love, give, share, create, and participate in productive activities that unite one to oneself, other humans and creation. Hence, to be human is to be "alive."

Being "alive" as human beings is to engage in productive activity or *non-alienated activity*. In non-alienated activity, I experience myself as the subject. Non-alienated activity "is a process of giving birth to something, of producing something and remaining related to what I produce."[7] My activity is "a manifestation of my powers, that

I and my activity and the result of activity are one."[8] To the contrary, alienated activity does not enable one to experience oneself as a subject of her/his activity. Rather, one experiences the outcome of one's activity as "something over there, separated from me and standing above and against me."[9] In alienated activity, I am *acted upon* by external forces rather than really acting. The "acquiring mode" of living sponsors alienated activity in which human beings are defined and measured by material things, leading to the objectification and "deadness" of human relationships instead of an "aliveness" characterized by non-alienated activity. The crisis of an acquiring mode is that it *supplants non-alienated activity (which is to love, share, and give) with life denying objects of alienated activity (the acquiring of material things), which vitiates and destroys what it means to be human.* This attitude or mode of living thus is not life giving. Instead, it robs us of our humanity.

One readily witnesses the religious legitimation of this acquiring mode that concerns itself only with the "bottom line," being the creation of wealth and accumulation of material things. This acquiring mode of living pervades much of the prosperity gospel movement in the United States and other fundamentalist forms of Christianity around the world that focus on what people materially possess as a sign of God's favor. Within the prosperity gospel movement, leaders "correlate wealth with the quality of one's faith and obedience in God; wealth and health are the results of unwavering faith."[10] Consequently, "those who experience chronic illness or financial duress must lack faith in God's eternal promises of riches and abundance for God's children."[11] To have faith is to possess *things* according to the logic of prosperity gospel. One's faith is measured by one's ability to acquire. Consequently, to not acquire material things or to be poor suggests that the individual has done something wrong. It signals a moral failure in the person, not a failure of ideology.

For sure, prosperity gospel teachings enable affluent persons to justify their extreme wealth in religious and/or theological terms. They are wealthy because they have done the "will of God." Their success is due to right moral action. As a result, many corporations and business leaders are never held accountable for exploitative practices that accrue wealth to them. When a corporation is able to avoid paying a living wage, healthcare, and more to employees who work forty or more hours a week, one must stop and interrogate such economic inequity and the distorted values that drive such economic practices.

Many Christian circles in the United States blame poverty on poor people. For some, part of the Christian responsibility is to increase wealth within society. For example, the religious right foregrounds the "dominion mandate" in which Christians are called to "rule" and "have dominion" within society according to the Bible. Because they argue that unlimited resources are available on God's earth to people who obey (which means persons who live "Christian" lives), poverty is then interpreted as deviance or a sign of disfavor with God. Most importantly, this Christian view ignores and under-estimates the real systemic inequalities that determine how wealth is created and distributed. Because such circles marry their rhetoric to free-market fundamentalism, poverty signals an absence of individual agency and hard work. The poor are culturally represented as not taking advantage of opportunities to lift themselves out of deprivation. Some conservative Christian leaders even equate poverty with a spiritual disease that can be conquered through prayer and tithing.[12] Such logic does not identify how inhumane economic practices of national and multinational corporations reinforce cycles of poverty for people across the globe.

The religious legitimation of this "acquiring mode" that concerns itself only with excessive profit has disastrous implications for laborers and workers around the world. One only needs to turn to sweatshops in Southeast Asia that pay workers pennies on the dollar to understand how inequitable and exploitative corporate practices are in other countries. These practices are either ignored or dismissed when we turn to the religious rhetoric that some Christian groups employ in speaking about poverty as personal irresponsibility, lack of faith, or spiritual disease. The acquiring mode of living that neoliberal market fundamentalism espouses is often framed in religious terminology, making challenges against such religious rhetoric even more difficult because it is cloaked "in the name of God."

Christian religious figures such as Creflo O'Dollar and Paula White often make statements about the source of poverty being due to a lack of faith, which ignore and dismiss why poor populations are often marginalized and deprived in the first place. For instance, poverty is deeply intertwined with racist and inequitable corporate practices in relation to immigration. In our national discourse surrounding immigration policy, Mexican immigrants are targeted as dangerous foreigners taking over "American" jobs with little to no discussion on the ways in which corporations bring Mexican workers to America in order to "cheapen" the labor pool. Even more deceptive, no one talks about the number one cause of job erosion and impoverishment of hardworking farmers and agricultural producers in Mexico which led many of them to the United States in the first place: the 1996 NAFTA treaty which directed almost all corn production to transnational US corporations, corporations small farmers could not compete with, leaving such farmers to economic devastation and dislocation. It seems to some that nothing is more risky than being poor in this country (and world for that matter). Religious statements that blame the poor reinforce this acquiring mode by attempting to ascribe worth and dignity to people in relation to what they have or possess. Even deeper, these statements also presume that the acquiring of wealth *says something about who is worthy or commendable and who is not praiseworthy within society.*

This acquiring mode then complicates discussions of human well-being and flourishing because it is fundamentally uncooperative in character. Individual material success and the acquisition of wealth become central values. To the contrary, social responsibility and justice become foreign and even hostile ideas to market worship. If the value of individual hard work is over-emphasized, then it becomes hard to see or understand how and why social conditions affect or impede people from well-being. This attitude reifies selfish formulations of material success so that structural explanations of deprivation seem non-sensical and a break from accepted conventional capitalist logic. Hence, the complication in discussing thriving and flourishing is not merely that wealthy people do not want to share but that *they do not see their responsibility and human duty as such.* This acquiring mode often *blinds* one from seeing her neighbor as central to the conditions under which her own humanity is actualized. In short, any other mode of living that is not grounded in acquiring things cannot be understood or embraced, as it defies the fundamental rationale of neoliberal capitalist society.

This attitude then distorts human meaning. If I am what I possess, then my worth is reduced to a thing, a mere commodity. My reason for existence as a human being is only in relation to material things and therefore, I do not experience myself as alive, as able to actualize myself and my human capacities to love, share, give, and create. Because a central impulse in human beings is to be loved and love, to experience care and give care, to create and self-actualize, this attitude and its commodifying tendency become crippling to the human spirit. It paralyzes the search for human meaning. It creates identity crises.

This acquiring mode fosters individuals who are not necessarily concerned with deeper religious or philosophical questions about human community, suffering, care, social trust, and more. Instead, such individuals are focused on how other people and things add to themselves as "salable" in order to move toward the "American Dream." Humans become instrumental means to each other as they pursue goals of wealth, power, and influence. Because this acquiring mode reduces human beings to things, people have no deep attachment to themselves or to others, not *because they do not care but because relationships are so thin and empty due to the cultural promotion and celebration of selfishness and narcissism.* Widespread indifference about poverty, gender inequality, racial injustices, ecological dangers, and more are then understood against this backdrop, which shapes and molds individuals who ground their identity in their possessions, in the things they have and the skills they can sell to "get ahead." Simply put, neoliberal capitalism (re)produces a commodity culture. Consequently, the ethical task is to re-orient human meaning beyond "things." The self needs to undergo radical transformation away from neoliberal consciousness in order to see oneself and others rightly.

The Problem of Money: Kierkegaard and the Self as an Ethical Task

The acquiring mode diminishes individual meaning and wholeness. The value and worth of the self is reduced to material ends. Religious and philosophical thinker Soren Kierkegaard provides a compelling concept of the self, rooted in a religious vision of wholeness and hope instead of money and material things. The religious "becoming" of the self, for Kierkegaard, should be seen as the ethical task despite the material clamor of society. I engage Kierkegaard with womanist discourse in order to explore constructive questions on the existential and spiritual crisis of the self generated by neoliberal societies.

Before elucidating his thought on money and the self as an ethical task, I want to address two concerns related to Kierkegaard's thought. The first revolves around the claim that his work is irredeemably misogynistic and therefore incompatible with feminist or womanist aims. For certain, there is a complex (and often ambiguous) relationship between Kierkegaard's work and feminism. On the one hand, he outright rejects the social and political equality between men and women throughout his pseudonymous writings and directly authored writings such as *Works of Love*. On the other hand, Kierkegaard expresses deep egalitarian aims as women are depicted as leaders of faith alongside men in *Fear and Trembling* (Mary, mother of Jesus, is heralded alongside Abraham as a harbinger of faith). While Kierkegaard cannot be identified as feminist or womanist, one must be careful to not rule out the ways in which aspects of his thought may promote womanist or feminist aims and ends. For instance, his discussion on the "role of witness" (I will turn to this later in this chapter) in critiquing social ideologies and practices align with womanist ideas of prophetic action in response to exploitative social structures and practices. Reducing Kierkegaard to a misogynist is highly problematic, and my intention is to appropriate particular aspects of his thought (religious inwardness and money as abstraction) within womanist discourse because it deeply resonates with womanist ideas of love of God, self, and neighbor within neoliberal societies.

The womanist idea of self-love is predicated upon the God-given right women of color have to self-actualize. This self-love is not a selfish love. Rather, it is a love that finds its origins in the love of the God/Divine (including all of creation) that extends outward in defining one's human worth and dignity, enabling one to affirm the humanity of one's neighbor as well. Womanist self-love is characterized by a relational self-understanding in which loving oneself is achieved through religious meaning (how God affirms the human subjectivity and identity of all persons).[13] As I address later, Kierkegaard's idea of religious inwardness toward wholeness, self-actualization, and love deeply align with womanist religious commitments to love God and self as the precondition for prophetic action and witness in broader society. I will also discuss how womanist discourse critiques and expands, in interreligious postmodern directions, Kierkegaard's concept of "God" and religious inwardness.

A second concern that emerges in relation to Kierkegaard's thought is its presumed lack of emancipatory aims, namely his scholarship's non-commitment to social change and political transformation. Some scholars might question how his "apolitical" work could be used in service to womanist and feminist aims when womanism directly advocates for social and political change. Soren Kierkegaard is often remembered as a theological and philosophical thinker who is focused on the religiosity of the individual, focused on how persons address intrapersonal matters that are fundamentally religious in scope. Consequently, he has been interpreted as an apolitical thinker who was not invested in questions of social togetherness and community. However, the concrete individual for Kierkegaard is always and already a product of society and history. Individuals are not to be seen as "unrooted" beings or autonomous from the communities that shape and form them; rather, individual existence must be seen within the moral patterns and processes of communal life. While Kierkegaard maintains that ethical judgment is made by the individual alone, he certainly sees such ethical judgments being influenced and impacted by who individuals understand themselves to be within their communities and/or societies.

Kierkegaard should not be interpreted as cut off from the political world and therefore unable to offer resources toward a critique of society. Kierkegaardian scholar and theologian David Gouwens notes that when one turns to Kierkegaard's focused attack on "Christendom" (especially in his mature writings), one sees his writings as countercultural and critical of the conservative establishment during his times. Gouwens notes,

> Kierkegaard's attack is indeed ferocious, his rhetoric is extreme, at times stark in its opposition to Christianity and worldly life. At the end he condemns marriage and procreation themselves as a contribution to the amount of original sin in the world. He criticizes Paul as well as Augustine and Luther on grace. On his deathbed, he refuses communion from any priest of the established Danish church. Theologically, one recent commentator sees Kierkegaard's attack as an assertion of radical individual ethical autonomy, a clear break not only with established Christendom, but with orthodox Christianity and with grace.[14]

Gouwens suggests that Kierkegaard can be read as offering a radical critique of existing religious and social structures that he felt were conservative and unhelpful to the religious life of love lived with and for others. In fact, Kierkegaard's thought, particularly near the end of his life, might be seen as showing how the ethical individual relates to the social, as he called upon the dismantling of the traditional-aristocratic hierarchies associated with the maintenance of Christian culture during his era.[15] His attack upon Christian hegemonic power must be seen within the context of political and social developments within the 1800s in which his otherworldly Christian vision "offered a social vision at odds with the liberalism and populism of his time."[16]

In fact, Kierkegaard's religious thought on the individual quest toward religious inwardness or wholeness challenged the dominant public theology during his era that saw the private and the public as separate and discrete spheres. Instead, he understood social religious witness and action as grounded in the individual who issues a public call to one's contemporaries and neighbors to morally act.[17] The departure point of social religious witness (such as Christian discipleship) is embodied within the individual that then bears witness within a community outwards toward the world. Hence, the individual and social were not articulated in dualistic terms for Kierkegaard. Rather, the individual and social were seen as situated on a continuum in terms of how Christians understand both their relationship with God and neighbor. Moreover, Jesus' life and suffering is central to how Kierkegaard understands the Christian witness, a theme I will return to later in this chapter. Hence, one might infer from Kierkegaard's theological writings that the quest for religious inwardness or wholeness of self (grounded in God/Divine) is simultaneously the impetus for prophetic action and witness.[18] The ethical task as the quest for individual wholeness then provides the grounding for a robust critique of society in Kierkegaard's work.

Similar to Kierkegaard, womanist theological discourse affirms that women of color's individual sense of wholeness and spiritual health is essential to their active laboring against unjust and unloving practices in broader society. While Kierkegaard's idea of the self as an ethical task strengthens womanist commitments, womanist discourse also critiques and enlarges Kierkegaard's conversation of individual wholeness not only through explicitly foregrounding women of color's experiences of wholeness (experiences that have been excluded within traditional theological and religious discourse) but also by conceptualizing Divine life beyond Kierkegaard's Judeo-Christian God. It is important to note that womanist perspectives point to what social obstacles may impede individual wholeness for women, which strengthens what prophetic witness may entail within society such as resisting patriarchy, class oppression, and racial injustice (actions not emphasized in Kierkegaard's thought). However, as I will discuss later in this chapter, Kierkegaard does not completely dismiss social impediments to religious inwardness or wholeness. He does intimate that the unrestrained pursuit of money hinders individual wholeness, although his critique here is not as comprehensive as womanist discourse in explicitly focusing on how women are unable to self-actualize due to inhumane racist, hetero-patriarchal economic structures. In addition, womanist perspectives privilege the multiple manifestations of Divine life that inform black women's spirituality, which debunks Kierkegaard's argument that individual wholeness can only be secured through a Judeo-Christian God (which I will expound upon later in this chapter).

As stated earlier, womanist perspectives on neoliberal economy might benefit from Kierkegaard's two concepts, money as abstraction and religious inwardness, because these ideas challenge the acquiring mode of society by foregrounding the *telos* toward which our actions are directed and find ultimate meaning: in the love of God, self, and neighbor (instead of material things). Kierkegaard is also an important conversational partner for womanist perspectives on economy because his work challenges the ways in which money and greed diminish community and stifle wholeness in individuals (rather than solely focusing on the structural inequities that the unrestrained pursuit of money creates). Kierkegaard offers a religious critique of capital, a critique that remains important to moving beyond equating human meaning to unrestrained consumerism. His religious critique of capital is not aimed at contemporary "free-market" capitalism per se but captures the ways in which human value is reduced to material possessions in order to secure status and worth.

This religious critique of capital shows up in Kierkegaard's discussion of "money as abstraction" in *Two Ages*. One might infer that one central argument of *Two Ages* is that the love of money and its distortion of social values and virtues within society are central problems that hinder any quest for religious inwardness or wholeness within individuals. In 1846, Kierkegaard published a literary review of a popular book entitled, *Two Ages* by Thomasine Christine Gyllembourg-Ehrensvard. This literary review consisted of three parts. While the first part reviews the story, the second part assesses the plot from an esthetical standpoint. The third part, entitled "This Present Age," is the longest section and provides a critical reflection on his societal age and its malaise and apathy toward wise action and "religious inwardness" due to the reckless pursuit of money. This third part is particularly significant to my religious investigation into the acquiring mode associated with our capitalist moment because Kierkegaard provides a religious critique of capital.

He identifies a central problem within Danish society in 1846 that led to a social and spiritual crisis: the problem of money overly defining social meaning and human value. Kierkegaard states at length the problem of money as "abstraction":

> So ultimately the object of desire is money, but it is in fact token money, an abstraction. A young man today would scarcely envy another his

capacities or his skill or the love of a beautiful girl or his fame, no, but he would envy him his money. Give me money, the young man will say, and I will be all right. And the young man will not do anything rash, he will not do anything he has to repent of, he will not have anything for which to reproach himself, but he will die in the illusion that if he had had money, then he would have lived, then he certainly would have done something great.[19]

For him, money is an abstraction in the sense that it creates an illusion on the meaning of life, as it is not grounded in the concrete actuality of what gives life meaning (i.e., love, community, health, etc.). Money is abstract in the sense that it only has meaning within an artificial context of economic exchange. It has no purpose on its own but only in relation to goods and services. Money can be properly understood as an artificial tool that is created to govern how goods are bought and distributed. This "tool" then has no intrinsic meaning and gives no insight into higher-level questions concerning human beings and the world in which they live.

However, as the aforementioned quotation by Kierkegaard discloses, money gives the illusion that it has a direct relationship to human activity. For instance, money is exchanged for the work we perform each day. When one works so many hours, one receives a certain amount of money in exchange for this work. Money then is seen as bearing a direct relationship to the value of one's work. However, work is an extension of one's human vocation as well as an extension of one's relationship to themselves and others. As one works, the meaning of such work is made complete in relation to the goals and aspirations of the worker. Work enables self-actualization and flourishing for the human being. Work's meaning is reflected in the joy, creativity, and passion the worker experiences as she performs her work. Yet, when reducing work to a monetary value, it re-shapes and forms the meaning of human work into an "abstraction" or an illusion in which money is understood as what concretely provides meaning to both work and life.

Kierkegaard laments that a young person actually believes in this illusionary quality of money and treats it as a "concretion" or reality that provides human meaning. In this instance, the possibility of "religious inwardness" is eclipsed in the young person as the search for material gain takes precedence. The religious inwardness that Kierkegaard refers to is found in one's discovery of God who provides all meaning to life, not money. Kierkegaard asserts,

This is the idea of religiousness. But the education is rigorous and the returns are apparently very small – apparently, for if the individual is unwilling to learn to be satisfied with himself in the essentiality of the religious life before God, to be satisfied with ruling over himself instead of over the world, to be satisfied as a pastor to be his own audience, as an author to be his own reader, etc., if he is unwilling to learn to be inspired by this as supreme because it expresses equality before God and equality with all men…[20]

The idea of religious inwardness for Kierkegaard is about an individual being satisfied, finding "rest within himself, at ease before God instead of in counting and counting."[21] When money is embraced as the ultimate and/or total meaning of life, religious inwardness is averted, it is rendered unachievable within the life of the individual. When money is the governing principle of value in society, it causes people to feel the anxiety of "counting and counting," never able to be at home or at ease with themselves as they are devoted to acquiring more and more.

For Kierkegaard, the modern times he lived in could be properly assessed as treating money as abstraction, which hindered the pursuit of religious inwardness. For him, acknowledging God cleared away the proclivity in using money as a form of power to dominate and regulate life's meaning, which created human slaves to material acquisition instead of individuals oriented toward love, ethical action, and community. The pursuit of money created an age that "flared up in the superficial," a society that has "no assets of feeling in the erotic, no assets of enthusiasm and inwardness of politics and religion, no assets of domesticity, piety, and appreciation in daily life and social life."[22] When money is the ruling principle of human meaning, one no longer understands her relationship to herself and her neighbor. Meaning itself is "flattened" and sociality is foreclosed as persons tend to envy their neighbor for what he has. This kind of society prevents persons from thinking about an ethics of relationality out of which they are able to fulfill what it means to be human, what it means to share life with and for one's neighbor before God.

Capital and money overstep their boundaries once they encroach upon the meaning of human life and ethical action. When monetary tools govern and regulate ethical activity, the experience of religious inwardness in the individual is hampered, leading to an impoverishment of individual ethical action as well as relationships among individuals in community. Moreover, a society of "counting and counting" creates a negative kind of individual, an individual that is oriented toward envy. But this envy is two-sided. This envy is "a selfishness in the individual and then again the selfishness of associates toward the individual" who possesses wealth.[23] Kierkegaard remarks that as enthusiasm can be a unifying principle in a passionate age oriented toward religious inwardness, envy can become a negatively unifying principle in an age that defines itself by the acquiring of money and capital.[24] This way of being holds the individual in captivity and disallows individuals to develop the type of character that enables wise action and ethical judgment. Instead, the character of individuals is formed by envy in which immoral ways of being such as mean-ness and dominating power form and shape the individual.

When turning to contemporary neoliberal economies, money is often worshiped as the provider of worth and value. For instance, when asked what they would like to be when they grow up, young people often offer up familiar responses on careers that are quite lucrative: lawyers, doctors, CEOs, and so forth. These career paths are not problematic in themselves. The real disturbing issue is that young people's imagination is uncreative because they have been taught to see value through monetary compensation. It is very hard to find youth who speak of being teachers, social workers, pastors, and writers because such occupations do not immediately conjure up images of material success. The commodification of career paths cancels out the possibility of vocational discernment among youth today. Money is treated as an abstraction in the sense that it is interpreted as a concrete reality that has value on its own. It is this faulty logic about money that hinders the quest for religious inwardness and identity in the individual as the individual is more concerned with acquiring things to gain human worth than leading an ethical life marked by compassion, love, and hope.

Consider how money is also worshiped above all else as the answer to life's problems. Individuals often feel as if a solution to their despair or loneliness is to *buy* material things such as cars, clothes, food, and even friends. One feels emotional pain and believes that collecting material items will alleviate their pain. To the contrary, such actions only exacerbate the pain one endures because the roots of one's emotional turmoil are existential. When money is treated as the end toward which human actions should be directed, individuals are unable to develop a "self" that journeys toward the knowledge of God and others, a knowledge that provides the grounding for a life of love and joy. Like Kierkegaard, a womanist religious critique of the acquiring mode recognizes that money is an abstraction that often over-determines meaning and value within societies, hindering individual wholeness and ethical action. Relationships among persons are severely diminished because our current neoliberal global economy attaches monetary value to non-market experiences such as friendship, love, and joy.

The ethical quest for Kierkegaard is not the acquisition of money (or acquiring mode) but religious inwardness. Kierkegaard's religious critique of capital and money is grounded in his articulation of the end goal, being religious inwardness out of which love for self, God, and others is experienced. This idea of religious inwardness is captured in his philosophical vision of human beings as "finite, historically situated beings whose primary task is to become whole persons."[25] His vision is concerned with the "self" becoming healthy and whole within a modern society that reinforces the sinful condition characterized by brokenness and fragmentation. In the *Concluding Unscientific Postscript*, Kierkegaard writes under the pseudonymous name of Johannes Climacus and remarks, "My principal thought was that, those of our time, because so much knowledge, have forgotten what it means to *exist*, and the meaning of *inwardness*."[26] He asserts that people have lost what it means to "exist humanly" because they are unable to see that the ethical task is the quest for authentic selfhood rooted in a vision of God who provides the conditions under which meaning of self is understood and actualized.[27]

It is important to note that the quest for "authentic selfhood" for Kierkegaard is not the same as the pursuit of atomic individualism.[28] His notion of the self is shaped and formed within the traditions and virtues of the community.[29] In *Either/Or*, Kierkegaard employs the anonymous narrator, Judge Williams, to describe authentic selfhood. Judge Williams describes authentic selfhood as responsibly choosing who one will be, which is rooted in God's purposes for one as a human being. This sense of authentic selfhood requires the embodiment of certain virtues such as faith, hope, and love but also involves the power of choice. Judge Williams cautions individuals to avoid making the wrong choices as one might gain material abundance but lose oneself (one's sense of peace, joy, dignity, etc.).[30] And these moral choices are made within the context of community. Atomic individualism does not consider the communal contexts out of which individuals morally act. However, Kierkegaard's idea of authentic selfhood foregrounds a certain "self-understanding" that develops within the individual based on the cultivation of character or virtue within communities.

Kierkegaard might be described as situated within the classical virtue tradition in that he understands the individual as a self who is shaped by particular virtues and exemplary traits. In order to avoid the unrestrained chase for money by the individual, he believed that the ultimate ethical moment is when an individual exercises freedom to "choose onself" (one's commitments and life purpose), making virtues necessary to the cultivation of an individual's character.

Womanist discourse also foregrounds the importance of virtue formation to wholeness and self-actualization within neoliberal contexts but acknowledges that social impediments often hinder the virtue formation process within individuals who endure oppression and marginalization. Those who are marginalized and subjugated often do not have the complete freedom to "choose onself," an unfortunate reality taken for granted in Kierkegaard's thought. Womanist scholars Katie Cannon and Melanie Harris have offered sustained treatment of how social, cultural, and economic systems affect conceptions of virtue ethics. Cannon persuasively contends that classical conceptions of virtue (i.e., Aristotle, Aquinas, etc.) tend to discount the moral agency of women, who were seen as less capable of being virtuous. Such patriarchal posturing within early virtue ethical theory conflicts with womanist virtue ethic projects, which foreground the diverse ways in which women of color cultivate virtue and moral agency within their daily contexts of hardship. Moreover, Cannon argues that the classical list of virtues (love, temperance, fortitude, etc.) and how they are cultivated within classical virtue ethics theory must be challenged. Cannon demonstrates that the "canonical virtues" that emerge within black women's lives may be different than the ones white male theorists often identify and privilege in philosophical and theological thought (Kierkegaard privileges faith, hope, and love). Unlike Kierkegaard, Cannon shows that black women's historical and current experiences disclose different virtues within the context of survival. These virtues are equally important to any discussion of faith, hope, and love as virtues.

For instance, by turning to black women's literary tradition, Cannon identifies three canonical virtues that black women have cultivated in order to exercise moral agency (that are not seen in traditional theological and philosophical accounts of virtue): invisible dignity, quiet grace, and unshouted courage.[31] Black women's suffering and historical struggles for flourishing alter the ground of moral life, challenging dominant Western assumptions about moral norms and agency. Cannon asserts that a description of virtues among black women must be grounded in the contextuality and particularity of their experiences of suffering in order to avoid the universalization of virtues and/or values often associated with Western discourse. She reviews Zora Neale Hurston's literary work as a moral source in inferring particular virtues and values that black women have employed within hetero-patriarchal, racist contexts from slavery through Jim Crow segregation in the United States.

In *Their Eyes Were Watching God*, Hurston introduces the reader to the protagonist, Janie Crawford and her embodiment of the virtue unshouted courage. Janie Crawford searched for a life of fulfillment through traditional patriarchal institutions of marriage and love. She searches for joy, happiness, and love, a way of being radically connected to herself and the world. She initially tries to find this connection through two marriages, which reflected hetero-patriarchal abuse and power, but ultimately defies these hetero-patriarchal conditions in order to experience wholeness and authentic selfhood. It is through her love affair with Tea Cake, a man 18 years younger than her, that she encounters love, connection, care, and compassion. She exercises unshouted courage within her patriarchal community, as she quietly refuses their advice to repress her sexuality with Tea Cake. Janie rejects the conventional sexual morality of her community, a heteronormative morality (sex only within the confines of marriage) that is deeply rooted in Western religious thought. She walks a fine line in rejecting the sexual norms of her patriarchal community in order to experience a path of self-discovery toward healing and wholeness. Unshouted courage was a virtue exemplified in Janie as she negotiated a life of wholeness that her wider community and its norms would not grant.

The virtue of unshouted courage is not a primary canonical virtue within Western theological and philosophical discourses. However, it is a primary theological virtue within Janie's experience as a black woman, an experience marked by suffering and struggle for self-actualization. The virtue of unshouted courage enables Janie to experience communion with God, others, and broader creation as she self-actualizes in and through her sexual and sensual body.

Hurston's work discloses that the virtue of "unshouted courage" has enabled black women to survive against tyrannical systems of oppression. "Unshouted courage" is about exercising a silent courage that may be interpreted as passive but is actually defiant. The roots of tyrannical abuse, in part, lie in repressing people's ability to exercise courage (in Janie's case, the community sought to repress her as a sexual subject). Janie embodied unshouted courage within the context of white racism and black patriarchy, which tried to prevent her from experiencing wholeness in and through her body. For Cannon, unshouted courage is a primary theological virtue (not merely a cardinal virtue as dominant virtue ethics classifies it as) for black women such as Janie, as this virtue has provided the conditions under which faith and love can be exercised responsibly for black women, in ways that do not reinforce their oppression or abuse under hetero-patriarchal oppressive systems.

Kierkegaard's account of virtues does not fully consider the particularity of women's moral agency when discussing the virtues and hence, movement toward wholeness and authentic selfhood for women. For Cannon, black women's virtues (such as unshouted courage) are often cultivated within the context of severe racial, gender/sexual, and class oppression, which demonstrates that the cultivation of virtuous character must take account of the social context in which moral agents (such as black women) are situated. Much traditional virtue ethics discourse does not integrate how oppressive social systems redefine *what counts as virtue* among disenfranchised individuals. In others words, oppressive contexts are essential to discussing the virtues.

Although a feminist philosopher and not a womanist scholar, Lisa Tessman also affirms the importance of social structures and conditions in discussing virtues. She argues that devastating social-structural conditions confronted by oppressed selves both limit and burden their moral goodness, affecting their possibilities toward flourishing. She elucidates two different forms of "moral trouble" prevalent under oppression and marginalization. The first is that the oppressed self may be morally damaged, prevented from developing or exercising some of the virtues. The second is that the very conditions of oppression require the oppressed to develop a set of virtues that carry a moral cost to those who practice them, traits that Tessman refers to as "burdened virtues." [32] For example, honesty as a virtue has been extolled in traditional virtue ethics theory. However, slavery in the United States demonstrates that honesty was often a complicated matter for slaves. Should one slave be honest to his master about an infraction another slave committed, placing that other slave's life at risk? What if the slave who committed the infraction was morally justified within an inhumane system, which allows one to reinterpret what honesty really means within the dubious moral matrices of slavery itself? When turning to contemporary culture, would a homeless mother with four children be decried as dishonest if she finds money and decides to feed her children instead of returning the money? Social-structural conditions might complicate how virtue is exercised, and standard virtues might even "burden" marginalized groups who may craft other distinct virtues to survive and experience quality of life.

Similar to Cannon and Tessman, womanist scholar Melanie Harris suggests that womanist virtue ethics establishes "moral agency for women and communities of color but also uses the histories, stories, and a number of 'nontraditional' sources from which womanist wisdom and morals can be gleaned."[33] Harris also contends that marginalized women of color's experiences (black women in her text) re-conceptualize discussions on the virtues. Harris intimates that the ethical self must be described in a more nuanced way by turning to the oppressed experiences among women of color if one is to chart out how such women experience inner wholeness such as the love of God, self, and neighbor. For Harris, virtues such as compassion, generosity, and audacious courage emerge as primary moral virtues for black women.[34] It is these virtues that have enabled black women to experience wholeness and well-being within unfavorable and repressive socio-economic and cultural contexts. While Kierkegaard's virtues of faith, hope, and love remain important, womanist virtue ethics allows one to see the diverse ways in which wholeness of self is experienced among women of color whose moral agency is often impeded by unjust social-structural conditions and contexts. Womanist virtue ethics therefore provides a necessary constructive critique of how virtue might be re-conceptualized within Kierkegaard's thought in order to include the diversity of human experiences toward authentic selfhood, particularly persons who are under oppressive gazes and systemic practices of inequality.

Womanist religious perspectives resonate with how Kierkegaard describes the ethical task as the journey toward wholeness within one's inner self through virtue formation, which enables individuals to resist the acquiring mode. The ethical life is the struggle to become a unified self rather than a fragmented self that is defined through the endless pursuit of material things. This process of becoming a unified self is understood in a twofold sense for Kierkegaard. First, the self seeks to be something more than a disjointed collection of competing desires and wants. The goal of the self is to seek a certain degree of coherence and integrity as one negotiates life's processes. Second, the self seeks a sense of coherence in order to experience a unity that endures over time. To be a self is to know who one is and what one's commitments and values are. A unified self enables one to live for something (i.e., for a cause, for God, for neighbor, etc.) that permeates all one does, which does not change on an hourly or daily basis due to popular opinion, expedient circumstances, or material reward.[35]

To become ethical, for Kierkegaard, is to become the person God created one to be. Being ethical then is not what one does necessarily but who one becomes. The ethical task is to self-actualize as a person who is aware of God as the source of the moral task. The ethical task is then religious in character. The ethical task in the highest form is grounded in a relationship with God in which the individual moves toward what she was assigned to become. God is simply the reality that stands behind this religious and moral obligation to self-actualize. The religious life allows one to realize the "highest good" in one's quest for religious inwardness, being wholeness within the individual. Developing religious inwardness in the individual is a process that involves religious knowledge of God and a relationship to God as God's creature.[36]

The ethical is primarily framed as religious in character as God is the source of the "ought." While Kierkegaard leaves open how one might interpret "the Absolute" or "God" within some of his texts such as the *Postscript*, many of his other works clearly maintain that he understands the ethical in Christian terms of sin and salvation. While he does not privilege Christian revelation in explicating the religious life in *Postscript* as he even claims that ethical religiousness could "exist in paganism," one must turn to his other works in order to uncover his deep theological convictions on the need for God, a need for God that he expresses through Christian language of sin and salvation.

I recognize that Kierkegaard's Christocentric language in relation to the ethical collides with the growing interreligious sensibilities within postmodern womanist religious thought. Many black women experience inner wholeness through non-Christian religious experience. One might argue that Kierkegaard's claim that ethical religiousness can exist in "paganism" still treats non-Christian religions as inconsequential and even inferior to Christian religion. This argument is justifiable. One might wonder how an atheist or humanist might be interpreted against Kierkegaard's claim that the self can only be rendered coherent in light of a Judeo-Christian God. What about black female playwright and poet Ntozake Shange's assertion of God being the Divine presence (not necessarily a Judeo-Christian God) found in black women when she states, "I found God in myself and I loved her/I loved her fiercely"?[37] Certainly, Kierkegaard's view collides with different Christian and non-Christian religious expressions of wholeness and well-being.

In Making a Way Out of No Way: A Womanist Theology, womanist postmodern theological scholar Monica Coleman critiques the Christian-centered language of both Western theological discourse and early womanist discourse, noting that black women reflect a diversity of religious experiences that should not be reduced to Christianity or the Judeo-Christian God. Coleman asks: when dealing with the religious and existential experiences of women of color, should they be religiously represented solely in Christian terms and Christian-influenced classical metaphysical understandings of the Divine? Western Christian theology and much of womanist theological thought not only privilege (without virtually any challenge) a Christological idea of God (which confines the revelation of God to Jesus alone) but also implicitly hold that all black women adhere to and can be described within the language and praxis of Christian ontology (i.e., metaphysical formulations of God as "Being" and "Substance" instead of process theological language of God as temporal, changing, and "becoming").[38]

Coleman states that a process womanist theology "does not require belief in the person of Jesus Christ or Christianity in order to explicate a doctrine of God, but is inclusive of various religious traditions and methods of liberation" in which black women participate as equal and fellow proprietors of freedom and justice.[39] She achieves a working example of this inclusion of non-Christian religious schemas in her turn to African traditional religions, emphasizing these religions' ability to adapt to their context and serve as a means of holistic life-sustenance (such as their syncretism of the religious worldviews of the oppressors with their own religious rituals and expressions as displayed in Santeria and other African diasporic religious traditions).[40] Coleman also proposes a Whiteheadian account of spirit possession as found in African religions, which strengthens her postmodern womanist theological project as being religiously plural and multi-vocal in relation to constructions of God. I infer from Coleman that any interpretation of religious experience impedes its own transformational thrust when it does not account for plurality and mutli-vocality within its models of God. Coleman calls for a postmodern concept of God that does not privilege and absolutize classical metaphysical formulas of God, making room for emerging creative possibilities on the nature of God and God's relationship to the world. Coleman's process theological turn renders visible the plurality of black women's experiences toward religious inwardness and wholeness, which challenges Kierkegaard's narrow conception of religious inwardness and its traditional formulations of a Judeo-Christian God.

As one can see, the point of contestation revolves around the nature of "the religious." For Kierkegaard, the religious is grounded in special revelation found in God's self-disclosure in Jesus Christ, grounding wholeness and authentic selfhood solely in a Christian conception of the Divine. While much of womanist religious literature does not undermine this religious proposition for Christian communities, this discourse does critique the universalizing impulses associated with special revelation in which such Christocentric theologies are imposed upon all humans throughout time, space, and place. When Kierkegaard asserts that an individual's self is "directed towards God," there is an absolute *telos* at play, which describes *all* of humanity as being directed and finding meaning in a Christian conception of the world and its patterns and processes. This assertion then becomes imperialistic and unhelpful in describing the concrete ways individuals find meaning and wholeness through non-Christian religious ways and modes of being. For womanists such as Coleman and Harris, the nature of the religious includes religious conceptions grounded in Christian, Islamic, Buddhist, and African traditional religious ways of being. The religious should be opened up to a diverse, multicolored way of imagining the Divine among human communities, as individuals search for meaning, hope, love, and joy.

However, one might respond to these womanist criticisms that Kierkegaard's reflections of "Religiousness A" (Natural Religion) and "Religiousness B" (Christianity) are highly nuanced. While Kierkegaard certainly grounds Christian faith in special revelation that overturns natural religiousness, he also understands Christian faith as the continuing attempts of any religiously reflective person to relate seriously to the highest good (although one might argue that the "highest good" is contestable). This nuance perhaps makes Kierkegaard deeply sympathetic to other religious expressions, while still maintaining his christocentrism.[41]

Kierkegaardian scholars may also argue that it is important to remember that the majority of Kierkegaard's intellectual works are committed to articulating a Christian witness within cultural, political and economic spheres of his era, as he is grappling with how to relate Christian identity to the public sphere. One might maintain that Kierkegaard's Christian language provides a resource for projects in Christian ethics, projects that are unapologetically Christian but not narrowly Christian (not dismissive of other religious traditions). Hence, one might conclude that Kierkegaard's idea of ethical religiousness grounded in Christian language can be helpful in thinking through ideas of wholeness and social critique of neoliberal practices for Christian communities.

These two rejoinders are partly justified. For certain, Kierkegaard's critique of money through a turn to religious inwardness is *radical and disruptive within his historical time period and social context* (for the reasons I mentioned at the beginning of this chapter). His project also makes room for exploring the Christian witness within society through grounding his argument in basic Christian theological terms and orientations of his day. Moreover, Kierkegaard's ultimate description of *God as love* in *Works of Love* may create room for non-Christian religious experiences that are grounded in love. Yet, one still cannot help but ask where non-Christian expressions are left in relation to religious inwardness as Kierkegaard ultimately sees God's nature and expression of love through God's self-disclosure in Jesus Christ. Kierkegaard's Christocentric language and its universalizing proclivities (whether Kierkegaard intends for this to be the case or not) cause doubt to linger over whether his notion of religious inwardness is fair to individuals who experience wholeness and authentic selfhood through non-Christian or nontraditional Christian religious expressions.

Despite womanist religio-cultural critiques of Kierkegaard's notion of the religious, Kierkegaard and much of womanist discourse agree that an important task is to understand the nature of the ethical in relationship to money, which enables one to not be determined by a world of "counting and counting" and free to respond to the Divine's gracious love. Kierkegaard's discourse on how religious inwardness forms morally virtuous selves does offer resources for a radical ethical critique of the acquiring mode of society and deeply resonates with womanist goals of love for the Divine, self, and neighbor. The self who moves toward religious inwardness is an individual who possesses the moral and ethical resources to critique social and political spheres that do not foster the good. Within Kierkegaardian and womanist thought, the virtuous formation of selves is essential to the wholeness of the individual self and central to the task of social transformation, although womanist articulations of the virtues substantively consider the social-structural conditions and obstacles that impede moral agents.[42] The individual self is created to evolve toward wholeness in order to self-actualize. Most importantly, the "public" character of the self becomes present through the process of religious inwardness. The ethical task is the individual's quest of living a morally virtuous good life with and for others. This quest toward religious inwardness grounds the ethical task of the self, which enables the individual to resist defining herself by the endless pursuit of money. Most importantly, the unrestrained desire for money can be identified as futile and meaningless when turning to what truly counts: the love of the Divine, self, and neighbor.

The Wealth of Religious Inwardness: The Role of Witness

Any womanist critique of the acquiring mode should also include a redefinition of what constitutes true wealth in light of religious inwardness and wholeness of self. Within the context of neoliberal societies, wealth is defined in monetary terms, feeding this acquiring mode. Instead, one can understand wealth more expansively, as a wealth of "inward assets" such as peace, happiness, trust, compassion, and hope. Drawing on Kierkegaard's work, one might infer that true wealth is the quest for authentic selfhood. As discussed earlier, the quest for selfhood is not the quest for atomic individualism. The cultivation of authentic selfhood is the pursuit of healthy individuality that finds its ultimate meaning in love of the Divine, self, and neighbor.

Religious inwardness leads to an internal wealth as it enables individuals to embody virtues that are central to experience wholeness. Such virtues shape the heart of the individual and allow individuals to see differently. This kind of sight is not physical but spiritual, a kind of seeing that reorients the individual toward the meaning of life itself. Kierkegaard holds love as the ultimate virtue that grounds the knowledge of God/Divine, oneself, and one's neighbor. In fact, love is a way of seeing. The vision of love is not merely what one sees but *how* one sees what one sees. In other words, the way the individual is shaped and formed is profoundly important to *how* the individual sees. The individual's formation through love is the basis for how such love is embodied and expressed within webs of relationality. This inward wealth then is grounded in a vision of love that re-forms individuals who come into loving, compassionate solidarity with humanity.

This inward wealth forms the virtuous character of the individual and sharpens one's eyes to see what is of greatest importance in life. Without the pursuit of religious inwardness, one's vision is narrow and myopic within societal systems. The acquiring mode frames how individuals see the world, themselves, and their neighbors. As already discussed, neighbors are seen in a utilitarian way, measured by their ability to meet our material goals or "social status" aims. However, virtues such as love or generosity reframe the world in a way that draws out the "ultimate good." Love reframes and expands our vision of ourselves and others so that we are able to trust and consider the interests of others. Love is not merely external acts (although there is an external component) but an internal attitude in which one's vision is re-ordered toward what is truly moral and ethical. And this love is not concerned with the results or "fruits" of such love.[43] The task is "loving forth" love in others.[44] For example, when being rooted in love, one can see the possibilities of the good in one's neighbor, even enemy, rather than embracing a radical distrust of others. One can also love without being desirous of something in return. To be certain, this internal attitude sponsored by love is not a naïve acceptance but an open-eyed ethic of right relationships that understands the call individuals have to love others without reservation.[45] This imaginative transformation of vision through love and other virtues reflects the internal wealth that is generated through the quest toward religious inwardness.

As stated earlier, this quest for authentic selfhood through religious inwardness is not without social and political implications. Kierkegaard's idea of religious inwardness is not only about an "ethics of interiority" divorced from external action. While religious inwardness is about the pursuit of wholeness through embodying virtues, it is also about how Christians live in the social worlds they inhabit. For Kierkegaard, the question was not *if* the religious formation of the individual affects broader culture but *how* the virtuous formation of the individual influences social relations.[46] As discussed earlier, the self as an ethical task is about *praxis*, the shaping of character that conditions and makes possible ethical action. Because the self is a "character-task," the self enters entire devotion to God as one seeks to live a life of hope and love.[47] The daily living of this life of hope and love is both actualized in our hearts and manifested in sets of relations. In *Works of Love*, Kierkegaard discusses at length how the love of God is made concrete with and for my neighbor. Therefore, social relations are constitutive of religious inwardness as one's religious journey is concretely manifested through the proper love of self and unrequited love of neighbor.

Because religious inwardness includes both an ethics of interiority (virtue or character-forming process) and the prophetic transformation of social relations into loving relations, moral imagination becomes essential to this task. In fact, how one faithfully and lovingly inhabits one's social world is a question of moral imagination. Similar to much of womanist thought, Kierkegaard's imaginative reflection on the gospels' portrayals of Jesus' life "gives him the standpoint for radical critique, from which he concludes that a believer may well be called not simply to grant priority to God over Caesar, but may be called to active opposition."[48] The ethical justification of radical critique to the established order is found through Christ's example, a moral exemplar who challenged elitist structures and practices that precluded and even oppressed the vulnerable and downcast. Kierkegaard's idea of moral imagination was a distinctively Christian imagination that enabled and empowered an active opposition to the present age where power and money distorted the true meaning of life, being the love for God, self, and neighbor. This kind of moral imagination that enables one to resist the established order deeply resonates with womanist religious projects, whether grounded in the moral example of Jesus or another religious figure.[49]

An individual who embodies active opposition to the established social order and its status quo is understood as a "witness to the truth" for Kierkegaard. The "witness to the truth" is the individual who has been formed by her experience of religious inwardness. The life of religious inwardness is supremely actualized through the knowledge of God, which opens up to a life of hope and love. The role of the witness "socially manifests rather than contradicts the life of faith, hope, and love."[50] In other words, Kierkegaard wants to ensure that religious inwardness is not just "hidden inwardness" in which one's spirituality or religious journey is unable to affect the present age. Knowledge of God cannot be evoked in order to ignore and/or dismiss social problems that threaten us as human beings. Religious inwardness cannot be used to "hide" from one's responsibilities to one's neighbor. One knows all to well how religion and spirituality can be used as an excuse for silence and inactivity. This inactive kind of religious inwardness is cowardly and not the heart of religious inwardness at all. The religious individual must transition from hidden inwardness to public stance.[51]

In *Practice in Christianity*, Kierkegaard attempts to critique hidden inwardness. He argues that such inwardness allows everyone to claim she or he is a Christian without any actions that manifests one's quest for religious inwardness. He claims that such inwardness is "so to speak, behind a jammed lock: it is impossible to find out whether all of these thousands upon thousands actually are Christians, for they all are that, so it is said, in hidden inwardness."[52] He is not asserting that one can be identified as a Christian solely through external actions. Rather, the virtuous formation of the self through religious inwardness *concretely and socially manifests* in one's works. As a result, one's action is an outgrowth of one's character, a praxis-oriented process, which belies interpreting religious inwardness as hidden inwardness.

Kierkegaard's reflection on hidden inwardness emerged from his frustration with the Danish church. During his era, everyone could be a Christian within the church without being accountable to what is *required* of an individual who journeys toward the knowledge of God (the knowledge of God being seen through Christ's example of hope and love). Kierkegaard offers a scathing social critique of what it meant to be a "Christian" during his time:

> I am not a Christian...The only analogy I have before me is Socrates. My task is a Socratic task, to revise the definition of what it is to be a Christian. For my part I do not call myself a "Christian" (thus keeping the ideal free), but I am able to make it evident that the others are still less than I.[53]

Here, he does not call himself a Christian because the church reflects dominant Christianity—and he disagreed with the silence and complicity of the church on a number of social problems then. Most importantly, he did not agree with the church's brand of spirituality, hidden inwardness, which allowed Christians to make excuses for their unwillingness to act. Womanist theological discourse initially emerged in order to critique the silence and complicity of the black church surrounding racism, sexism, classism, and more. The majority of womanist religious literature today (representative of different religious traditions) has promoted the significance of individuals being witnesses to the truth. Prophetic moral action is the call womanist discourse makes. Consequently, religious inwardness is deeply connected to prophetically addressing social problems that inhibit people's ability to self-actualize and flourish.

Kierkegaard challenges the church to develop the social implications of inwardness, implications that lead away from hidden inwardness or inaction. The journey toward religious inwardness is about developing an appreciation for the way faith shows up in the public sphere. As one can see, Kierkegaard certainly sets the stage for a relation between the public and private as well as the consideration of a strong religious role in the political sphere.[54] However, this relation is not reduced to each other. The private is not reduced to the public. The Christian has the responsibility of understanding how her private journey of religious inwardness relates to the public sphere and how the public sphere inhibits or encourages the quest for religious inwardness. In fact, for Kierkegaard, the moral protest we observe in *Two Ages* debunks how the public sphere inhibits religious inwardness through treating money as the source of ultimate meaning. Being a "witness to the truth" then means being able to describe, understand, and embody what it means to be an individual who is oriented toward prophetic action in the social sphere.

This role of witness enables prophetic action as well as public stances. As discussed, it is critical to remember that Kierkegaard provides a stark contrast between Christ and the world. Being a witness is a call to imitate Christ in the present age. Such imitation is not merely a deontological ethics. Christians are not called to live out some set of rules in order to claim a certain "Christ-likeness." Rather, Christians imitate Christ's life and character, being formed and shaped by Christ's witness to come into solidarity with the suffering of the outcasts, poor and lowly people, workers, laborers, and more. Womanist theologian Delores Williams reminds us that this "imitation" of Jesus is embodying his ministry to the marginalized, which collides with the established order that scorns the vulnerable. As Jesus is the truth, we must *be* the truth. Truth is not found in propositional beliefs but modeling one's life after Jesus' example through a virtuous heart and prophetic action. As Kierkegaard states, "Truth is not a sum of statements, not a definition...but a life."[55] Being a witness therefore engenders prophetic action and public stances as it allows an individual to hold herself accountable to others publicly. Religious inwardness encourages social responsibility rather than selfish individualism. Religious inwardness creates the requirement that one publicly bears witness to the truth. The religious individual must resist giving up and collapsing in front of the power structure. She must be a witness and embody prophetic action. Being a "witness" is the final and fullest expression of the individual before God/Divine.

Moreover, I argue that being a "witness to the truth" also invites other non-Christian religious individuals to develop a certain awareness and moral imagination on what can *be*. Being a witness to the truth is about a religious imagination that provides the conditions toward the possibility of seeing something different and better. Kierkegaard' thought and womanist postmodern religious scholarship do not care if moral imagination is interpreted as idealistic and "unachievable." In fact, "reality" in relation to moral imagination is irrelevant. What matters is that the individual is able to participate in an inward deepening of what is possible, what can be. The individual, in this instance, becomes a "witness" to the truth of what can be. The witness is able to see an aperture, a new opening to something different, a new way of seeing.[56] The witness, through her journey of religious inwardness, is able to discover a vocabulary that grounds and enables practices of quiet grace, love, hope, and togetherness in the public realm. For Christian communities, Jesus' prophetic witness generates the basis of social critique, as Jesus can be interpreted as a sign of offense to the established order.[57] For non-Christian communities, moral exemplars such as Mohammed or Buddha may provide the basis for generating a social critique of society and its acquiring mode.

The wealth of religious inwardness is the call to be a witness to the truth. This idea of wealth counteracts the meaninglessness associated with a life defined by money and excessive materialism. This wealth offers individuals internal assets marked by love, community, and trust rather than monetary assets that reduce human meaning to *things*. Religious inwardness provides the conditions under which wholeness of self might be achieved, a mode of being that is frustrated by the alienated activity and acquiring mode sponsored by neoliberal economies.

3

Loss of the Erotic

The previous chapter affirms that neoliberalism numbs our ability to feel deeply, passionately, and compassionately about life. We are unable to resist the acquiring mode or be a "witness to truth" because neoliberal forces breed a sense of apathy and inefficacy in us that we can transform broader society. The alienated individualism that neoliberal ideology presumes as "given" frames our ways of relating to each other. Neoliberalism anesthetizes an individual's longings, yearnings, and desires for connection and community in favor of acquiring things and material objects. As a result, the self needs to undergo radical transformation, from an acquiring mode to a giving and sharing mode of being.

This chapter explores how the erotic, as a religious and/or spiritual good, enables the transformation of self and society away from the alienating proclivities of neoliberal culture. Drawing upon American theologian Paul Tillich as well as black feminists Audre Lorde, Alice Walker, and Toni Morrison, I argue that the power of the erotic as a religious and/or spiritual good must be recovered in our societies in order to foster connection and belonging. Traditional notions of the erotic tend to equate this term with the pornographic. Lorde and Morrison challenge this traditional understanding of the erotic. Instead, the erotic is about deep-shared feelings, sensation, and connection with and for each other that wake us up to love, freedom, and pleasure. The erotic is about self-expression and connection rather than repression and disconnection from one's deepest feelings of love and togetherness. Black feminist and womanist religious and cultural thought provides rich counter-discourses on the power of the erotic in our neoliberal capitalist structures. I turn to two novels, Toni Morrison's *Sula* and Alice Walker's *By the Light of My Father's*

Smile, in order to demonstrate how the power of the erotic can shape communities that are pulled toward each other through connection, desire, and freedom rather than pushed away from each other through fear, apathy, and disconnection. Recovery of an erotic imagination is one condition under which persons can resist neoliberal forms of disconnection, disembodied action, and emotional numbness in order to embody values of empathy, care, and compassion. We must tap into the erotic dimensions of human meaning, flourishing, and fulfillment.

The Erotic: A Religious Question

Much of traditional Western philosophy and theology attempts to evade or contest that the body is a prerequisite to the religious quest for human meaning and wholeness. Erotic energy and relationships are often not seen as what constitutes the religious search. This dismissal by traditional philosophies and theologies is rooted in the problem of duality in which mind/soul is esteemed over body, contemplation over corporeal materiality, and intellect over emotions. This failure to include *eros* or the erotic as a vital dimension of bodies-in-relationship is due to how the West has interpreted the body—at best, as secondary to the mind and at worst, as corrupt and sinful. Early Greek philosophy out of which Western theology grew saw the body and emotions as something to be tolerated as one searched for a higher morality grounded in the life of the mind and intellect (reason). For Plato, his theory of "ideal forms" maintained a strict division between the perishable, imperfect physical world and the perfect, eternal ideal world. For this philosopher, the physical world is marked by change and corruption while the ideal world is characterized by perfect forms and true knowledge. In fact, Neo-Platonists used this distinction between the physical and the ideal to argue that the soul is perfect but trapped in an imperfect body. Because the body belongs in the physical realm, it is the root of evil. As a result, the soul seeks to "break free" from the body so it can live into its true perfection, which is in the realm of ideal forms.

Consequently, the quest for the "highest good" is not in the physical world (which includes the body); rather, the quest for the highest good can only be secured through the "non-body," being reason, mind, and intellect. Body, emotions, and feelings hinder the quest for true knowledge associated with love and justice. The body and the erotic therefore were not construed as religious goods that could foster communion with the Divine, oneself, and others. Rather, they were interpreted as forces to "tame" or "mortify" (Paul's words) in pursuit of the religious quest.

Influenced by Platonic thought, Western theology also reinforced this dualism in which the body was seen as separate and even antagonistic to the mind and rationality. Thinkers such as Augustine, Aquinas, and Calvin saw the body as a potential distraction from union with God, particularly the sexual dimensions of the body. For traditional theologians (most were men), the erotic was something to be feared and avoided as this force complicated one's pursuit of salvation. The erotic was seen as compromising the religious quest. Moreover, the erotic was equated with sex itself and, more specifically, a pornographic rendering of female sexuality. The erotic was denounced as "lust of the flesh" that should be avoided at all costs in order to embody perfect obedience and virtue before God.

Most of Western theology has focused on the synergy between *agape* and *philia*, being anxious about the proper place of *eros*. Agape and philia are seen as non-threatening concepts that promote unconditional, brotherly care, juxtaposed to *eros*, which is often interpreted as intense, emotional, irrational, fleeting, and even dangerous. One can easily turn to Christian scriptures in which Paul warns Christians about the lust of the flesh, the problem of the body and its erotic nature as something to "mortify" or kill for the sake of higher spirituality governed by the mind and spirit. Agape and philia even ground ideas of love and community within most contemporary liberationist and postcolonial theologies. For liberationist theologians such as James Cone and James Evans, agape is inseparable from God's being so that any deviation from agape distorts the authentic Christian conception of God.[1] Agape (and even philia) then facilitates a way of being in the world. Throughout much of the history of Christian theology, there has been little consideration of how eros relates to conversations of love because of the dominance of the agape motif.

However, eros and agape should not be seen as antithetical and oppositional to each other. Instead, these two can be seen as constituting the ontological unity of loves. Love is a crucial category of religious reflection across multiple religious traditions. While many religious thinkers want to establish an absolute gap between eros and agape, American Christian theologian Paul Tillich held out the possibility of eros being indispensable to the concretization of other loves such as agape. Tillich delivered a set of lectures at the University of Nottingham in England and at Union Theological Seminary in

Virginia, refining his conception on the ontological unity of love.[2] In 1954, he devoted a chapter to the "Ontology of Love" in Love, Power, and Justice. In that chapter, he tried to explore a clear definition on the ontological character of love by engaging the interrelationships between the different types or "qualities" of love.[3]

Tillich refers to love as "the moving power" as well as "the foundation of all social and political power structures and source of all moral norms."[4] In Tillich's first volume of Systematic Theology, he reviews the classical types of love, in which such loves are often categorized into "lower" and "higher" loves.[5] Tillich takes issue with this strict categorization in which eros tends to be traditionally classified as a "lower" love in relation to agape, which is a "higher" love. He argues that eros and agape must be seen as expressions of the "same ontological drives toward union."[6] For Tillich, there is no absolute gap between eros and agape as agape within the Christian tradition is enfleshed in and through the body ("the word became flesh"). Womanist theological ethicist Eboni Marshall Turman intimates this in her book Towards a Womanist Ethic of Incarnation, in which she infers that the incarnational dimension of agape is only realizable in and through bodies-in-motion, bodies that dance and pull toward each other in full expression of beauty, love, and unity.

For Tillich then, love is a force that "catalyzes the movement from unrealized, abstract being to being actualized in differentiated forms of existence."[7] Tillich seems to suggest that eros actually enables agape to fully actualize, as such love is manifested in and through the flesh. Even Divine love within Christian traditions depicts love as being actualized in and through the body (incarnation) in efforts to reunite in harmony, peace, and care. Eros provides passion and deep feelings in diverse embodiments of love, including agape. Love is one, despite its diverse and plural manifestations, and the erotic supplies the drive and passion toward union with ourselves, each other, and all of creation. Eros must be reclaimed and reconnected to religious thought, feelings, and practices. When eros is rejected as that which connects us to ourselves and each other, we are unable to see the profound religious dimensions of eros.

Consequently, eros and agape need not exclude each other. Rather, as theologian Alexander Irwin notes, "The ontological unity of these loves must be recognized as the basic condition of love's expression in human life."[8] When one recognizes the underlying unity of these types of loves (not as "lower" and "higher" types), one can reject the abstract, pure notion of agapeic love that seeks to free agape from its erotic feelings and realities. One can also reject an agapeic love that seeks to free it from the body, from the corporeal materiality of existence itself. Eros and agape must be reconciled, a conceptual move I render more explicit in the following chapter.

When foregrounding a more expansive concept of eros as a driving force that seeks to unify and connect all of creation, one is able to clearly surmise that the erotic *is not* the pornographic, nor should it be reduced to sex. The erotic must be reconsidered. Instead, the erotic is about shared deep feelings, sensation, and connection with and for each other that wake us up to love, freedom, and pleasure. The erotic is about self-expression and connection rather than repression and disconnection from one's deepest feelings of love and togetherness. While the body, sexuality, and sex are dimensions of the erotic, the erotic is not to be reduced to any one of these three dimensions. The erotic is a life source and unifying power that creates intense, passionate connection between the world and us.

Womanist theologian Karen Baker-Fletcher asserts that much of Greek literature understood eros as a "unifying force." Unlike *epythemia* (only physical desire), eros included passion and desire for the beloved. Eros was a desire for union with the sacred, being that which is beautiful, good, and true.[9] The sacred is uncovered and found in those whom we love passionately, in the work we do, in the ways we dance and cook, as well as in Creation that loves us back in all its beauty.[10] For Baker-Fletcher, eros is a desire for union with ourselves and others (including Creation) in order to be satisfied in body and soul. The erotic, then, has the power to "heal the soul and bones."[11]

One important aspect of Baker-Fletcher's thought on the erotic is how she extends it to ecological love. For her, the sacred includes *all* of creation. Within much of Western theology (particularly in Christian traditions), the sacred tends to be anthropomorphized, excluding the ways in which non-human beings participate in Divine activity. Erotic feelings foster connection and unity within life, which includes both human and non-human beings. This widening and enlarging of the concept of the Divine allows one to understand how eros relates to a drive toward union and wholeness with all that is sacred, beautiful, and true. Baker-Fletcher's ecological turn remains important within neoliberal societies that numb us to the sacred in creation, as our environment is increasingly objectified for consumption and use. The erotic must include how the environment reveals Divine activity and why our connection to the physical world is critical to our own wholeness and well-being.

We must reconsider the erotic as a power that unites, heals, and connects us to the deepest parts of who we are in the world. Black lesbian feminist and cultural theorist Audre Lorde notes that the erotic has been "made into the confused, the trivial, the psychotic, the plasticized sensation."[12] It is rendered psychotic and irrational (and therefore, dangerous) because it is understood as the pornographic which objectifies and abuses human bodies and earth bodies. However, Lorde responds that the erotic is the opposite of the pornographic. She asserts, "But pornography is a direct denial of the power of the erotic, for it represents the suppression of true feeling. Pornography emphasizes sensation without feeling."[13] Lorde helps one understand the distinction between the pornographic and the erotic, as the former is life-denying, objectifying, and abusive while the latter is life-giving, uniting, and healing.

The erotic is a passionate life force and creative energy that fuels all of our endeavors and loving acts of labor in the world. The horror of neoliberal societies is that it defines the good and beautiful in terms of profit rather than in terms of human connection and care, which robs us of erotic value and power within our ways of being and living. We are emotionally numb to ourselves and others, unable to feel anything because our false "good" is bound up with the reckless pursuit of money and its concomitant alienating ways of acting (social distrust, lack of care, etc.). The numbness of feeling that neoliberal society produces cuts us off from the emotional, connective power needed to transform our societies into just and compassionate communities.

The erotic should therefore be celebrated in *all* of our endeavors such as writing a poem, dancing, thinking through ideas, protesting unjust structures, and pursuing excellence in one's work. We are fully connected to ourselves, our own humanity, when we tap into the erotic that gives meaning and deep feeling to what we create and share with and for each other.

When the erotic is not present, we are unable to employ the creative power needed to transform our world. For instance, neoliberal systems often reduce work to a bear necessity, a duty that enables one to earn money to survive and provide for the ones we love. In this case, the joy and passion associated with work is emptied. One experiences work in an objectified way, not as a creation or extension of oneself as discussed in the previous chapters. Lorde remarks that emptying work of the erotic is like "blinding a painter and then telling her to improve her work, and to enjoy the act of painting. It is not only next to impossible, it is also profoundly cruel."[14] The issue at stake here is not just the doing of one's work but is the question of how fully one can *passionately feel in the doing* of one's work. Work enables us to connect to our own capabilities to feel with deep satisfaction our own creative acts as human beings. As Lorde remarks, our work might be understood as a conscious decision and "longed-for bed" which we enter gratefully and which we rise up empowered.[15] Consequently, one must resist neoliberal systems of oppression that succeed in numbing our deep desires for fulfillment and flourishing.

The erotic is feared (and interpreted as the pornographic) because it entails the kernels of protest and subversive action against neoliberal oppressive systems and practices. Black feminist sociologist Patricia Hill Collins notes that the erotic provides the energy for change.[16] This power that emerges from the erotic must be annexed in neoliberal systems for structures of oppression to function, regulate, and control. The repression in these systems teaches people to "love small" rather than "love big" as love opens people up to vulnerability and transformation in themselves that they can direct toward the wider world. When people "love small" (whether this subject of love is a person, idea, etc.), potential sources of power as energy that flow from love relationships are diminished and attenuated.[17]

When one embraces the erotic and begins to deeply feel different aspects of their lives, a person will demand more from herself and from society. We start to expect joy and justice from our life-pursuits within the context of social, cultural, and economic institutions. We begin to awaken to our capabilities as human beings called to give, share, and love. Our erotic knowledge then empowers us.[18] The erotic becomes "the lens through which we scrutinize all aspects of our existence, forcing us to evaluate those aspects honestly in terms of their relative meaning within our lives."[19] We refuse to settle for the status quo, the numbness, and apathy associated with neoliberal cultural malaise. The erotic begins to color our lives with shades of "what can be," contrasted to the imprisoned context of our neoliberal present. The erotic gives us permission to say "yes" to our longings, yearnings, and cravings for love, vulnerability, joy, connection, and justice. It allows us to live from the inside out.

Neoliberal societies teach us to reject the importance of the erotic in sustaining our power for transformation and healing. Moreover, when we look away from the erotic, we create contexts where we will treat each other as objects of satisfaction that lead to the pornographic, the abused, and the absurd.[20] Instead of allowing the erotic to create a context of mutually satisfied and empowered subjects, we will create contexts of objectifying power relations that are bent on abuse and domination.

It is important to note then that the erotic is a deep part of the religious quest, particularly in articulating a "power in right relation," which rejects the "power-over" model associated with neoliberal societies. Jewish and Christian feminists have done well in demonstrating the role of the erotic in dismantling racism, patriarchy, and heterosexism. For example, Jewish feminist religious scholar Judith Plaskow has employed the idea of eros to describe a new theology of sexuality from a Jewish perspective. While I have argued that the erotic should not be reduced to the sexual, sexuality certainly is a critical dimension of the erotic. Plaskow recognizes this, contending that we remain alienated from ourselves when we are unable to value our human sexuality as a divine good.

Plaskow asserts that, "our sexuality is a current that flows through all activities that are important to us, in which we invest ourselves."[21] She identifies activities that employ sexuality, such as intellectual exchange and common work as these experiences are "laced with sexual energy that animates and enlivens them."[22] This sexual energy, for Plaskow, is what creates communal bonds. In fact, for her, these communal bonds are erotic bonds.[23] These communal bonds are grounded in deeply shared feelings rooted in connection and affective ties. One cannot talk about emotional bonds within the context of community without simultaneously discussing what grounds such bonds: erotic feelings and practices that draw hearts, minds, and bodies together. If one understands the erotic as the driving life force that unites and heals, communal bonds certainly are constituted by erotic feelings and sensibilities. Plaskow then establishes that the erotic, and more specifically sexuality, should not be seen in isolation from our human activities but the force that animates and emboldens all that we do.

Yet, Plaskow notes that sexuality has been deeply repressed and devalued within much of Judaic religious thought, especially women's sexuality. She acknowledges that erotic thoughts and feelings have been recognized in Judaism but this recognition has usually expressed itself as deep suspicion and even hostility of the erotic and sexual. Plaskow argues that this suspicious gaze in relation to the sexual and more broadly, the erotic, is due to what has sat at the center of Judaic law: hetero-patriarchy. Men, for the most part, have been shapers of Judaic laws.[24] Consequently, the goal of many of these laws and statues has been to restrain the erotic and sexual, particularly among women as women's sexuality has been seen as both dangerous and powerful. For Jewish male religious leaders, women's bodies needed to be controlled in order to maintain both patriarchal religious purity and control within society. She lifts up that a deep-seated ambiguity toward sexuality "underlies the extensive rabbinic legislation enforcing the separation of the sexes," although such rabbinic legislation "acknowledges the sexual power of community and the continuity of sexuality with other feelings."[25] This contradiction was undergirded by a more primal fear: the power of female sexuality.

For Plaskow, the ambivalence within Jewish religious thought about sexuality discloses the need to defend and preserve hetero-patriarchy, which meant controlling women's sexuality, erotic feelings, and bodies. The goal was to restrain the dangerous power of sexual impulses, particularly in men who were "seduced" by women. One can just turn to the numerous stories in the Torah in which women are depicted as leading men astray due to the erotic and sexual (Eve, Jezebel, Delilah, etc.). Plaskow seeks to reclaim the role of sexuality as a power that women can employ to deconstruct and challenge hetero-patriarchal systems that deny women the power to connect to themselves and others. The erotic for Plaskow is pregnant with subversive possibilities in relation to fighting hetero-patriarchy.

Carter Heyward is a Christian lesbian feminist theologian who has also demonstrated that embracing the erotic helps to challenge and dismantle systems of "othering" (whether one is talking about racial, gender, or sexual others). Drawing on the work of Audre Lorde and Dorothee Solle and other lesbian feminists, Heyward identifies the erotic as a desire or longing "to taste, and smell and see and hear and touch one another," which shapes our forms of connection and togetherness.[26] It is a yearning to be involved in each other's feelings, lives, and bodies.

For Heyward, the erotic most importantly is a relational movement. At first, the erotic is a movement of our sensuality (our entire moral/intellectual/emotional/sexual self) toward wholeness that "draws us more fully to ourselves."[27] Heyward asserts that because eros is our most "fully embodied experience of the love of God," the erotic allows us to experience God through our bodyselves, creating a mutually enhancing relationship. The erotic is connected to the Divine, which enables us to more fully awaken to the divine spark planted within us, which is love. I discussed earlier the importance of understanding the incarnation as a concrete demonstration of the value of the erotic in Christian traditions. Heyward affirms this interpretation of the Christian tradition and argues that eros reconnects us in ways that are healing and unifying.

Moreover, eros is the urge and movement toward mutuality and right relationship with others. Eros urges one toward mutuality and "rightness in relation," which strengthens our capacity to make connections among others that are truly life-giving, caring, and loving rather than selfish and abusive. Heyward doesn't understand mutuality as some sort of "fair exchange" within a strict economic model. Rather, she understands mutuality as "sharing power in such a way that each participant in the relationship is called forth more fully into becoming who she is – a whole person."[28] Here, I understand Heyward's understanding of mutuality to be related to the psychosocial dimensions of the erotic and how it enables us to actualize as human beings. I return at the end of this chapter to how the erotic addresses the social-structural dimensions of neoliberal societies in which mutuality also must have a reciprocal and "fair exchange" component in order to resist structural injustices.

As one can see, a number of feminist discourses have articulated the erotic as a religious and/or spiritual good that can foster radical connection as we experience self-actualization. Moreover, the erotic empowers one to resist apathy. The erotic empowers persons to work toward the transformation of their social worlds. The erotic is a unifying force at the intrapersonal, interpersonal, and social-structural levels. Black feminist and womanist perspectives have done well in recovering the importance of the erotic in challenging neoliberal ways of being. I now turn to how black feminist and womanist discourses have illuminated the unifying and spiritual importance of the erotic: through literature.

The Erotic as a Unifying Force: *Sula*

Black feminist and womanist studies have turned to black women's literature as a way to explore the spiritual importance of the erotic. Within such literature, the erotic has been a driving life force among black women, creating connection, purpose, and self-actualization for these women. Toni Morrison's novel *Sula* provides a vivid account of how the erotic binds two women together as well as the complexities and contradictions that emerge when one is not accountable to the power that the erotic grants. I think *Sula* is one of Morrison's more under-appreciated novels, which explores the power of the erotic.

The novel focuses on two main characters, Nel Wright and Sula Peace, who have been bonded together since children. It is through their relationship early on that these two women move deeper into their desires for freedom and authentic selfhood. Nel and Sula represent the range of life choices and possibilities that black women possessed in the middle of the twentieth century in the United States. Set in Medallion, Ohio, a small rural town called the "Bottom," this story chronicles the life choices both women made, choices that, in large part, are shaped and grow out of the erotic relationship they share with and for each other. From 1919 to 1965, we watch Nel and Sula grow and mature into adults in a racist patriarchal society that offers them a proscribed range of choices. We watch both women shape themselves in light of sexuality, erotic power, evil, and love.

Sula and Nel represent two different sets of life choices that black women make toward self-discovery and integration within their proscribed societal context. Nel opts to embrace conventional morality as she fashions a life characterized by the patriarchal model of marriage in the Bottom. As a girl child, Nel fantasizes about "lying on a flower bed, tangled in her own hair, waiting for some fiery prince."[29] While Nel at one point had dreamed of leaving the Bottom and traveling around the world as a child, she chose the traditional model of marriage along with the security and stability it brought. Because Nel still desires to be self-determined and free within the deepest parts of herself, Nel's life as an adult is marked by stagnation, repression, and passivity, as she merely *exists* in the Bottom.

In contrast to Nel, Sula chooses to *live* rather than exist. As a child, Sula's fantasies are erotic, passionate, and sensuous as she dreams of galloping "through her own mind on a gray-and-white horse tasting sugar and smelling roses."[30] Sula chooses not to be dependent upon social norms like her mother Hannah and grandmother Eve. As an adult, Sula is a fiercely independent and sexually free woman, experiencing life on her own terms. She is an active woman who rejects the patriarchal gender norms of her day in which she sees marriage as a trap to women's economic and sexual freedom. She rejects the limits and restrictions of female domesticity. The narrator says that Sula "lived out her days exploring her own thoughts and emotions, giving them full reign, feeling no obligation to please anybody unless their pleasure pleased her."[31] Her life choices are feminist in the broadest sense of the term, as she sought to be self-determined within a sexist society.

It is important to note that Sula and Nel's sets of life choices possess both possibilities and limitations. For Nel, she seeks security, direction, and community in order to live life well. Her choice in living a traditional life of marriage reflects her desire to connect and be present to the people she loves. However, Nel is deeply repressed. Her decision to have security and community overwhelms her need to self-actualize as an independent self-determined sensuous and erotic being. She is unable to live passionately as her life is driven by formality rather than deep passion and connection.

For Sula, she is independent and understands her erotic power to live life fully and without apology as a black woman. Sula grips life by the throat and forces it to give her the multiple desires she possesses. She lives a life of curiosity, unpredictability, and dangerous joy. Yet, Sula is directionless and at times, becomes unaccountable to her erotic power, an unaccountability that ultimately destroys her friendship with Nel. Both women's life choices entail gains and losses.

Nel and Sula's female friendship is joined by the erotic. When Sula returns to the Bottom after being away for many years, the narrator reflects on the nature of their friendship. Nel realizes that Sula's return to the Bottom was like "magic." For Nel, Sula's return for her was like "getting the use of an eye back, having a cataract removed. Her old friend had come home."[32] Sula gave Nel a new sight, a new way of seeing herself as a passionate erotic being with aspirations and dreams in a racist, sexist world. Sula was the person who had made Nel laugh, "who made her see old things with new eyes, in whose presence she felt clever, gentle, and a little raunchy."[33] Sula brought Nel home to herself. Likewise, Nel was the "first person who had been real" to Sula.[34] Sula has "clung to Nel as the closest thing to both an other and a self."[35] Because Sula had "no center, no speck around which to grow" due to her tumultuous childhood, Nel has been that one reality Sula found meaning and solace in.

In fact, Nel and Sula could not be distinguished from one another, as their union was so close. The narrator asserts that Nel has lived through Sula's past and present perceptions so that "talking to Sula had always been a conversation with herself."[36] Even Nel's love for her husband Jude has become "a bright and easy affection, a playfulness that was reflected in their lovemaking," because of Sula's return to the Bottom and back into Nel's life. They were inseparable, as a "compliment to one was a compliment to the other, and cruelty to one was a challenge to the other."[37]

The reader is able to clearly see how the erotic defines the friendship between Sula and Nel. Their physical connection is profound as they are two parts of the same personality. The yearning and longing that each other experience in and through each other's bodies enables them to see themselves anew in the world, a world that denigrated black women. Nel and Sula are able to see beauty, love, and friendship within themselves, which radically energizes and colors their lives. As stated, it is through Sula that Nel can reclaim the lovemaking and playfulness with her husband, Jude. And it is through Nel that Sula feels there is a such thing as a "real human being" (meaning loving human being). As black women, they teach each other to desire and move toward self-determination. This driving force toward union with the beautiful and loving undergirds their friendship and makes possible moments of joy as black women in the Bottom (characterized by poverty and despair).

However, we watch their friendship experience a fateful turn as Sula has sexual relations with Jude (Nel's husband). Nel finds Sula and Jude naked in bed and severs all contact with Sula. Eventually, Jude leaves Nel and moves to Dayton, Ohio. What's most telling is the reason why Sula violated Nel in such a grave way. The narrator remarks that Sula "had clung to Nel as the closest thing to both an other and a self, only to discover that she and Nel were not the one and the same thing."[38] But what does Sula mean by Nel and her not being "one and the same thing"? The narrator brings us further to what Sula might mean. Sula acknowledges that she "had no thought at all of causing Nel pain when she bedded down with Jude." However, Sula charges Nel with changing into "them" once she and Jude married. "Them" are the other townspeople that were quite content *living without passion and openness toward the world*, opting to live in fear of what one might lose by abandoning convention and traditions. "Them" were bursting forth with "skinned dreams and bony regrets." And "them" also included women who "without men were like sour-tipped needles featuring one constant empty eye."[39] Nel had become "them."

For Sula, she and Nel had never experienced any division between themselves (they were "one self") until Nel's marriage, which made Nel become like "them." Sula recognizes that Nel's marriage disrupted the union she and Nel experiences so that Sula was "ill prepared for the possessiveness [she felt] of the one person she felt close to."[40] Sula knows that "Nel was the one person who had wanted nothing from her, who had accepted all aspects of her," which now made Sula want "everything, and all" from Nel because of "*that*," being Nel's erotic and unconditional love.[41] But for Sula, Nel no longer wanted to be that, as it was "too dangerous." Sula now felt "Nel belonged to the town and all of its ways," which were characterized by a "closedness" to life.

One might argue that Sula is the personification of evil after turning on Nel in this way. I would suggest that a more complex reading of Sula involves acknowledging her inability to manage the profound erotic connection that Nel and her possess. She wants all of Nel. Nel did not want this. Jude stood in between Nel and Sula, as Sula believes that Nel changed once she married. I interpret this novel as Sula's attempt to remove Jude, which delves more deeply into the Janus-faced nature of Sula's motivation. She is unable to find a life-giving way to make Nel fully hers, so she resorts to painful, emotionally violent action. However, Sula's actions are motivated by a deep longing and yearning she has to secure her "other half." The narrator suggests that in Sula's strangeness, "her craving for the other half of her equation was the consequence of an idle imagination" [in regard to Jude].[42]

Sula desires all of Nel but she deeply violates Nel's trust and love by sleeping with Jude. For certain, part of Sula's illicit affair with Jude is simply her desire to conquer and consume men, a way of reclaiming her strength and power. As Sula asserted herself in the sexual act, "particles of strength gathered in her like steel shavings drawn to a spacious magnetic center, forming a tight cluster that nothing, it seemed, could break."[43] Yet, Sula eventually realized that this kind of power was the *pornographic* rather than the erotic strength she gained from simply being in authentic union with Nel. Sula eventually discovered that consuming men as "pig meat" left her with "a loneliness so profound the word itself had no meaning." It left her with the "death of time."[44] The complexity of motivation involved in Sula's betrayal of Nel hits at the heart of Sula's traumatic past and how this past shaped her. Sula being interpreted in this light avoids reducing her to pure evil over and against Nel's pure goodness. One is able to see the flawed humanity of Sula as well as the power of the erotic as she searches for meaning, wholeness, and authentic selfhood.

Some scholars such as black feminist scholar Barbara Smith have argued that *Sula* can be read as a lesbian novel. Smith contends that *Sula* works as a lesbian novel "not only because of the passionate friendship between Sula and Nel but because of Morrison's consistently critical stance toward the heterosexual institutions of male-female relationships, marriage, and the family."[45] While I admit that this reading is certainly a creative possibility, I think that this interpretation may miss the ways in which the erotic binds people together, in ways that *resist labels or categorizations*. Even in non-sexual friendship between women (or men), the erotic can be powerfully satisfying among persons so that union is felt as something that frees one to be at home with oneself. It is Sula's belief that she sees herself more clearly in and through Nel, which leads her to pain and panic as Jude's presence reinforces the disruption of this unprecedented bond. The friendship these two women share opens them up to the complexities of life such as pain and joy, sorrow and happiness, oppression and liberation. As discussed earlier, the hunger for self-actualization with and for each other is a deep component of the erotic and Sula and Nel experience this dimension together. Consequently, to simply reduce Sula and Nel to a lesbian relationship would miss the complexities of how the erotic functions and manifests within both sexual and non-sexual bonds.

Nel eventually realizes this powerful and enduring connection she has with Sula despite Sula's actions. Nel visits Sula as she is on her deathbed, which produces a half-hearted reconciliation. But this awareness for Nel is made complete when Nel visits Sula's burial site. As Nel is standing there, she begins to uncontrollably cry as the narrator says that Nel's loss of Sula "pressed down on her chest and came up into her throat."[46] Nel says, "All that time, all that time, I thought I was missing Jude." She further sobs, "We were girls together...O Lord, Sula...girl, girl, girlgirlgirl." The narrator ends the story that "it was a fine cry – loud and long – but it has no bottom and it had no top, just circles and circle of sorrow."[47] Even in death, Nel feels Sula. There union is made complete.

I have talked at length about the power of the erotic between Sula and Nel. However, Sula and her erotic capacities unify Medallion as the townspeople fear her and are able to define their own goodness over and against her "evil ways" (sexual ways). The residents could simply assert moral purity by defining themselves against who she was, by simply being different from Sula. As a pariah "after everyone's husbands," Sula provides the communal cohesion to the Bottom as the residents are able to experience their own moral rightness (read: unlike Sula). They felt they needed to love and protect themselves from Sula (or what Sula represented), particularly wives who feared Sula as a seductress. Sula's embodiment of the erotic challenged the racist, hetero-patriarchal structure, which limited women to the home. Sula defies such conventional morality without apology. In fact, Sula challenges the very environment and community that molded and shaped her. Her experimental life asserted that women could be defined by choice and self-determination, despite the cost. Nel is able to identify her source of grief over the many years since she severed ties with Sula. Her grief is not because of Jude's abandonment. Rather, her deep grief is because she awakens to the lost years of being without Sula, as Sula's actions simply reflected her tragic and traumatic childhood. Nel acknowledges that Sula tried to *the best of her ability* to live a life informed deeply by erotic power and passionate living.

Sula teaches one something about the power of the erotic in all of its complexities as a binding and unifying force among oppressed black women. As black feminist Hortense Spillers notes, "Sula is both loved and hated by the reader, embraced and rejected simultaneously because her audience is forced to accept the corruption of absolutes and what has been left in their place – the complex, alienated and transitory gestures of a personality who has no framework outside of moral reference beyond or other than herself." Sula does not represent evil but embodies the contradictions of erotic relationships. Sula unapologetically transgresses hetero-normative gender roles, seeking to "make her own way" in a misogynistic world that denied her personhood as a black woman. She also exercises her erotic agency within the parameters of being a poor black woman. Race, sex, and class certainly shape how agency is asserted. Her erotic agency is healing to Nel who is able to reclaim her sensuous, playful, and loving side in Sula's presence. However, the oppressive white, patriarchal gaze that Sula disrupts through her erotic embodiment is simultaneously the same gaze she internalizes about herself and eventually Nel. Sula doesn't believe that black men can be life-partners with black women, leading her to objectify the many black men she slept with. Moreover, she denigrates Nel for attempting to achieve authentic partnership with her husband Jude.

It is the erotic that creates "voice" and agency for these two black women, Sula and Nel. The erotic "un-silences" the voices of these women as they attempt to find meaning and move toward wholeness in a racist, hetero-patriarchal society. They do so imperfectly but with a genuine intention toward freedom and authentic selfhood.

The Erotic as a Spiritual Good:
By the Light of My Father's Smile

Alice Walker's *By the Light of My Father's Smile* is also a literary work
that foregrounds the erotic as a *spiritual* life force. This novel tells the
story of two daughters who endure and overcome the sexual repression they experience by their father. In the early 1940s, anthropologist
Senior Robinson (his full name is never given) and his wife, Langley,
desire to study the Mundo people, an endangered wise, egalitarian
community of mixed-race African/Indian ancestry in the remote
Sierras in Mexico. Being a black anthropologist in the United States
in the 1940s, Senior Robinson is simply unable to ascertain funding
due to structural racism. He pretends to be a Christian missionary
to receive funding as an anthropologist in order to study the Mundo
people in the Sierras. However, he becomes seduced by the "power of
the cloth," which leads to deep contention within his home, especially
in relation to his two daughters, Susannah and Magdalena.

He uses patriarchal power to repress his daughters burgeoning
sexuality, particularly Magdalena, which leads to bitter confrontation, division, and resentment. Magdalena's life forever changes when
she is caught with her beloved boyfriend (Manuelito) as a teenager
and violently beaten by her father, Senior Robinson. From that day
forward, Magdalena harbors in her heart bitterness, resentment,
unforgiveness, and hatred for her father. Susannah also becomes
estranged from her father in order to stand in solidarity with her sister Magdalena. Senior Robison attempts to block his two daughters'
exercise of the erotic, which has disastrous consequences. However, it
is through the daughters embracing of erotic agency that they are able
to reconnect with the heart of life, being love and forgiveness.

One infers throughout this novel that the celebration of sexuality
and the power of the erotic are central to the experience of the Spirit
and the formation of the authentic self. The book opens with a raw,
sensual lovemaking scene shared between Susannah and her female
lover, Pauline. Senior Robinson is dead but is present as an Angel
watching over Susannah. He narrates the sexual encounter his daugh-
ter has with Pauline, an encounter full of erotic openness, playfulness,
and pleasure. Pauline is an older woman that finds strength and power
in erotic agency, particularly her sexuality. She is very well read and
"cared only for the bold, the brave, the brazen."[48] She was like women
who "knew they were trapped and resolved to fly out of one trap after

the other, full of anger and heightened libido."[49] Early in life, Pauline believed that sex was a great power to "have over others," as she used sex "to give pleasure, ruthlessly, and leisurely take it."[50]

Yet, Pauline's perspective of sex is complicated by her history of rape. At the age of fifteen, her mother, father, and brothers "got her drunk" and left her alone with a young man who raped her, resulting in her getting pregnant (and subsequently, being forced to marry her raper). After this event, Pauline did not feel at home in her own body, distrustful of men and her own ability to love and be loved. She is jaded by the conventions of her society that would force her to marry and build a life with the man who sexually violated her. This shaped Pauline's experience of self, as she is alienated from her emotions and her body.

Pauline goes on a journey of loving her body that leads to her finally leaving her rapist/husband, Winston. After Pauline births her son, she meets a woman named Gena, who becomes her lover. Pauline says that Gena offers sexual intimacy of an "incredible nurturing quality," the kind of affectionate sex that seemed designed to reconnect her to herself in order to keep her alive.[51] This "orgasmic freedom" enabled Pauline to liberate herself, to come home to pleasure, affection, love, and self-worth. Pauline admits about orgasmic freedom, "Once I experienced it, I felt I had been reborn."[52] Pauline further states about the erotic and orgasmic freedom, "It was a revelation. That I, lowly me, somehow had this precious thing, I knew instantly what it meant. It meant I was not forgotten by Creation; it meant that I was passionately, immeasurably loved."[53] In and through the erotic, Pauline believes that love is a possibility and is awakened to the vibrancy and vitality of life itself. Pauline is able to appreciate the mystery of love and its diverse manifestations associated with pleasure and the body.

Spirituality, for Pauline, was profoundly connected to this erotic revelation about herself. In fact, her exercise of erotic agency connected her to the Divine, being Creation, as she attempted to experience authentic selfhood. Prior to meeting Gena, her value of self was jaded by the denigration she experienced at the hands of her sexual abuser. She did not see herself as worthy of love or pleasure. Once Gena opened her up to her true self-worth through the erotic, Pauline saw the *divine in herself*. She did not look outside of herself for revelations of divine beauty such as love, compassion, and truth. Instead, she turned inward, recognizing that her erotic knowledge enabled her to uncover the secrets of life, being joy and trust associated with living a life of wholeness.

Pauline also notes that this orgasmic freedom "has been a male right...since the beginning of patriarchy."[54] Pauline seems to be arguing that her "coming home to herself" was grounded in the recovery of her voice, her erotic voice, which had been muted when she was raped. Patriarchy had justified her rapist, as sexual agency was bound up with male entitlement and even violence. Her being "reborn" was coming into full voice and agency through the celebration of her body. It was after this experience with her erotic power and agency that Pauline planned her escape from her husband. For Pauline, this reclamation of erotic power then is not only a personal victory but also a challenge to patriarchal structures that repress and violate the central core of women's humanity. After they make love in the opening scene of the book, Pauline encourages Susannah to pursue her burgeoning quest toward wholeness and healing through her erotic agency.

We then learn about Susannah's journey toward erotic liberation. Susannah, having married her husband Petros at a young age, begins to realize how insidious patriarchal institutions are in obstructing women's erotic voice and agency. It is while Susannah is visiting her husband's relatives in Greece, that she recognizes the far ranging consequences of patriarchal domination. She meets Irene, a dwarf, who has been forced to live in the back of church by authorities because of her difference. Against Petros' knowledge and wishes, Susannah visits Irene everyday while she is in Greece. Irene discusses with her the violence women have undergone in Greece such as public stoning. Susannah attempts to talk with Petros about such patriarchal violence but he is repulsed by this information, denying that his country does such things. Susannah begins to contemplate Petros' overt denial of gender violence in his own country.

Yet, a turning point for Susannah is when Irene does a "reading" about her future. Irene tells Susannah, "You are on a journey to your own body" as "someone who left her body long ago, when you were quite young."[55] Irene reminds Susannah that she is coming home to her body not her "mind," as living inside of one's head can often disconnect them from the urges, sensations, and longings that are associated with the pursuit of the true and beautiful in life. Irene says to Susannah, "[You are on a journey] to your own skin, the way it shines, the way it glows, smells, absorbs the light."[56] Irene further states that this "absorbing of light" was about Susannah reconnecting to her "inner man," as her inner voice was lifting her "into the carriage of her own body," which would allow her to take charge of her life. She was being beckoned to come home to a spirituality that placed the body and the erotic at the center of this journey.

It was then that Susannah began remembering the wisdom and egalitarianism of the Mundo people her parents had studied and written about. For instance, in Mundo life, when a women got pregnant, her pregnancy was considered a shared experience by the father so that the "father-to-be took to his bed with labor pains and all his buddies gathered around him to offer up support. Sometimes the father's cries drowned out the mother's."[57] The Mundo people also did not lie. They knew the power of a lie and its power to generate deep domination, violence, and inequality. Interestingly, the Mundo people never accepted the lie about "original sin" within Christian traditions (through eating the forbidden fruit). They concluded that perhaps original sin was "one of the biggest lies that has unraveled the world."[58] For the Mundo people, the idea of "original sin" had created all kinds of male hierarchies that relegated women to inferior cultural spaces (i.e., Eve deceived Adam).

Moreover, the Mundo people saw spirituality as only being able to find expression in and through the body. Even Manuelito (Magdalena's lost lover) states when he dies,

> The first thing that happens when you die, is that you have a burning desire to urinate. You have nothing to pee with, you understand, just the desire to do so. Among my people, we are told this is what happens, and so I was not very surprised. It is understood that spirituality resides in the groin, in the sexual organs. Not in the mind, and not in the heart. It is while fucking that you normally feel closer to God.[59]

It was this egalitarian disposition of the Mundo people that Susannah remembered as she began this quest for meaning, wholeness, and healing through her body.

Susannah's sister Magdalene was not as fortunate to find healing for her soul while living on earth. As discussed earlier, Magdalena's life forever changes when she is caught with her boyfriend as a teenager and violently beat by her father, Senior Robinson. From that day forward, Magdalene harbors in her heart bitterness, resentment, and hatred of her father for not only physically beating her but also for ripping out of her arms the beautiful experience of love she found through her body with her boyfriend, Manuelito. As the years passed and she grew into an adult, Magdalena assuages her heartbreak and anger toward her father through over-eating, becoming obese. Even though she becomes well educated and develops a career as a successful professor, she remains broken and her weight reflects her depression and sorrow.

On a flight some two decades later, Magdalene and Manuelito see each other again and re-ignite their love. After experiencing love again through her erotic encounter with Manuelito, Manuelito is hit by a bus and killed. Magdalene is driven so deep into depression that she eats herself into coma, has a heart attack, and dies. It seems as if Magdalena never receives wholeness and healing that she so desperately craved. However, when Magdalene dies, she enters the Spirit realm as her ancestors did (mother, father, and Manuelito). It is here that she is reconciled to her father and mother, which points to eccentric spiritual opportunities for love and healing beyond the grave.

Senior Robinson acts as an Angel watching over his daughters, even watching over them while they make love. I can imagine the shock and even repulsion a reader might experience at the thought of a father observing sex among his daughters. Wouldn't this be akin to incest? Not necessarily for this novel. Near the end of the novel, Manuelito (now dead and speaking from eternity) describes a ceremony that the Mundo people perform for lovers who are joined together. In order for the lovers to prepare to make love, the mother and father arrive singing with "sweatgrass, feathers, and eggs" (signs of fertility, creativity, and bountifulness) and "kiss in all five places" before sending their grown child to their lover.[60] The mother and father kiss their grown adult child in all five places: the ears, eyes, nose, mouth, and "the place where life begins." The Mundo people celebrated the purity of sexuality and the erotic. They did not see the vulva and phallus as vile or pornographic but as deeply spiritual. Hence, this kiss was not a kiss of perversity but a kiss of celebration, extolling the body and its sexual organs as spiritual and pure (pure as the eyes, nose, ears, and mouth).

For the Mundo people, kissing in all five places was a sign of deep respect for sexuality within this community. Hence, when a woman enters into the bedroom to make love, she does so "by the light of her father's smile." Patriarchal norms that seek to repress women's sexuality and erotic agency had no place in the Mundo tribe. This elevation of the erotic as a primal life force that should be celebrated rather than feared sits at the heart of this story. In order for women to fully exercise their erotic agency, hetero-patriarchal ideologies and structures must be challenged and dismantled. Moreover, in order for women to experience healing and wholeness, they must be reconciled to the beauty and power of their bodies and the erotic.

One is certainly left with lingering questions over whether this literary decision that Walker makes is more harmful than good. Certainly, Walker's decision to allow the father (as an angel) to watch over his daughters while they have sex may open her up to the charge that she promotes incest, even sexual abuse between father and daughters in this novel. I must admit that Walker's literary choice here is very risky. Walker certainly wants to cast a vision about sexuality, sensuality, and the erotic that are freed up from the pornographic and framed as a creative, spiritual good for individuals and communities to celebrate. She wants to envision a different world where sexuality and sex are not feared and interpreted as corrupt but discerned as a life force that creates union and connection among humans and all of Creation. Yet, does the benefit of introducing this new vision of sexuality outweigh the costs associated with obscuring and rendering moral ambiguous the problem of sexual vouyerism through Senior Robinson's indulgence of his daughters sexual conquests? I don't think these questions have one-dimensional answers. But, the reader must keep in mind that Walker is attempting to delineate new erotic realities that can ground humanity characterized by spiritual communion, care, love, and bodily appreciation.

Challenging Neoliberalism: The Erotic as Political

Morrison's *Sula* and Walker's *By the Light of My Father's Smile* certainly demonstrate that the erotic politically challenges the passionless and numb ways of being that are a part of neoliberal culture. The erotic connects deep feelings with wise responsible action. In fact, the two novels that I analyzed disclose that the erotic can shape moral behavior and fuel socio-political engagement with the world.

In part, the erotic is political because it is just not a private experience. It is also shaped by and in movement toward another person, idea, or object. Because the erotic is fundamentally an energy relation that orients itself toward mutuality, it can interrogate the non-mutual, hierarchical relations sponsored by neoliberal societies. For Susannah, the erotic calls her beyond the boundaries of herself in efforts to ask questions about structures within broader society that do not nurture the actualization of one's humanity. Susannah not only is able to question women's subordination in her worlds but also is able to affirm deep within herself her bisexuality as a spiritual good. She is able to publicly affirm her queer sexuality, despite the church's teachings on this issue. For her, the erotic grants the capacity for countercultural public/political action.

The erotic as a source of *political knowledge and action* is what so many black feminists thinkers affirm. Responsible action is cultivated by erotic knowledge. Eros is a mode of cognition and a way of gaining deep insight into the worlds we inhabit. Erotic knowledge is a form of wisdom that puts us in touch with the deepest levels of our lives. Because the political sphere is about how we organize basic resources in order to live well together, erotic knowledge contributes to this organizing.

For example, erotic knowledge contributes to the movement for a living wage. The living wage movement in the United States contests the paltry minimum wages that working classes receive, which often does not allow them to stay above poverty level line. While CEOs make money in the millions, janitors, secretaries, and other blue-collar workers often work in order to survive. Moreover, women often do not have proper healthcare coverage and benefits, which exacerbates their poor economic conditions (and the conditions of their children). This huge disparity in income is unsettling. Erotic knowledge moves beyond the abstractions associated with the living wage issue (statistics and figures). Erotic knowledge privileges opportunities for a mother to communicate her experience on how an absence of living wage in her life alienates her from her work and violates her sense of human dignity as a worker. This mother might also share how her children are affected, as she might struggle to pay for daycare, good education, and more. It is through the hearing of this mother's story that shared feelings can be cultivated between that mother and her hearers. This mother's story, concrete struggle, and emotional pain connect her to others, prompting others toward responsible political action to seek a living wage. True knowledge of this mother's suffering cannot simply be gained in abstraction. Knowledge of her condition must also be experienced through shared feelings. This mother's story might touch and transform the deepest and most intimate places of other people, resulting in a movement—that is, *movement* toward each other in support of collective well-being. The erotic, in this case, sponsors connection that becomes the grounding for protest and political action.

Moreover, grounding our analysis of social and political conditions in the erotic can help one grasp the gender dimensions of the erotic. In relation to the living wage movement, poor to working class women are deeply impacted, often through the absence of childcare and healthcare associated with minimum wage jobs (and these women are the primary caretakers of children). A concept of healthy erotic relations can be used in assessing what is wrong with our present neo-liberal socio-economic order, such as gender inequity in relation to living wages. Concepts of healthy erotic relations measure the depth of alienation within neoliberal life and point to areas in which funda-mental change is necessary within political life.

The experience of the erotic is also a combative energy of revolt within political spheres. As Audre Lorde states, "In touch with the power of the erotic within ourselves...we begin to give up, of neces-sity, being satisfied with suffering and self-negation."[61] Lorde further states, "Charged with the anger at injustice that belongs to the deep-est nature of eros...our acts against oppression become integral with self, motivated and empowered from within."[62] A unique contribution of black feminist literature is that erotic feelings *awaken and sustain the anger needed to spur the fight against multiple oppressions.* These theorists connect the "the work of love and justice" to the "power of anger" on personal and political levels. Through erotic knowledge, we resist and refuse social, economic, and cultural humiliation from racist, hetero-patriarchal authorities. The erotic as an energy of revolt is deeply subversive because such erotic feelings threaten established hetero-patriarchal power relations in political and economic spheres.

For instance, healthy visions of erotic relations might counter oppositional forces against same-sex marriage within the United States. To say that one is a lesbian is to make a statement that is both personal and political as LGBTQ identities are seen as overhaul-ing heterosexual social structures. As Foucault reminds us, there is a "history of [hetero]sexuality" at play, a history that has been cultur-ally produced to support the economic, social, and cultural status quo. Heterosexuality has been secured and sustained through "dis-course and social practices – romance, marriage, weddings, family values, traditions, eugenics, and social purity campaigns, to name a few – that have been variously organized and articulated depending on the social formation."[63]

Within the political and economic spheres, erotic knowledge chal-lenges traditional interpretations of marriage as simply religious institutions, as marriage is an *economic* institution that secures het-ero-patriarchal ends. Around the world, marriage involves transac-tions of money or land in which families are required to pay to seal the marriage. Who you marry is often the most determining aspect of your future for many women around the globe. In different countries, who poor women marry has everything to do with their survival. In many countries, women are not even able to hold property or make a sustainable wage to live. Because women are the primary caretakers of the poorest group in the world being children, they are constantly forced to think about how they will make ends meet. Consequently, marriage is primarily seen as a financial transaction that guarantees the future economic stability of oneself and one's children.

While marriage in the West such as the United States is often primarily seen as a spiritual and/or social institution that secures happiness or personal fulfillment, marriage is still largely an economic institution that secures financial benefits that one does not have access to as an unmarried or divorced person. For instance, marriage grants the opportunity for a couple to share employer benefits such as healthcare, benefits that are critically important to one's physical well-being. Marriage also enables a couple to save money on car insurance. It is general knowledge that a person's rates can go down once they have "tied the knot" (assuming that both persons have a safe driving record). One knows the tax-break benefits at the end of the year that are often granted to those who are married.

The continuing national debate surrounding same sex marriage discloses that *economics* is at stake. Heterosexual compliance is built into economic structures and institutions in the Unites States such as marriage. Marriage can be seen as a capitalistic institution that is grounded in particular hetero-norms. While I am in no way arguing that the meaning of marriage is reducible to the economic, the economic is often under-emphasized in conversations surrounding marriage as an institution that offers particular financial benefits based on heterosexual privilege. Same-sex marriage then is not just about the future social fabric of the United States but also about the economic future of same-gender loving people. Same-gender loving persons not only want to have the opportunity to love whoever they desire but also want to break the "glass ceiling" on who is allowed to benefit from marriage as an economic institution. When discussing the possibility of same-sex marriage, one can clearly see that heterosexuality is deeply linked to the neoliberal structuring of marriage.

Yet, one must return to the relationship between patriarchy and heterosexuality in order to understand how hetero-normative matrices condition current neoliberal systems. Patriarchy "refers to the structuring of social and economic life—labor, state, and consciousness—such that more social resources and value accrue to men as a group at the expense of women."[64] Patriarchy, as a form of social organization, has been integral to neoliberalism's exploitative social relations in order to "maximize" profit. In fact, patriarchy is readily seen in the contradictions neoliberalism presents to what it means to be a woman. Women are "contradictorily positioned in contemporary capitalism as free workers and citizens, yet devalued as females, such as the unpaid labor of women."[65] Neoliberalism's privileging of the value of individual hard work is belied by the social expectation that women should primarily serve others as wives and mothers. Neoliberalism values the autonomous subject, yet women are expected to provide "most of the necessary labor that is essential to our collective survival although it is rendered invisible within the value system of commodity exchange."[66] What is important to patriarchies is that they generate a social organization that splits between public wage economy and unpaid domestic production, both regulated by the value of excessive individualism.[67] Unfortunately, because women tend to be concentrated in the unpaid domestic area, they often are unfairly penalized within patriarchal organizations. As of 2013, women are still being paid only 77 cents to men's dollar. Even within corporate settings, women continue to pay a price in terms of a loss of earnings simply for being a female within a hetero-normative society.

Yet, women are not only negatively positioned in relation to patriarchy but some men are negatively positioned within patriarchal structures. Due to issues of race, class, and sexuality, women are often positioned differently to each other as men are often positioned differently in relation to one another. For example, two women (a black woman and white woman) may work at a corporation ran by a white man. One might argue that both women encounter patriarchy. While this initial observation may be true, their experiences are qualitatively different within the patriarchal and hetero-normative context of this corporation. Historically, black women have not only been positioned negatively in relation to white men but also in relation to white women. While both women may experience patriarchy, the black woman also experiences herself as a "raced" person who negotiates her identity in way that the white woman does not have to do as the white female worker possesses white privilege, a privilege the black women is not afforded. Consequently, patriarchies arrange and structure the experiences of these two women in different ways.

Similarly, men encounter this same "differential" within patriarchal, hetero-normative contexts. Two same-gender loving men may encounter homophobic attitudes and practices within many social contexts. Both men experience brute forms of violence within a context that demands and requires them to be "straight." To not be hetero-sexual is to be disciplined and punished for a deviant sexuality. However, the white same-gender loving male and Hispanic same-gender loving man are positioned differently within such hetero-patriarchal hierarchies. The white gay male still possesses white privilege within a system that constructs and reward whiteness, although heterosexist discrimination remains an oppressive experience for him. To the contrary, the Hispanic same-gender loving male does not have white privilege. In fact, he experiences racism not only within wider society but also within the gay community itself from gay white men. This example also shows how men are as vulnerable as women within patriarchal, hetero-normative systems.

By asserting that men and women are distinct and opposite sexes who are naturally attracted to each other, heterosexuality then becomes essential to patriarchy. Women's position under the hetero-normative gaze is "a subordinate other, as sexual property, and as exploited laborer."[68] Her position depends upon this heterosexual matrix in which she is described as a man's opposite. If "man" is the epitome of strength then "woman" is quintessentially soft and demure. If man is fundamentally rational and sexually virile than woman is emotive and less virile. As a result, hetero-normativity helps to secure the regulation of women's bodies, labor, and desires. Even same-gender loving desires are structured and interpreted against these essentially "natural" ways of being, leading to the pathologizing of gay, lesbian, bisexual, and transgender desires and identities. Clearly, heterosexuality creates gendered regimes that inhibit the diversity of sexual identities from being embraced within social and economic life. This history of sexuality is structured in dominance.

Erotic knowledge then interprets this hetero-patriarchal history as socially and culturally produced, rather than norms instituted by God or some Divine Being. It is the erotic that energizes us to revolt against the production of hetero-patriarchy in the economic, cultural, political, and religious spheres of neoliberal society. And this revolutionary energy does not subscribe to a hierarchal "power-over" model but to a healing, creative "power-with" paradigm. This kind of power confirms the oneness we all desire to experience, which is both spiritual and political.

I think it is important to remember that the erotic as political does not assume a naïve "oneness" or unity. Lorde reminds one that the erotic and its quest for connection among persons is not an unqualified affirmation that we agree on everything. Rather, it is the struggle to respectfully work together toward justice even in the midst of our differences. The erotic is never about "perfect" uncorrupted connection as the erotic is constantly being colonized within neoliberal structures of dominance, which transforms it into the pornographic. However, the language and experience of the erotic can offer resources in challenging and combating the numbness and loss of yearning to be with and for each other.

4

Love as a Concrete Revolutionary Practice

In this neoliberal moment, love is seen as apolitical and unrealistic. Love is often used in confusing and sloppy ways, which leads to a disbelief in love itself. Some simply interpret love as fantasy. As discussed in chapter 2, because love is seen as a commodity that benefits one's bottom line (one's own interests, social status, financial agenda, etc.), love remains suspect and undesired within personal and social dimensions of life. Some simply "write off love," arguing that it does not exist. Love is seen as impossible within personal relationships and broader political life. This cynicism of love within social and political communities is a tragedy. In part, love is often relegated to the idealistic because it is understood in abstract terms rather than as a practice. Love is a concrete revolutionary practice that integrates the ways in which *eros* enables an "enfleshment" of *agape* and even *philia*.

This chapter explores the radical potential of affect, being love. Employing black feminists such as bell hooks, Alice Walker, Audre Lorde, and Jennifer Nash, I suggest that love is not merely an ideal sentiment but a concrete revolutionary practice. Love is a *movement*. It *is movement* toward each other.[1] For black feminist and womanist religious perspectives, love has been a practice of self-actualization as well as a strategy for constructing compassionate political communities. Black feminist and womanist thinkers assert that love can birth new moral worlds in response to the pathologies of neoliberal societies. They do not hold love and the political as antithetical concepts or realms.

The analytical and political importance of love must be grappled with because love is a concrete revolutionary practice that makes room for an affective politics needed to resist neoliberalism. I argue that love grounds an *affective politics*, which is a cultural politics of emotions that seeks to align the emotions of political subjects with certain political causes and commitments. An affective politics grounded in love empowers political subjects to emotionally connect to commitments oriented toward democratic flourishing. In order to theorize an affective politics, I explore the limits of theories of intersectionality and argue for "assemblage" theories in conceptualizing love as a practice of radical democratic possibility.

Revisiting Love as Radical Political Practice

Love is a concrete practice in the sense that love's embodiment is expressed in sets of practices oriented toward individual fulfillment and human flourishing. Black feminist bell hooks asserts that love is more than a feeling; it is a practice. By practice, she means concrete sets of actions that persons commit to as a way to enable nurturance and growth in oneself and others. These concrete sets of action such as affection, care, compassion, and mutuality constitute love. She clarifies that affection or care is only one ingredient of love. She states, "To truly love we must learn to mix various ingredients – care, affection, recognition, respect, commitment, and trust, as well as honest and open communication."[2] For her, practices, such as respect, care, and trust, reflect love as a practice within communities. Love is not a mere sentiment or an abstract idea. Love is rooted in a set of practices that are undergirded by intentionality and choice.[3] I infer that for hooks, talking about love as a practice enables communities to speak about love alongside accountability, responsibility, and concrete actions that enable flourishing and fulfillment for oneself and others. One can only know love through actions that honor people's movement toward freedom and self-actualization.

Yet, hooks does not merely leave love in the realm of interpersonal relations. She also speaks about the political dimension of love. She laments the lack of "an ongoing public discussion and public policy about the practice of love in our culture."[4] For her, love impacts how we fashion political communities and implement policy programs. She offers an example concerning the impoverished status of children's rights within the United States. She argues that the absence of children's rights is a fundamental question of love in a society. Children deserve to be engaged with compassion, respect, recognition, and care in order for them to flourish. Engaging children in these ways is the realization of love, for hooks, and is simultaneously deeply political. Children can only be treated with justice if a society has an overarching vision of love that shapes and guides their laws, public policies, and cultural sets of practices.[5] Love is then a political and policy force because it shows up in how we organize and behave as political communities. Without love, political communities are unable to engage the profound importance of neighborly care, no matter who that neighbor may be, which forecloses possibilities of a truly just society. Hooks affirms the importance of recognizing the political dimension of love, contending that love is not merely oriented toward the self but also oriented toward the neighbor.

Christian, Jewish, and Black religious traditions have explored the concept of neighbor love as the grounding of human flourishing. Within Jewish and Christian traditions, a number of scholars speak of love as a practice and not merely an optimistic idea or ideal. Jewish religious thinker Abraham Heschel helps one understand that the Hebrew Bible is a story or history of a covenant of love between the Divine and the Divine's children (Israel). The relationship between God and God's people is expressed through a history of practices in which God practices mercy, forgiveness, and care despite the unfaithfulness of Israel. Within Judaism, the meaning of God's love can only be ascertained within history, a history that reveals God's actions and practices toward the Jewish people. In fact, part of God's practice of love, for Heschel, involves erotic aspects and emotional fulfillment, as the metaphor of groom and bride is constantly applied to God and Israel in the prophetic literature of the Hebrew Bible (although one might critique the bride/groom metaphor for its hetero-patriarchal language).[6] While bride/groom metaphors certainly reinforce hetero-patriarchal arrangements, Heschel intimates that the erotic remains critical to how Hebrew scriptures discuss love as practice.[7] In other words, what love is and does can only be grasped and understood through its concrete mode of expression as revealed through practices of mercy, forgiveness, justice, care, and compassion. The Hebraic conception of love is not an abstract, ideal vision of perfect relating. Instead, love *is a history* of practices between God and humanity (and among human beings within community). For Jewish thought, love always creates its own history and this history reveals practices that open up new forms of community and ways of being.

Christian traditions also disclose love as a history of God relating to humanity through concrete actions and practice. Mercy, forgiveness, justice, and reconciliation in Christian thought are not just formal ideas of what love is but are concrete practices that point to what *love requires*. Love is actualized in and through these concrete actions and ways of being. Moreover, Christian thought understands Divine love through the history of Jesus. Christian faith sees the story of Jesus (whether one has a high or low Christology) as central to understanding new forms of human existence in terms of what human beings are capable of *being*. As womanist theologian Delores Williams reminds us, this question of *being* sits at the heart of Christian traditions, as these traditions elucidate what love is through action and practice.

Black religious traditions have also centered love as a practice. African-American religious thinker Howard Thurman articulated love as the grounding of his vision for God and human flourishing. Grounding his religious thought in Christian personalism, Thurman posits that the inward movement of the soul is grounded in God, which makes possible the unification of all life. Thurman laid heavy stress upon love, writing at length about the interconnectedness of life throughout the entire cosmic structure, including animal and plant life. One's very consciousness is connected to that of others. Beyond this metaphysical connection, however, Thurman strongly emphasizes the importance of knowing and *loving other people concretely*. He acknowledges that love manifests itself through concrete actions. Love has physical implications.[8] In his essay, "Mysticism and the Experience of Love," Thurman describes the necessity of knowing another person's "fact" in order to truly love her or him. He says, "To speak of the love for humanity is meaningless. There is no such thing as humanity. What we call humanity has a name, was born, lives on a street, gets hungry, needs all the particular things we need."[9] It is through love as a practice that we come to understand love more deeply. Feeding the hungry, offering shelter to the homeless, and so forth for a particular person is love, for Thurman. Love is something that must be acted upon and practiced.

For Thurman, love does require us to develop a general sphere of acceptance that will allow us to love anyone with whom we come in contact, but the emphasis is always on loving in the particulars. And this love is the grounding of community and hope. He asserts that God is the source and grounding of this experience of love, which for him, is the necessary counter-experience to systems and cycles of violence and hatred in the world. Thurman invites humans to cultivate the inner life, develop character, and share the foundational belief in a call to community and harmony. This incarnation of love through the religious encounter (expressed within community) and concrete practice (practices of care, mercy, forgiveness, justice, etc.) then can confront systems of oppression, violence, and dehumanization. Other

African-American religious thinkers, such as James Cone, Martin Luther King, Jr., Kelly Brown Douglass, and Shawn Copeland, have addressed the necessity of love being seen as concrete practice, which inaugurates liberation and human flourishing.

What has been unique about black feminist and womanist discourses (as well as black religious traditions more broadly) is that they transform ideas of intrapersonal and interpersonal love into a theory of justice. The Combahee River Collective Statement speaks to love as a practice of justice when it notes that their intersectional politics emerges "from a healthy love for ourselves, our sisters, and our community which allows us to continue our struggle and work."[10] For black feminists and womanists, love *is a politics* of claiming, embracing, and restoring marginalized, subjugated subjects (such as black women) within personal and political relationships. Love as a political practice is about how love moves through the self in efforts to produce new forms of political communities with affective bonds that draw individuals toward one another. Love is not simply a private affair (as we saw in the previous chapter on the erotic). Love is also public as it provides the conditions under which its forms enable individuals and groups to live together (i.e., respect, compassion, empathy, etc.).

What do I mean by a love that moves through the self (self-love) and outward to the political? Womanist Alice Walker suggests that self-love is the departure point for other forms of erotic, sensual, humanistic, and spiritual loves. For Walker, a womanist subject "loves other women, sexually and/or nonsexually," along with loving music, dance, food, the moon, the Spirit, and roundness.[11] In other words, sensuous, erotic, spiritual, and humanistic loves proceed foremost from self-love. But self-love is not about selfish love. For her, self-love is about turning oneself away from the insignificant and the frivolous in order to pursue "the serious." Walker notes that the womanist agent acts "grown-up" as she is "responsible. In charge. *Serious.*"[12] This subject orients herself toward serious things, which implies a level of social engagement that transcends the self. It is through her sense of self-love that she recognizes the importance of becoming socially engaged to ensure the "survival and wholeness of the entire people."[13] For Walker, the womanist subject then embodies a radical curiosity about the world as she seeks to make a contribution beyond her own interests, needs, and desires. For the womanist agent, self-love is about the labor of self, a labor that also recognizes the profound importance of communal wholeness.

Black feminist and womanist thinkers intimate that a black feminist-womanist politics requires that the black feminist/womanist subject (in and through self-love) works on self *and* transcends the self.
This politics is a radical articulation of how the self and the political are inextricably intertwined. This work of the self to transcend
the self in order to ensure "the survival and wholeness of the entire
people," is difficult but necessary for a black feminist-womanist politics. The black feminist-womanist agent committed to self-love must
learn how to train the self to see in new and different ways, which
challenges the self to also move beyond one's own interests in order to
engage the social world toward justice-making.

For both black feminist and womanist discourses, part of training
the self toward socio-political engagement is cultivated through an
affective politics. When I speak of an "affective politics," I refer to the
cultural politics of emotions and how emotions work to align political
subjects to certain causes and political commitments. How do emotions move in and between bodies in efforts to live more humanely
and justly? Drawing on black feminist Jennifer Nash, I use this term
to "describe how bodies are organized around intensities, longings,
desires, temporalities, repulsions, curiosities, fatigues, optimism,
and how these affects produce political movements (or sometimes
inertia)." [14] As explored in the previous chapter, love as understood
through the *interplay between agape and the erotic*, is about bodies
that are moving toward each other with desire, longing, curiosity, and
intensity. It is in and through *the body* and its emotions that love and
subsequent commitments associated with love become possible.

Feminist political philosopher Martha Nussbaum reminds one
that public emotions have large-scale consequences in terms of a
nation's ability to progress or digress.[15] Emotions are often ascribed
to aggressive totalitarian or dictatorial regimes that sidestep reasoned
discourse. Emotions are seen as dangerous to democratic political
liberalism, which makes it impossible to acknowledge that even liberal democratic models are constituted with citizens who are driven
by emotions.[16] As a result, one must ask how emotions either support or undermine efforts toward societal flourishing. Emotions can
offer new vigor and depth as a nation moves toward goals of equality,
inclusivity, and equity or emotions can derail democratic pursuits,
fostering intolerance, and deep division.[17] Even political philosophers
such as John Locke and Immanuel Kant understood the significance
of emotions, as emotions were not just impulses but "contain cogni-
tive appraisals that have an evaluative content."[18] Emotions do not

just reflect impulsive, unscientific claims about something (an idea, person, object, etc.) but reflect how individuals evaluate and morally weigh something such as an idea, value, institution, or person. Understanding public emotions gives us insight into what drives and repels citizens. All democratic societies must ask how their political culture and their cherished values (such as freedom, equality, and justice) can be sustained over time. Values like empathy for the needy, anger at injustice, and joy for equality are examples of how emotions work to further solidify democratic commitments toward flourishing. Political principles not only need reasoned debate but also need *emotional support to ensure their stability over time.*[19] In order to guard against intolerance and injustice, all societies must cultivate sentiments of understanding and compassion to fight hegemonic structures.

Historically, a number of political and religious leaders have understood the profound importance of public emotions in underwriting causes for justice and well-being. One reason why President John F. Kennedy, Martin Luther King, Jr., Ella Baker, and Mahatma Gandhi were such great political and social leaders is because they understood the centrality of public emotions in political projects. These individuals touched the hearts of citizens and inspired feelings of political efficacy in the masses to envision peaceful and compassionate societies. King knew that segregation was an accepted "fact" among most white Americans in the twentieth century. For whites, Jim crow was a matter of law. King galvanized protests that re-shaped public emotions about segregation. The non-violent marches and protests entered the homes of all Americans, as people watched on their televisions images of blacks being brutally beaten and violently arrested by white policemen. People were repulsed at the violence they witnessed. Greater outcry denouncing segregation in the United States began to take root. The tide began to turn as white liberals protested in solidarity with African-Americans. King knew that hearts needed to be changed alongside the law. The re-shaping of public emotions was central to the work of the Civil Rights Movement.

King's non-violent methods, however, were grounded in Mahatma Gandhi's philosophy of non-violence, *satyagraha* meaning truthforce. Indian historian Ramachandra Guha describes Gandhi's philosophy of *satyagraha* as oriented toward actively protesting with the truth to change the hearts of one's oppressors. For certain, Gandhi believed that laws supporting the caste system in India needed to be transformed. But he believed that without changing the hearts of oppressors through the truth, the real revolution would remain unachieved. The techniques and methods of civil disobedience, for Gandhi, sought to attain justice not through armed struggle but through voluntarily suffering in order to shame those in power.[20] Gandhi knew that if the masses were to submit to non-violent protest through *satyagraha*, they needed to *emotionally connect* to the movement. Anger toward the caste system was not the only emotion Gandhi sought to cultivate in the masses. Compassion for one's oppressor was the other emotion he sought to cultivate as this emotion would sustain the non-violent movement and keep the masses from resulting to armed struggle. One can see that our collective life is indeed organized around affective experiences, which calls upon us to rethink the place of an affective politics. Neoliberal regimes certainly organize the affective experiences of individuals and communities, experiences that cause persons to choose alienation and rugged self-interest due to the zero-sum logic associated with hyper-competitive ways of being. Because neoliberalism cultivates particular kinds of emotion such as radical self-interest, fear of the other, and distrust in systems due to greed, an affective politics of love is needed to counteract these ways of being.

Black feminist and womanist discourses understand this affective aspect of the political realm and assert an affective politics that takes seriously love in its many concrete forms as a revolutionary practice. There are intimate connections between the emotional and political, between the subjective and social as "politics and history manifest themselves at the level of lived affective experience."[21] The body and its emotions are central to justice work as it determines how our longings, desires, and intensities align with political projects to secure freedom, equality, and equity. It's through the body and its emotions that persons are able to rebel against oppressive structures in efforts to discover new values and modes of relationships to replace old ones. Political struggle and justice work are not just against something but *for something* as well, which means an affective politics is critical to challenging and resisting neoliberalism as a political and cultural project that produces disastrous forms of melancholia. Black feminist and womanist traditions then articulate love not merely as a regulative ideal but as a concrete revolutionary practice that fashions an affective politics in creating more just and compassionate political communities.

Love as a Practice of Celebrating Difference

The experience of love is normally not complicated when we love someone who is similar to us but rather when one is called upon to lovingly exist in community with one who is unlike us. We often do experience compassion or concern for people *like us*. However, people who are different from us are often interpreted as deviant and even dangerous (especially if this difference conflicts with established religious and/or cultural norms). Because social division, conflict, and angst often accompany issues of difference, an affective politics of love is committed to celebrating difference as something to be valued rather than feared.

One way of talking about problems of difference within societies is through investigating how individuals exercise compassion and empathy toward others. Drawing on a long philosophical tradition, Nussbaum offers a basic structure to how compassion and empathy are exercised and experienced among humans. According to Nussbaum's account, compassion has three necessary parts or "thoughts." The first "thought" that an individual has in relation to compassion is the thought of seriousness. In experiencing compassion, an individual believes that the suffering of the other person is non-trivial and urgent. If an individual believes that the sufferer's cries are insignificant, she will not necessarily feel compassion but apathy and indifference.[22]

A second thought associated with compassion is non-fault. We generally do not feel compassion for individuals when they are at fault for their present situation of suffering. If suffering is self-generated, we might even feel disgust or anger. When we feel empathy, we believe (at least in theory) that a suffering individual is not to blame for their unfortunate predicament. If one is seen as guilty of one's suffering, empathy is withheld. As discussed in chapter 2, the poor in the United States are often seen as culpable for their poverty, which prevents many American citizens from feeling compassion for the poor. We simply do not feel compassion for people we blame. Even if we feel compassion for someone like a criminal, it is limited as the suffering is self-inflicted.[23]

A third thought associated with compassion is the thought of similar possibilities. People tend to feel compassion for suffering individuals who are similar to them. People are able to place themselves in the shoes of the suffering person because people can potentially imagine themselves in that position. The suffering individual evokes strong emotions from us as they represent our lot in life and what is most important to our concepts of flourishing and well-being.

There are examples from the behavioral sciences to corroborate the claim that humans tend to express empathy for those who are socially or culturally similar to them. Social psychologist Daniel Batson does important experimental work on compassion to prove that we tend to show concern for people most like us. In his experiment, Batson instructs students to listen with imaginative participation, to the hardship of another student they do not know.[24] In this study, the students experienced compassion for the student they did not know, even desiring to discuss ways to help the suffering student's plight. Batson then instructed another group of students to only consider the technical, factual aspects of the suffering student's plight without the student's story, and the emotional connection was not the same. In fact, the emotional connection had been diminished. Batson inferred that we feel compassion not with strangers but with people we relate to, people who are similar to us rather than different from us.[25]

However, there is a certain complexity associated with compassion among human beings. For example, an individual might exercise profound compassion for strangers who have been victims of an earthquake or hurricane (such as the hurricane Katrina in New Orleans in 2005). However, it is important to remember that these strangers are still seen as victims, as persons who are not blameworthy as their predicament is caused by forces outside of their control. The point here is that there is always a complex set of factors that may give rise to feelings of compassion. However, compassion and empathy overwhelmingly tend to be experienced among individuals and groups who are fundamentally alike. Difference then presents a challenge to the basic ways we experience compassion as human beings. Difference challenges how we might understand compassion as social animals. If people or ideas are foreign or alien, they simply do not "count." This problem of difference is the central obstacle in relation to developing compassion within a heterogeneous society.

In addition, the animal and behavioral sciences help one understand how in-group behavior affects capacities to have compassion and concern for people who are fundamentally different. Dutch primatologist Frans de Waal provides a case study on compassion and concern among mice, which might shed light on human behavior in relation to care and compassion. On June 2006, a research team at McGill University administered painful injections to some mice, which induced squealing and profound pain in the mice.[26] In the cage, there were also mice that had not been injected. If the non-pained mice were in the cage with pained mice they had previously lived with, they showed visible signs of being concern (such as being upset). If the non-pained mice were in the cage with pained mice they had not previously lived with, the non-pained mice were unaffected. They did not show the same kind of emotional concern. The experimenters surmised that the emotional lives of mice show social complexity. Familiarity among the mice was directly correlated to how compassion and concern were exercised. In fact, familiarity was a prerequisite to compassion and empathy among the non-pained mice.

This case study offers parallels, even if provisionally, between animal and human behavior in relation to compassion and concern for others. Similar to mice, humans also exhibit "in-group" behavior when it comes to compassion and care. Compassion is an important way of grasping the complexities and challenges associated with difference within societies. Similar to philosophy and the social sciences, religious and theological discourses have also engaged concepts of love in order to articulate under what conditions practices of love are possible.

Neighbor love has been a central concept among various religious traditions. However, neighbor love has been subject to different interpretations. What constitutes neighbor love? For instance, within Christian traditions, one might argue that Paul's term for love, *agape*, possesses political dimensions.[27] In this instance, love is not seen as a private sentiment or singularly characterized by emotional feelings. Agape is not just an affective love that reflects my own narcissistic desires to be loved. Echoing in some ways Kierkegaard in chapter 2, this love expresses itself publicly through how I relate to my neighbor, to what I am willing to *give* to my neighbor without a *quid pro quo*. The acquiring mode of neoliberalism calls upon individuals to see love as a commodity that can be bought and sold. However, as I have already discussed, the interplay between agapeic and erotic love can never be understood within the exchange logic of neoliberalism as this love rejects narcissistic reciprocity as the grounding of loving relations. Neighbor love is political in the sense that it is public, relates to my neighbor, and forms the basis of social relations. This love is also self-giving in the sense that it is not driven by the self's ego to receive attention that solely affirms one's own desires and needs.

Yet, *who* is my neighbor? It seems that loving one's neighbor is not solely loving someone who looks like me, acts like me, or is the bearer of the same traits and rights as myself. This neighbor could easily reinforce a neoliberal form of narcissism that demands one's neighbor be similar to oneself and therefore, lovable. As Zizek notes, only a love that has been exposed to the "monstrosity" of the neighbor can be agape in the truest sense of the term.[28] This monstrosity is related to how foreign and alien the neighbor appears to be, so that my encounter of my neighbor strikes me as a monstrous encounter. I might even find the neighbor repugnant and offensive as I am unable to relate myself (my worldview, moral orientations, and so forth) to my neighbor. My neighbor and I may not share a life-world out of which we might establish the basic terms to identify with each other. We are therefore unable to experience an intersubjective or symmetrical relationship. In this instance, we have no way of domesticating the experience we have with our neighbor.[29]

Within some interpretations of love, the "neighbor" takes on a generic meaning in which she is simply interpreted as one who is a human being and made in God's image like me. In this account of love, the focus is on similarity and familiarity as the grounding of loving relations. I love my neighbor because he is a human being like me. While this account is certainly true, it misrepresents what's at stake in conversations on neighbor love. There is a certain complexity concerning the idea of the neighbor because some neighbors I encounter are so foreign and alien that I am unable to establish a positive relationship between them and me. My neighbor's face is not the face of familiarity but the face of a radical stranger who I may fear or even hate. As Zizek notes, what is missing in these sanitized versions of love is the idea that I encounter the neighbor with a "disguisting tic or grimace."[30] The neighbor is not someone I can exercise empathy with as I encounter the neighbor in all her "alien monstrosity and inhuman excess."[31]

As a result, love is respect and care for a neighbor in the particulars, not simply a "universal" abstract love, which can actually ignore loving a particular neighbor in all his alien or foreign specifics. One may make the statement of "loving everybody" but this declaration does not necessarily grapple with loving a particular neighbor who might represent what stands at the unconscious (or conscious) periphery as foreign and monstrous to me. This type of neighbor love then does not enter through abstract declarations of "loving everyone" but starts by singling out the neighbor that appears alien to me, the neighbor who I love in the midst of her obvious differences. It is with this neighbor that a more general love can start. This kind of neighbor love is intrusive and subversive to neoliberal ways of relating and being, as an individual must encounter her neighbor on the neighbor's own terms. To love in this way is an affront to the exchange logic and value within neoliberalism because this kind of neighbor love makes no demand to reciprocate. This love is "violent" to neoliberal systems in the sense that it seeks to overthrow current dehumanizing ways of being.

Zizek asserts that within the neoliberal capitalist order, the revolution toward love of neighbor and radical inclusion seems "violent" to present neoliberal forms of relationality. Neighbor love demands the opposite of neoliberal rationality, which is rabid self-interest and self-preservation (to the exclusion of others) as first rules. It's not just that this revolution to love a particular neighbor is too much but that this demand forces us to experience ourselves as mistaken and complicit when we exclude *who* the neighbor really is. The neighbor is an individual who is similar *and* radically different from me. Love is only present when the neighbor is expanded in this way.

Another reason why neighbor love must begin with the acknowledgment that some neighbors are encountered with a "disgusting tic or grimace" is because hierarchal domination and injustice are often built upon the disgust of neighbor due to that neighbor's differences. Disgust as a political emotion is often not addressed within religious and theological discourses but remains essential to understanding how hierarchy and power gain their legitimacy within cultures. A key tool of subordination and oppression is projective disgust of those who are viewed as different and therefore inferior. This projective disgust is often centered upon the bodies of "different others." Projective disgust is "a disgust for a group of other humans who are segmented from the dominant group and classified as lower because of being (allegedly) more animal."[32] Projective disgust involves some act to humiliate and denigrate. The "disgusting" group is dirty, smelly, seen as subhuman. Yet, the groups who are ascribed to these elements of disgust do not have these properties at all, as this narrative is a device of elite groups to oppress and disenfranchise.

For example, in India, the caste system was legitimated by emotions of disgust that held social and political sway in nation building. The lowest caste (or uncaste), the "untouchables," were seen as defiled, impure, and dirty because their labor involved cleaning latrines and disposing of corpses. The untouchables were then segregated and disenfranchised, not accorded their civil liberties and human rights as citizens in India. This interpretation of the lowest caste as "untouchable" and dirty was false as it served the interests of the ruling caste. Even Gandhi, who earlier in his life didn't publicly challenge the caste system in India, later repudiates the emotions of disgust that legitimized the horrific structural discrimination of the untouchables. During the cholera epidemic, Gandhi pointed out that the lower castes were cleaner and at less risk than the upper castes in India, as the lower castes defecated in fields far from their homes, while the upper castes defecated into chamber pots that were then poured into gutters outside their windows.[33] Disgust, as a political emotion, was powerful in justifying and legitimizing the political caste system in India.

Similarly, segregation in the United States is another example of how disgust was employed as a political emotion in order to discriminate and disenfranchise African-Americans. It was a common fantasy that African-Americans smelled worse than whites and that their bodies would contaminate pools, water, food, and so forth. Separate water fountains, bathrooms, pools, and schools were created to avoid the contamination of white bodies by black bodies. Jim Crow laws were codified and sustained through emotions of disgust among the white population, as black bodies were tainted and animalistic. Southern whites often had visceral loathing for black bodies and segregation laws refused humanity to these bodies at a very basic level. The political emotion of projective disgust then structured an entire society in which the United States and its sense of identity were bound up with this demarcating emotional line of difference. Ethnic difference is then not seen as something to be valued but something that represented dirtiness, inhumanity, and defilement.

Women and sexual minorities also have a long history of being subjected to projective disgust around the world. Women's body fluids alone in relation to menstruation and childbirth have been seen as impure and defiling. Women's bodily vulnerability has been interpreted in ways that have led to deep subordination of women in the social, economic, and political sphere. Same-gender loving bodies have also been seen as disgusting and nasty, particularly transgendered bodies. Transgendered bodies have been met with profound violence as such bodies have been interpreted as sites of perverse, sadistic, and deviant behavior. Some people are physically repulsed by the sight of transgendered bodies. LGBTQ people are seen as contaminating the "body politic," or national political community. This has played out, for example, in the United States in which same-gender loving individuals are interpreted as defiling the religious purity of the national community. Religious fundamentalists of all persuasions argue that same-gender loving people invite sin into the national political community, exposing society itself to contamination and social death. Such arguments however reveal the political emotion of projective disgust that is used to create laws and policies against same-gender loving communities.

Projective disgust creates radically segregated worlds, which targets vulnerable populations such as ethnic minorities, women, sexual minorities, and the disabled. Projective disgust causes societies to create and implement laws and policies based on stigmatization and division. Projective disgust operates within daily lives at the intrapersonal level and also within political communities at the structural-systemic level. It requires a devaluing and fear of difference. In fact, it uses difference to humiliate and denigrate, blocking equal political respect.[34] Projective disgust is about nation building as it provides a tool upon which the elite and powerful can segregate, stigmatize, and subordinate as a *matter of law*. Projective disgust poses problems not just for development of the individual but for development of society. A society is unable to experience flourishing if repugnance of others different from ourselves is used to create hierarchal structures that denigrate and divide.

Within religious and theological discourses, neighbor love responds to such emotions and practices at both personal and political levels. Neighbor love is both personal and political, as it represents a revolution against political emotions that sponsor projective disgust and hence, radical injustice and structural subordination of vulnerable groups. Because projective disgust hinders practices of connection and compassion, love is not merely giving oneself over to a universal, abstract law to love, but a love that demands an encounter with the strangeness of the neighbor, which simultaneously reveals the strangeness in ourselves as estranged from the grounding of both God and each other.

In order to resist projective disgust and its denigration and devaluation of difference, black feminist and womanist projects lift up difference and alterity as the departure point for practices of love. For example, Walker uses a flower metaphor as a way of discussing the celebration of difference, which forms the foundation of womanist praxis. Walker writes, "As in: 'Mama, why are we brown, pink, and yellow, and our cousins are white, beige, and black?' Ans: 'Well, you know the colored race is just like a flower garden, with every color flower represented'."[35] The womanist agent is invested in the representation and celebration of "every color flower," which shows the radical investment that womanist projects have in celebrating difference. The garden/flower metaphor is employed by Walker, as she knows that black communities have an array of "different colors." Historically, the history of colorism within black communities reflects the problem of projective disgust as darker-hue blacks were met with denigration and humiliation from both white society and light-skinned blacks. This history of colorism (which was nothing more than internalized racism among blacks) undermined the celebration of difference, even within oppressed black communities. For Walker, this metaphorical dialogue about the beauty of diverse flowers demonstrates what's at stake for womanist projects: difference in all of its various manifestations (racial, gender, color, class, sexual, etc.) remains essential to self love and love of others.

Rejecting the *projective disgust of difference is the central transgressive quality of Walker's womanist subject, not necessarily any ontological claim about black women's experiences as such.* Black women's experiences are indeed central to Walker's womanist project as black women's experiences have constituted "difference" within white feminist and black liberationist discourses, discourses that have treated black women's experiences with projective disgust. Walker exposes the truth that women of color's perceived or actual "differences" have been treated with contempt (exclusion, injustice, and so forth). Consequently, what stands at the heart of a womanist affective politics is not so much an ontological claim solely centered around the exclusive analysis of black women's experiences as such, but rather battling and confronting hegemonic ideologies and practices that denigrate and devalue difference through projective disgust (of which black women's experiences have been subjected). I know that this way of reading the womanist project and its affective politics conceptually differs from how womanist theology and ethics have analytically interpreted womanism. However, I think my reading is in keeping with how Walker presents and describes this conceptual term and project.

Lorde also understands the black feminist project as training the self (through self-love) to turn away from the fear of difference in order for healing, liberation, and flourishing to be possibilities. While Lorde certainly addresses the structural-systemic issues that block black women's well-being, she also addresses the deleterious psychosocial aspects of black women's lives that undermine their own well-being such as the fear of difference. Lorde states that black feminists must learn how to "value recognition within each other's eyes as well as within our own, and seek a balance between these visions."[36] It is the black feminist and/or womanist subject who labors to transcend the self's fears in order to embrace difference and see this difference as constitutive of one's sense of flourishing. Similarly, black feminist June Jordan asserts, "If I am a black feminist serious in the undertaking of self-love, it seems to me that I should gain and gain and gain in strength so that I may without fear be able and willing to love and respect, for example, women who are not feminists, not professionals, not as young or old as I am, women who have neither job nor income, women who are not Black."[37]

For Jordan, the act of self-love (labor of self) is also a political act and process of embracing difference, of "becoming more expansive in one's conception of political community."[38] One can infer from Jordan (and even Lorde) that part of the labor of self through self-love is transcending one's fears of difference, which means that the self may need to work against itself (in terms of its fears) when undertaking this serious task. The self is then able to recognize the need for a politics organized not around the appearance of sameness and homogeneity but around the complexity and vibrancy of difference.[39]

Black feminism and womanism foreground an affective politics that takes seriously self-love as the departure point for possibilities in building creative political communities that celebrate difference rather than denigrate difference. Projective disgust and its unjust, hierarchal ideologies and practices create negative political emotions that undermine the practice of love and care. Love is a concrete labor of actively reorienting the self and pushing the self to be configured in new ways that may be both difficult and challenging.[40] Love is a practice of celebrating difference as it helps one "live into" one's own humanity through valuing rather than fearing the perceived or actual differences of others. Neoliberal social and cultural formations are not merely fashioned by structural and policy injustices but are (re) produced through undemocratic political emotions based on fearing differences. Political cultures must tap into the power of affect and love in creating strong, vibrant, and democratic political communities that are not governed by projective disgust. Moreover, love can enable our social, economic, and cultural institutions to shift from greed, egoism, and aggression to forms of care, compassion, and trust. Love enables one to transcend narcissism associated with the singular focus on the self in this neoliberal moment. A part of this transcendence is seeing difference as something to be valued rather than destroyed.

Love as a Practice of Radical Democratic Possibility

Love can be a practice of radical democratic possibility in that an affective politics changes the grammar of justice. Crafting political communities of difference is a revolutionary undertaking, as persons are called upon to work on behalf of self and sometimes against the self (in terms of the self's fears about difference and alterity). Working on behalf and against the self is important because the language of love is often deployed in hegemonic ways. Some groups claim that they are "acting out of love" when they bring harm to people who are different from them. Some groups use love as a justifier for their projective disgust. These statements of "acting out of love" then actually function as claims to power in order to sustain ideologies and practices of injustice. For instance, religious fundamentalists often claim that they "love the sinner but hate the sin" when they oppose LGBTQ freedoms and rights. These groups argue that love drives them to oppose "unnatural relations, lifestyles and orientations" associated with LGBTQ persons. However, such claims belie the disenfranchisement LGBTQ persons experience in economic spheres of society as well as the persistent social humiliation they suffer. These fundamentalist groups are unwilling to acknowledge the profound structural/political harm (and personal pain) their ideologies and policy stances have generated for LGBTQ persons. In other words, love cannot be used as a practice of disenfranchisement that forecloses democratic possibilities for all persons within our political community.

My goal is to explore meta-theories that enable us to speak of love in political terms, as an affective politics. The vast majority of black feminist and womanist religious literature has employed theories of intersectionality, which may not help one theorize an affective politics in the midst of differences. In part, theories of intersectionality attempt to promote democratic possibilities for vulnerable populations (i.e., poor black women or immigrant women of color) through offering a more complex construction of identity in light of difference (identity is often about the ways in which multiple identity markers such as race, class, gender intersect in shaping identity itself). For instance, public policies that may attempt to remedy racial injustices on behalf of black communities often do not consider how race intersects with class in structuring the life-chances for particular members within these communities. The affirmative action policies of the 1980s were deeply critiqued, as these policies were ineffective in helping poor blacks secure employment and educational opportunities. Critics argued that affirmative action policies tended to help a group of blacks that already had middle class social standing. The black middle class was already well educated but needed formal barriers to be removed to create greater opportunities for them. However, poor blacks often were not even able to take advantage of affirmative action opportunities in relationship to college admissions because many of these African-Americans had already been deeply disenfranchised during their early education years, making them unprepared to thrive at the collegiate level. Affirmative action policies tended to rely on a race-based identity politics, which failed to ask how class affected large groups of blacks from accessing such opportunities. The intersectional identities of poor blacks made it hard for them to benefit from this policy. Intersectionality then became critical to helping one re-think the challenges of identity politics in relation to policies.

For certain, theories of intersectionality have been essential to addressing structural injury (structural injustice) on behalf of oppressed communities. Moreover, this theory has been central in calling for diversity management and inclusion based on diverse identities. Intersectionality calls for social recognition of difference in order to address structural injury (whether this injury is economic, racial, gendered, sexual, or so forth). Through challenging structures and policies that inhibit well-being and flourishing, intersectionality seeks to create democratic possibilities by foregrounding difference.

Yet, one might raise the question on the limits of intersectionality when articulating an affective political community that seeks to remedy injury *in affective terms* as well, something intersectionality is hard pressed to address because it focuses on materiality and structural injury in relationship to identity (social recognition and/or redistribution). Queer theorist Jasbir Puar offers a groundbreaking analysis on the limits of intersectionality and how a "theory of assemblage" might help ground an articulation of affective political communities. For Puar, a theory of assemblage suggests a different set of metaphors for identities within the social world such as mosaics, patchwork, heterogeneity, fluidity, and temporary configurations. Within this theory, there is not a fixed, stable ontology for the social world and its multiplicity of identities (as theories of intersectionality assume). Rather, identities (such as race, class, sexuality, gender) are complex, fluid configurations that can properly be characterized as discursive practices and expressions, which means that identities are social constructions generated by material and linguistic conditions rather than ontological assertions.

As a result, the theory of assemblage avoids essentialism and reification of identities such as race, gender, and sexuality. For instance, sexuality is not an actual ontological category as such; it is linguistic expression that *appears* to describe ontology (something intersectionality does not address). One might even argue that "sexuality" is a category that emerges out of colonial agendas and imperial projects during the modern period to advance hetero-normative economic and cultural systems. The coining of the term "homosexual" certainly reinforced a hetero-normative regime of epistemic violence, a way of "othering" sexual subjects who did not comply with heterosexist cultural and economic institutions upon which power was built and preserved. Consequently, assemblage theory does not think of race, sexuality, gender, and class as a combination of interrelated parts, as these "interrelated parts" would then have their own ontological grounding as they interact (or "intersect" with each other).[41]

For certain, assemblage theory would not say that race, class, gender, and other categories do not exist. Such categories (as discursive practices and expressions) *do exist* and perform a certain kind of social-structural work, creating systems of racism, patriarchy, and heterosexism, among other systems.[42] But these categories are not fixed points of ontology. Puar suggests that such "categories – race, gender, and sexuality – are considered events, actions, and encounters between bodies, rather than simply entities and attributes of subjects."[43] Puar seems to suggest that encounters between bodies can reflect hegemonic and oppressive energy or liberative energy. Racism or sexism as encounters and events reflects patterns of relations that are rooted in hegemony and domination. Assemblage theory turns to the kind of social-structural *work these categories do* in creating structural events of hegemony (racism, classism, patriarchy, etc.). Therefore, assemblage theory does not support these categories as ontological but as discursive practices that create encounters, events, actions, and sets of relations that oppress and dominate. Such discursive practices are "assembled" in different ways to fashion hegemonic encounters and events between bodies within structural relations of power.

As a result, one might look for how such categories are assembled within structural configurations to oppress particular groups, without reifying and essentializing those categories (categories grounded in ontology). As one might anticipate, assemblage does not focus on identitarian politics as a way of addressing social recognition and structural injuries as intersectionality does. Instead, assemblage focuses on how categories (as discursive practices instead of ontological distinctions) sponsor *encounters and events between bodies* that disclose structural patterns of power relations. How these discursive practices and encounters are assembled will constantly differ, which means hegemonic systems of oppression and how one addresses injury is *based on complex, fluid encounters and configurations of systemic violence rather then identity claims for social recognition alone.*

Unlike intersectionality, a theory of assemblage makes room for how bodies and emotions are affected in relation to systemic violence such as projective disgust that undergirds hegemonic structures such as racism, heterosexism, and classism. For Puar, assemblage underscores "feeling, tactility, affect, and information."[44] Because assemblage theory is concerned with diverse structural encounters of systemic violence (material and psycho-social violence) among bodies, assemblage is better poised to remedy structural injuries in *affective terms* within political communities. For Puar, intersectionality and assemblage *do not need to be understood as oppositional. But they are frictional,* as assemblage is interested in affect, movement and futurity and intersectionality is more focused on identity and inclusion into liberal political community in the present.[45] I would argue that assemblage theory can even be seen as supplemental to intersectional work, if one desires to talk about remedy in affective terms within political communities. But one might ask: how is the work of intersectionality (and its focus on identitarian politics to remedy structural injury) *practically* different from assemblage theory (and its focus on affective political work such as love and future movements of care)?

When employing theories of assemblage, an affective politics offers a powerful re-conceptualization of the public sphere that is different from intersectional work. In theories of intersectionality, the public sphere is associated with groups that may have intersectional identities but these identities are nevertheless constituted by fixed points (race, class, gender, etc.). Race, class, gender, and so forth tend to be conceptualized on a formulaic grid in which such categories themselves remain unquestioned. One can turn to the ways in which race has been interrogated within postmodern discourse. Blackness, for instance, is deeply questioned in the United States in which African immigrant, bi-racial, and queer black communities contest blackness as an essentialist category with one specific meaning. How might this impact identity politics within black communities that presume to speak for all "black folk" (whoever these "folks" might be now into the twenty-first century)? How might the Black public sphere(s) be reconstituted in light of the deconstruction of blackness itself? Intersectionality doesn't seem to help resolve this problem in which the category of race itself is deeply problematized because intersectionality relies on these basic categories as tools for constructing "intersecting" identities (and inclusion of such identities into justice work).

On the contrary, the theory of assemblage organizes political communities around heterogeneity, variety, and difference *in relation to bodies and affect* rather than around fixed categories that fashion intersectional identities of difference. This is an important point because we "keep ourselves open to all forms of affective [political] life that have not solidified into institutions, organizations, or identities."[46] Affective political work generates a public sphere and concept of political community that gathers and finds meaning in and through new collective forms of affective relationality that are not easily captured by intersectionality. With assemblage theory, we are able to not only chart encounters between bodies that reflect hegemonic relations of power but also capture events between bodies that reflect new patterns of caring and compassionate relationality. We are able to envision how a love politics creates a political community based on public feelings and practices of love. Love (as a practice and labor of self discussed earlier) forms the basis of new forms of affective collectivities. This political community "is not based on shared identity or sameness but on a conception of a public rooted in affective affiliation and a shared set of feelings."[47] While these new publics and new forms of relationality might be tenuous and even fleeting, such publics are marked by love (and its associated practices) rather than by identity alone. These publics also may not be readily accessible and available to memory and sustained through past collective activity, often prerequisites of political communities based on identity. Political communities based on affect would open up possibilities for new configurations of affiliation in order to sponsor practices of compassion, empathy, joy, and so forth.

In addition, political communities based on affective affiliation are important, as political communities should not solely be based on reforming injury (structural injustice) within the public sphere(s). Political communities also must be based on affect and care to address forms of projective disgust that inhibit democratic possibilities toward visions of flourishing. When de-centering identity as the privileged foundation of the public sphere, love is able to transcend the logic of injury, which is at the heart of calls for identity politics.[48] The concept of injury is central to identity politics because "politicized identities generated out of liberal, disciplinary societies, insofar as they are premised on exclusion from a universal ideal, require that ideal, as well as their exclusion from it, for their own perpetuity as identities." Insofar as intersectional projects solely focus on privileging identity toward social recognition, justice work is more or less about inclusion into a political system as it is. Intersectional projects are about the call for recognition and reparations for structural injustices. On the contrary, an affective politics doesn't solely focus on the remedying of injury as the *end goal*. An affective politics also desires the public to be a site "where selves laboring to love are oriented towards difference and towards transcending the self to join collective action."[49] As a result, an affective politics re-imagines the public sphere(s) as a site organized around visions of care, tactility, and compassion rather than organized solely around shared identity that demands the recognition of injury as the end goal.

Grounding a political community in affect rather than identity also re-conceptualizes the idea of remedy in relation to harm within the public sphere(s). Instead of depending on the neoliberal state for remedy of injury as intersectional projects often do, a love politics asks what internal resources affective political communities have in readdressing harm such as projective disgust. While intersectionality rightly thinks about the remedy of injury in structural-systemic terms (through the state), affective politics recognizes the limits and even complicity of the state in sponsoring neoliberal projects of harm and injustice, which leads political communities to articulate the affective dimensions of healing fissures, divisions, and injustices within political communities. As stated, I am not denying the important justice work that intersectional theories have done in securing redress of injuries. However, *political communities are more than the sum total of injuries associated with identities*. The only way to dream of new collective forms of relationality is through affect and care, which opens the future up to societies that can address, on deep levels, structural forms of projective disgust.

I want to note that histories of projective disgust and its concomitant hegemonic structures often create deep wounds in the national political community. These past wounds make it impossible for certain groups to trust other groups who have been oppressors or violators. When turning to political communities within the United States, one only has to think of Native American genocide, American slavery,

Jim Crow laws, Asian American discrimination, Mexican subordination through immigration laws, and so forth to grasp the bitter histories that wound and separate groups. While the language of injustice is important in describing these atrocities, I also think that the language of tragedy captures the affective dimensions of these unfortunate histories. These various periods throughout American history have created a national tragedy in which trust, respect of human dignity, and care have been destroyed. It seems that one might question if a national political community's belief in love and care *can survive* such disasters that affect the inner lives of all citizens.

How can an affective politics of love emerge when the lingering consequences of national tragedies are yet present? Must we only expect "toleration" of citizens we oppose? Are justice, forgiveness, and reconciliation possible within national political community given these tragic histories that bitterly divide us? Even today, such histories of projective disgust reinvent themselves through debates over affirmative action, immigration, welfare reform, gender equity in pay, criminal justice, and more in which the wounds of the past break open again. Strong political emotions often inform how conflicting groups see and respond to each other within political communities. National tragedies of this sort create a great weight within nations, making difficult any affective politics grounded in empathy, understanding, and care.

Surviving great national tragedies requires an affective politics of love. If people are being asked to sit down with groups they consider offensive and/or inferior, they need a *strong reason* beyond principles of liberal democratic procedures. Liberal democratic procedures are important in sustaining freedom and justice. However, such procedures do not supply individual and groups with the kind of motivations and intentions oriented toward new futures of understanding, compassion, and trust. People within political communities must be moved by a deep care for one another in order to make a different future possible and sustainable. This affective politics certainly reminds us of the historical and contemporary pain and suffering caused by bitter histories of projective disgust. These histories are identified as a tragic loss for *everyone*, as it inhibits national political communities marked by new democratic futures of care. Deep structural harms wound oppressed communities and distort the humanity of the oppressors. As political communities, this ongoing struggle we have to heal the fissures and divides are as necessary as remedying structural injuries. Without such healing, the reinvention of new systemic forms of projective disgust will simply persist.

As one can see, an affective politics is invested in the future as a locus of democratic possibility. Love (along with care, tactility, etc.) becomes a practice(s) of democratic potentialities. In and through an affective political community, love becomes a radical concrete revolutionary practice fully grounded in the present but open to the unknown possibility of the future, a future which requires imagination. It invites affective political communities to creatively imagine new revolutionary ways of being. It potentially creates new social and political scripts that are not within the grid of neoliberal rationality and governmentality. It provides hope. An affective politics provides the conditions under which political communities can "imagine a world ordered by love, by a radical embrace of difference, by a set of subjects who work on/against themselves to work for each other."[50] An affective politics inaugurates democratic possibilities toward political communities rooted in care and love. It is also a critical response to systemic violence such as projective disgust (which is often labeled as unharmful "preferences" or biases within neoliberal society).

Love is a concrete revolutionary practice that sponsors an affective politics, creating new political communities that open us up to futures of democratic possibility. Addressing harms associated with projective disgust is equally essential as remedying structural injustices. I am interested in delineating how an affective politics of love productively addresses the social harms associated with projective disgust within neoliberal societies. Remedying projective disgust through an affective politics redefines the grammar of democratic possibility for healing and flourishing within political communities. Love is a necessary practice in order to challenge our neoliberal order, and we must acknowledge that we are bereft as societies without love.

5

Hope as Social Practice

Within much of classical Jewish and Christian discourses, hope is often articulated as a belief in super-ordinary interventions into the present order (i.e., supersessionist logic seen within much of Jewish and Christian religious thought). I argued in chapter 1 that Benjamin and Zizek (to some extent) tend to employ apocalyptic language in order to envision social transformation. They use supersessionist logic. I do not want to interpret hope through employing supersessionist logic, as it may not enable one to theorize the conditions under which hope is possible within the worlds we already inhabit. For certain, supersessionist logic such as apocalyptic language can be defiant and subversive to hegemonic structures. However, such logic does not attend to the complex, social practices that shape and inform what is possible in our neoliberal moment.

I advance that a pragmatic politics of hope emerges at the site of *mundane and ordinary lived experience*. Hope may be understood as a social practice. I employ the work of religious studies scholar Vincent Lloyd, as he helps one understand the importance of grounding a pragmatic politics of hope in mundane and everyday lived experiences. In order to demonstrate this argument, I turn to a feminist religious movement, Madres de Desaparecidos (Mothers of the Disappeared), as this movement embodies a pragmatic politics of hope at the site of everyday lived experience, being motherhood. This movement not only offers a thick description of hope as social practice but also demonstrates that both agapeic and erotic loves can ground practices of hope.

Hope Revisited

Hope might be understood as a social practice. In particular, black feminist and womanist discourses have emphasized social movements among women of color who practice hope. For women of color around the world who lead social movements, hope is located in the ordinary and mundane practices of their everyday lived experience. Hope is not merely abstract theorizing but is rooted in the messiness, complexity and ambiguity of lived experience, practices, desires, and longings for alternative worlds *located in the present*. Religious Scholar Vincent Lloyd states "only once that complex texture of the social world is acknowledged can we understand the usefulness of religious language in naming practices of political significance."[1] One practice of political significance is hope. In order to understand hope, we must turn to how *people live and actually hope* (as a practice) rather than abstract religious theorizing about hope.

Understanding hope as a social practice is important because traditional theological discourse, such as Christian discourse, has articulated hope in ways that depend upon supersessionist logic. Supersessionist logic involves the idea that the world is made right from the outside rather than from within.[2] Under supersessionist thought, there is an overturning of the old world with a new world, which communicates a radical break and discontinuity between the old and new world. According to this logic in much of Jewish and Christian theologies, the world is fallen and broken, needing a redemptive force from the outside in order to make itself right. Within supersessionist logic is the problem of *enchantment*, that there is a perfect world that completely breaks from the present world we possess.[3] For certain, when re-envisioning new worlds, we must see and talk beyond the social worlds we inhabit. However, as argued in chapter 1, new possible social worlds are envisioned from within the present. We therefore do not need to turn to an abstract "perfect" future located outside our social contexts in order to experience hope. In fact, hope is the stuff of the present. It is how we practice commitment to projects of love and justice that offer us new visions of hope.

Understanding hope as a social practice oriented toward love and justice resonates with immanent theologies. I probed the limits of apocalyptic eschatologies within Christian discourses in chapter 1, arguing that womanist theologies posit a realized eschatology as a way of locating redemptive possibilities from within rather than outside the world. When one focuses on modes of redemption from outside the world rather than analyzing modes of religiously living and acting from within the world, one misses how people remain faithful through practices of hope within their complex daily hardships and struggles. In this instance, hope is not about metaphysical propositions concerning Divine life. Rather, hope is about *how people employ rituals and practices in exercising faith* as they fashion new possibilities toward love, justice, and freedom (which may or may not include how people employ overarching metaphysical religious propositions in order to flourish).

My way of speaking about hope as a social practice contrasts with much of Christian theology's discourse on hope in which supersessionist logic sits at the center. For example, Christian theologian Walter Brueggemann offers an interpretation of Micah 4:1–5, describing these passages through an ethics of hope. Yet, he describes hope in supersessionist terms. To be clear, Brueggemann's broad intellectual work in biblical studies has rejected supersessionist models in relation to bibilical hermeneutics. For example, within much of Christian theology, the "Old Testament" is seen as being made complete by the "New Testament." Judaism is merely understood as a precursor to Christianity in which Christianity is seen as the culmination of God's final disclosure in Jesus Christ. In fact, Christians have historically interpreted themselves as God's new chosen people, replacing the Isrealites of the Old Testement. In this instance, supersessionism is understood as a replacement theology of sorts in which Christianity supercdes Judaism through a "new convenant." I am not referring to this idea of supersessionism, which Brueggemann rightly challenges and debunks.

Instead, I am referring to how Brueggemann speaks about human and social flourishing in reference to Micah, which is grounded in a Divine intentionality and action that precipitates and initates new possibiliites toward flourishing. He envisions God as the *source and grounding* of what is possible without any attention to how the empirical world of social practices actually offer the conditions towards the possibility of flourishing. In reviewing his interpretation of Micah, I am contesting his urge to privilege the necessity of an outside Divine force in initiating and propelling new worlds and possibilities instead of the richly textured world of social practices among oppressed groups.

For Brueggemann, in the book of Micah, one is met with sobering and sad news: Jerusalem has been destroyed due to the exploitation of the city through corrupt leadership. For certain, Micah's listeners encounter the city in a state of disrepair. Listeners see the city as filled with many injustices, in utter ruin.[4] The fresh imagination of a new city is revealed to Micah. Micah claims to bear divine intention in offering up new imaginative possibilities of a new city despite its present ruin. Micah claims that in the promise of God, the city is not defined by the dominant imagination, which interpreted the city as irredeemably lost and destroyed. The city is not confined to this *way of seeing*. Instead of destruction, the city would be re-imagined through divine intention for the city to flourish.

Brueggemann contends that Micah describes hope for Jerusalem, despite the city's destruction. First, Jerusalem will be the rallying center once again for people from around the world, unlike the present moment in which Micah speaks where Jerusalem had not welcomed different nations (4:1–2). Second, people will assemble in Jerusalem and YHWH will be recognized as dispensing justice among the nations (vs. 3), unlike the present Jerusalem that had perpetuated radical injustices against the vulnerable. Third, the nations in response to Torah teaching will begin disarming in order to forsake war (vs. 3), unlike the fully armed Jerusalem that met destruction. Fourth, the people of the land will live modestly (hence, language of sitting under one's own vine and fig tree) in order to not provoke war (vs. 4), which clashes with the greediness and material exploitation that led to the destruction of the city. Finally, the new city will acknowledge the religious liberty of other people (their right to serve their gods) without Israel yielding its loyalty to YHWH (vs. 5), which contradicted the current Jerusalem and its intolerance of other faiths.[5]

Micah's hope toward the flourishing of the new city encourages the residents to reject the dominant interpretation of the city, a view that accepted the permanent disrepair of Jerusalem. In the book of Micah, one can see the deep contradiction between the city articulated by the established ideology and the city imagined through the divine promise Micah communicates. Unlike the city associated with the dominant ideology, the new city grounded in prophetic imagination has one source: YHWH. The prophetic imperative "is that listeners will sign onto this alternative imagination and act accordingly."[6] The book of Micah imagines a new possibility, and this possibility toward human flourishing is connected to both Divine promise and one's neighbor. As discussed, this new vision of flourishing includes the neighbor (who is radically different from the Jewish people and outside of YHWH as a non-worshiper of the Torah) as a legitimate heir to this divine promise. The city imagined by the prophetic tradition of Micah involves poetic imaginative acts that contradict the greedy and tribal ideologies of the established city that laid in ruin. Micah communicates that a new choice can be made and this choice begins with hoping in a Divine imagination and intention.

Brueggemann notes that the work of hope (as seen through prophetic imagination) is "to dislodge the 'giveness' of claims of established ideology. If that 'giveness' is dislodged, then alternatives become thinkable and chooseable."[7] Human flourishing needs hope and moral imagination in order to envision new social and moral worlds, new ways of being that actualize our humanity. However, for Brueggemann, such hope and imagination are *not directly present or accessible to the senses but rely on the anticipation of something to come outside of the current world.* This new world is initiated through Divine intention and action. He asserts, "My thesis is that the hard work of imagination (that claims divine rootage and divine propulsion) is a fundamental precondition for a society that can flourish."[8]

Brueggemann employs the Jewish story of Micah as a way of discussing hope and moral imagination but this discourse depends upon supersessionist logic. To be fair, Brueggemann seeks to *draw out norms* in relation to hope. This conversation about norms is rooted in particular metaphysical propositions grounded in Divine life that can never be relativized like care of the poor, injustice of economic exploitation, interreligious acceptance and peace, and so forth. Such norms enable us to say what we ought to do and how we ought to ethically live. Normative visions enable moral justification of justice actions in the face of horrific injustice and oppression. Brueggemann is correct to posit the importance of norms that ground moral projects oriented toward freedom and justice. However, the problem with Brueggemann's analysis is that the empirical world does not feed into how such a normative world is possible (or whether this normative vision is commendable). Presumably, we might reasonably agree with Brueggemann that the normative vision he foregrounds through Micah is something to be ethically preferred. However, *how* Brueggemann gets there forecloses the question of how we go about commending certain normative visions and orientations more broadly. We indeed act in relation to norms but there is always a gap between norms and how such norms are implemented and/or re-assessed in light of social practices. Oftentimes, we are forced to re-think our normative orientations themselves in light of social practices.

People actually navigate the "gap" between norms and social practices within the context of their real-lived experiences, which means that transcendent theological narratives may not help us move toward "the stuff" of hope as this narrative may be detached from social practices in present contexts. I understand hope not as belief in particular religious propositions, but as a virtue, disposition, and practice to remain committed to liberative projects of human flourishing despite the messy, contradictory, viscous, and complex experiences of life.

Most importantly, Brueggemann's description of hope through Micah does not allow the empirical world to feed back into his discussion of hope as the inauguration of this new world is primarily initiated and actualized *through Divine agency.* To be certain, there is something to be gained from the rich vision of hope we find in Micah. However, my concern is that any vision of hope that does not engage the empirical world loses its critical force. Transcendental visions of hope not rooted in the messy experiences of our social worlds as well as human agency risk slipping into melancholic fixation and fantazised but ever-distant "New Jerusalems."[9] I am not advocating for stepping outside of norms (as we are unable). Instead, I am interested in how we critically "bracket" social norms in order to consider how social practices inform our justification and/or potential re-evaluation of such norms.

I also understand Brueggemann to be using the story of Micah as a form of prophecy about a Divine future to come, which breaks into history. Prophetic utterance is deeply associated with hope as it articulates what one might *hope for.* In Brueggemann's instance, prophecy is understood as an overarching Divine vision of justice that critiques present forms of injustices. This transcendent vision is couched in metaphysical terms in which norms of justice are derived from *a priori* knowledge about Divine intention. Hence, for Brueggemann's form of prophecy, there is a *je ne sais quoi* that stands behind prophetic speech and utterances. Prophetic speech speaks from "on high," representing an ultimate reality that is absolute.

However, similar to philosopher and black religious scholar Cornel West, I do not agree that an absolute, singular divine reality (and its moral imperative) stands behind prophetic speech. Prophecy does not "have unique access to the pure future, pure past, or the pure normative,"[10] as Brueggemann's idea of the prophetic seems to draw upon. Prophecy is about "calling out the gaps between social norms and practices that account for the tragic nature of social life," and marshaling the strategies of tradition, liturgy, religious practices, and more as a means of coping with this tragic condition.[11] As a result, prophetic speech may reveal multiple conditional futures that can be accessed based upon how we choose to "close the gaps" between our norms and practices. Prophetic utterance (and therefore hope) does not stand outside of the social practices of human beings but rather is found in the ordinary, mundane practices of life.

Prophecy is virtuous speech that "persuades its listeners to take part in such thinking and acting" in order to make the "invisible visible." Lloyd speaks about the importance of the prophet in that the prophet's words do not represent a singular Divine intention and reality. Rather, the prophet "must refuse the hegemony of the visible."[12] The hegemony of the visible are those dominant norms that suppress and attempt to render invisible the everyday social practices that oppress and marginalize certain individuals and groups, disclosing the tragic dimensions of life itself. The hegemony of the visible erases the quotidian daily practices of vulnerable populations that give rise to suffering and hope, pain, and resistance. This understanding of prophecy reveals the potential violence of norms (hegemony of the visible) and why liberative social practices are essential to critiquing death-dealing normative visions in order to fashion more humane visions of hope, justice and human flourishing that confront hegemonic realities. For example, Martin Luther King's vision of a racially inclusive society was not based on his "mere dreaming" or grounded in a singular Divine reality. Rather, King's vision for racial justice and reconciliation was deeply informed by the cadre of "mixed" communities (black and white people) around the United States that had been modeling what a community of love looks like across racial lines. King was very familiar with movements that were modeling integrated living such as Koinania Farm.[13] For King, these movements and their social practices already pointed to what was prophetically possible for broader America.

Black feminist and womanist thinkers I have mentioned such as Karen Baker-Fletcher, Monica Coleman, Melanie Harris, bell hooks, and Alice Walker have discussed hope as sets of collective practices rooted in religious forms of moral protest among marginalized women of color. These thinkers articulate hope as resisting and protesting the hegemony of the visible. These discourses also aspire to represent the ordinary lives of women of color who hope in extraordinary ways. For the black feminist and womanist, one cannot speak about hope without turning to the richly textured world of social practices women of color inhabit. It is through these women's worlds that societies might learn what a politics of hope requires. Radical practices of love (agapeic and erotic), justice, and freedom create the grounding for prophetic utterances to emerge.

Because black feminist and womanist perspectives privilege practices and social movements among women of color in exploring hope, I turn to a particular religious movement among women of color who embody hope as a social practice. This religious movement discloses marginalized women's everyday social practices and forms of moral protest from which they express hope. Madres de Desparecidos or Madres de Plazo de Mayo not only provides an insightful case study on why turning to social practices among women of color remains important in describing a pragmatic politics of hope but also demonstrates that their politics of hope is driven by a rich interplay between agapeic and erotic love.

Mothers of the Disappeared

Every Thursday afternoon at 3:30 p.m., mothers and grandmothers of "disappeared children" march in the Plaza de Mayo, known to be the place where the Argentine presidential palace resides. These mothers and grandmothers not only remember and mourn their dead and abducted children but also challenge the Argentinian military power that performed these human atrocities. For these mothers, the ethical necessity of publicly lamenting the dead interprets Argentina's past as catastrophic, bearing witness to the piles of young bodies that cry out for justice. These mothers' private acts of mourning the unjust deaths of their children quickly transformed into public declarations for justice.[14] These mothers, called "Madres de Desaparecidos" (Mothers of the Disappeared) or "Madres de Plazo de Mayo," used their political organizing and Christian spiritual activism to transform the corpses of their children into national emblems of unfulfilled democratic promises for justice within Argentina.

The Madres movement is a women's movement that emerged in the 1970s to protest the abduction of their children during the Dirty War of 1976–1983 in Argentina. The Dirty War emerged out of a series of military coups due to severe economic depression in this country, largely engendered by global economic expansionism. Neoliberal capitalist processes and growing disparities between the rich and poor played a role in why political tyranny emerged, complicating the experience of freedom Argentinians experienced during the early 1900s. The abduction of children was due to the ways in which particular families politically dissented and critiqued the inequitable economic conditions and oppressive political decisions of the ruling military government in Argentina. To be sure, neoliberal economic logic (austerity measures, the dismantling of Welfare State, and increasing foreign investment), in part, was responsible for the economic devastation and subsequent political dictatorship that took root in Argentina. Mothers of Plaza de Mayo as a global women's movement interrupted and disrupted the undemocratic and non-egalitarian program undergirding the Argentinian government and its aims to align with the exploitative neoliberal values of global capitalism. The Madres brand of Christian activism was both political *and* spiritual as they protested through marches, chants, and prayers. While the Madres cannot be termed "feminist" in the sense that they were not interested in directly challenging the gender system and the sexual division of labor, they were committed to the preservation of life by demanding their rights as "traditional" women to secure the survival and memory of their children. In fact, by joining together, these mothers were unintentionally creating a new form of political participation, outside the traditional party structures and based on love, care, and cooperation. Our present global economic structure does not value these norms but instead, privileges alienating norms such as competition, isolation, and rabid individualism. These insidious neoliberal values prevent economies of solidarity from forming out of which love, compassion, equity, and human flourishing can be realized.

This movement also demonstrates that hope is best described through ordinary, everyday lived experiences among individuals and groups. For the Madres, hope is not ascertained through supernatural interventions into the world. They do not rely on any outside forces to remedy the violence and evil they experience at the hands of a rogue military regime. Rather, they depend upon their everyday practices of motherhood and how their embodiment of motherhood subverts the dictatorship's neoliberal practices of division, hatred, violence, and projective disgust toward those who dissent. These women's embodiment of motherhood inaugurates a politics of hope and love, which also enables these women to envision an alternative democratic future of care. Before I discuss the Madres' social practice of hope through motherhood, I discuss the historical backdrop and national political situation out of which these mothers were responding.

Totalitarian Neoliberal Markets and the Madres' Response

In 1976, Argentina's collapsing economy and external indebtedness set the national stage for the "Dirty War," a term used to describe the mass abductions and killings of children and young adults through methods of torture and rape underneath the Argentine military dictatorship. Throughout most of the twentieth century, Argentina's vast wealth was concentrated in the hands of a few elite with enormous amounts of land. Wealth was equated to land in which "three quarters of it was owned by fewer than 2,000 individuals, as late as 1970."[15] When industrial planning eventually was proposed and implemented in this country, it was done in a haphazard way. Because big international companies, most of them British, had been influential upon Argentina's economy throughout the twentieth century, industrial growth stagnated.[16] Big business and foreign corporations were privileged over the working class in Argentina's economy, which reflected gross disparities between the rich and poor.

By the 1940s, there was a large working class that struggled with worsening conditions, including low wages, poor working conditions, poor housing, and more. Moreover, this large working class had no political parties to represent their class interests. Labor activist Juan Peron came to political power, winning the presidential vote of the working class population by promising to improve worker's conditions such as shortening working hours and raising the minimum wage.[17] Peron was swept into power not only by his championing of the working person but also by his new girlfriend-turned-wife, a popular actress named Eva Duarte who would eventually be affectionately known as Evita (Eva Peron).

However, Peron was no revolutionary. His goal was not to give power to the working class. Instead, his political aim was to get the working class to give power to him so that he could champion their economic and political cause.[18] He encouraged the working class to embrace a socialist vision wherein Argentina could thrive. Yet, even Peron's administration collaborated with and gave more power to big businesses, which did little to improve the long-term economic well-being of the working class. Many political factions such as the Montoneros became dissatisfied as there were an increasing number of bankruptcies and a continuing decline in the real income of the working class.[19] Wealth continued to be concentrated in the hands of the few as Argentina moved into the 1960s and 1970s. After Peron was exiled and returned to rule right before his death, Argentina was descending into economic and social chaos as extremist and terrorist groups emerged in response to the policies of Peron's government, particularly violent policies and military tactics that tried to suppress dissent. After Juan Peron's death in 1974, his third wife Isabel Peron came into power to extend the Peronist vision of championing worker's rights, although the country descended further into social and economic chaos and violence.

In March 1976, the military Junta overthrew Isabel Peron and the Peronist government, suspending Congress and installing their own Supreme Court appointees. This military junta banned all political parties, interest groups, and even labor strikes. All potential political solidarities were declared subversive by the junta.[20] The military junta under General Videla gained initial legitimacy in Argentina due to the senseless and random violence of various political factions. The economic and political system in Argentina was at a dead end. No one could articulate an alternative other than the military government that came to power through a coup. The new military regime in 1976 initially promised to restore the rule of law and order, which included the respect of the democratic rights of citizens. This is what all citizens wanted to hear. The regime promised to rebuild democracy.[21] But these promises never materialized.

Instead, the military regime passed a series of laws that eventually led to the militarization of the Argentine state itself. Some of these laws included imprisoning anyone for ten years who "propagated subversive material or material that was offensive to the military."[22] The regime justified this law by arguing that Argentina was in a "state of emergency" and in a state of war (due to violence among political factions) in which the military justified the usage of extreme methods. They called such methods the "process of national reorganization."[23] The idea of the military seizing temporary power for purposes of establishing national order and stability in Argentina was not new. In fact, prior to 1976, this had happened before. Yet, whenever the military stepped in prior to 1976, it was seen as a temporary intervention to restore order and to hand power back over to the political arena for civilian rule. Under Videla's military rule, this sentiment was no longer shared. Instead, high-ranking military leaders understood their power as permanent, which led to this military dictatorship repressing and destroying all dissidence and critique.

Because the military junta supported a regime that continued to deny social and economic justice to the masses, many dissidents emerged, primarily young professional who challenged the political, social, and economic measures the junta put in place. Because the military regime was attempting to advance a neoliberal economic agenda that further liberalized trade and opened the country up to world markets, many domestic companies could not compete with foreign imports, investment and production in Argentina. The junta's economic policies sought to privatize key industries that had previously been under state protection. While Argentina certainly had stressful poverty levels (around 9%) before the military took political power, poverty and unemployment grew at an astronomical rate as the junta reorganized the economy along neoliberal lines. In order to fund these changes, the military also borrowed money from abroad, money that came with high interest rates. This huge debt burden along with neoliberal economic policies underwritten by the IMF and World Bank further exacerbated an already declining economy, which led to young dissidents who critiqued the social and economic policies of the junta.

Young professionals who publically disagreed with the junta were immediately kidnapped and/or murdered. Initially, these young people who disappeared were articulated as part of violent extremist factions by the military regime. They tried to depict those who disappeared as socially deviant and subversive in an attempt to isolate the families of the disappeared who were speaking out against the crimes of the Argentine military regime. But this was not true. The disappeared were mostly university students and young professionals who were dedicated to improving the lives of the economically vulnerable and poor in their country. These young adults were activists who desired change and social transformation in their country against the backdrop of radical economic and cultural inequalities. Many of these young professionals sought to promote social change through teaching small children in shantytowns or organizing laborers to demand equality of pay. In short, they were social reformers who called upon the people to hold the government accountable in ensuring equity and equality for all Argentinian citizens.[24]

Those who were abducted or eventually murdered by the military government were interrogated in secret. The military carried out raids in unmarked cars not only to obliterate the identities of the disappeared but also to leave the disappearances unacknowledged.[25] The fear of the military led to complete silence throughout the country about what persons saw or heard. People were afraid to acknowledge what they had witnessed, fearing for their lives as well as the lives of their loved ones. This fear and silence made the disappearances possible. In fact, such disappearances could only be made complete by the "disappearance" of citizens' testimonies on the brutal, inhumane atrocities done against thousands of young people. In fact, an English paper *Buenos Aires Herald* remarked that neighbors and cemetery workers saw security guards bring six or seven bodies to bury almost once a week while the military anti-terrorist campaign transpired.[26] This is the military backdrop of terror against which mothers and grandmothers searched frantically for their beloved children in 1976. At first these women were largely apolitical, searching desperately for their children who remained missing. They were simply overwhelmed and crushed by the weight of their heartbreaking predicaments. They contacted political officials, visited hospitals, and showed up at schools. These mothers often joined together in efforts to ask political and religious leaders for help in finding their missing daughters and sons. However, they received no help or answers. It was out of the mothers and grandmothers desperation that they began talking among themselves about ways to find out answers to their questions. They *were not looking to start a political movement or moral protest. They simply wanted their children back.* However, they realized that this simply was not what the military government wanted. These mothers and grandmothers came to the realization that if they wanted to secure answers, they would have to politicize what had begun as deeply personal tragedies. They would need to morally protest the junta, using their spirituality to frame the evil committed against their children.

As mothers and families began to look for their disappeared children, the junta tried hard to cover and deny such activities. The military not only denied their role in the disappearances but also generated a social script that blamed the mothers as somehow negligent or irresponsible for their children's disappearances. These mothers were seen as morally deviant, unable to perform their protective duties and obligations as mothers. Moreover, the children were seen as "getting what was due to them" as the military simply framed these children as part of extremist groups, part of larger terrorist agendas. The images and master narrative that the military junta spun was used to galvanize public support for the junta and against all people who questioned the government in relation to these disappearances. The junta tried to remind the public that Argentina was in a state of sickness in terms of socio-economic stability and needed to be brought back to health, which meant "ridding the body" of all elements (subversive people) that continued such sickness.[27] Mothers of the disappeared were depicted as "mad" and "crazed" by the military as a way to render them illegitimate, lacking credibility. The junta's unjust rationale initially trumped the mother's protest for justice, as most citizens simply wanted to bring stability and social order back to Argentina.

Geographies of Dissent

Because these mothers were initially not welcomed into the halls of governmental power in relation to these abductions and killings, they claimed the geography of dissent, which was the Plazo de Mayo where Argentina proclaimed its independence from Spain in 1816.[28] On Saturday afternoon of April 13, 1977, the first demonstration was held. Fourteen women decided to show up and march at the Plazo de Mayo, knowing the inherent danger in publicly challenging the government. Each woman wore flat shoes in preparation to run if they needed to.[29] They also wore white headscarves to represent their purity of love for their children and for their beloved country that had gone astray from its democratic promises. They found this first day of protest to be unremarkable as the plaza was somewhat empty. It seemed that activity was not present on Fridays and they needed activity in order to draw attention to their protest against the inhumane abductions of the military state.

After minimal activity in the plaza over the next few Fridays, the mothers decided to change the weekly protest to Thursdays in the plaza to attract more attention. This plaza was the heart of Buenos Aires political and economic center. In defiance of the military regime that ruled by terror and repression, these women courageously marched in the streets and city square of Plazo de Mayo, reminding the government that truth would prevail. They knew that their country was wrecked by violence and the people rendered mute due to fear. Women of the disappeared came out of these violent shadows of repression and fear in order to make visible injustices that were veiled by the military dictatorship.

In the beginning, the mothers simply marched counter-clockwise along the plaza. This act of marching in the plaza was to disrupt the unquestioned sphere of military dominance and rule. Because of fear, the military regime's actions were left unquestioned. In fact, the propaganda that the government published to discredit these mothers also fueled people's unwillingness to question the genocidal actions of the government, opting to believe that these women were ultimately responsible for the missing status of their children. One often saw business leaders and politicians hurry through the plaza or cross the street to walk on the other side to distance themselves from these mothers. The mothers ignored such propaganda (as well as the reactionary, fear-based responses of the citizens) and came to the square in order to tell their story of violent undemocratic repression.

As the mothers returned to the plaza weekly, they began holding up cardboard pictures and images of their disappeared children.[30] Because the military had invoked a social script that was theatrical (posting billboards and marches depicting these mothers as crazy), the mothers organized one of the most visible, theatrical counter-resistant movements in the world, using the same sense of performance to challenge, shame, and undermine the government's action.[31] They knew that by marching at the Plazo de Mayo on Thursday instead of the weekend, they would be making a spectacle of their cause, rendering themselves visible as a powerful and potent dissenting voice to the government.

These women fashioned one of the "most visible political discourses of resistance to terror in recent Latin American history" through using their bodies to challenge the disappearance of their children's bodies.[32] If women's bodies could be sexually terrorized by the military regime, women's bodies could be organized to stand in defiance of such inhumane practices. These women's positioning of their bodies in spaces of power (Plazo de Mayo) is significant as the military regime sexually tortured women's bodies to render them powerless within a totalitarian, capitalist machine. This positioning of their bodies in spaces of power was also driven by their deep-shared feelings and yearnings to secure freedom and justice for their beloved children and dissenting neighbors who were being persecuted by the junta. One might describe the Madres as driven by an erotic energy in that they sought to cultivate a deep love for justice and democratic freedom within Argentine's citizenry. These women's positioning of their bodies in the sphere of power advocated that Argentina needed communities that were pulled toward each other through connection, desire, and freedom rather than pushed away from each other through fear, apathy, and disconnection. This erotic charge was present in these mothers' public cry for justice and national togetherness within Argentina. They incarnated a politics of love through actualizing their cries for justice in and through their bodies.

At first, the mothers were of minimal interest to the police. However, as the demonstrations grew in number over the next few months from fourteen to a few hundred, two or three vanloads of police would arrive, and the mothers would be identified as well as forced to leave.[33] As the numbers grew, the police began arresting them and often held these women at police stations up to 24 hours. Despite police brutality, the informal movement grew. Mothers, grandmothers, sisters, aunts, and even some men who had not experienced the abduction of their children came and marched with the mothers of the disappeared. It was no longer a movement concerned with the fate of immediate family members or relatives but concerned with ensuring that the protest against the government was heard. This was quite a breakthrough in the movement as people had previously preferred to only be associated with the mothers if they had lost an immediate relative. The names "Mothers of the Disappeared" and "Mothers of the Plazo de Mayo" did not emerge out of this movement but were names locals called these women as they persistently marched in the plaza in efforts to find their disappeared children.[34] This name began to resonate with the madres.

The only way to find out about this movement was through word of mouth in 1977. The newspapers remained silent about the mother's protests, excluding the *Buenos Aires Herald* (which also had a restricted readership).[35] Although the madres had minimal press, people who had missing children found these mothers. They came to the meetings the mothers held in churches and other locations to attempt to get information on their missing loved ones. Many persons that initially came to merely inquire about particular individuals often stayed with the mothers and volunteered their time as writers of letters, drafters of petitions, and more.[36] Some citizens were stepping forward and standing in solidarity with the women, acknowledging their suffering and the sinister role the government played in carrying out these killings.

The government feared their potential and growing influence as what had begun as 14 women marching in the Plazo de Mayo grew into hundreds of women. These women's offices and homes were raided. Police on horses even attacked these mothers with iron chains one day as they marched in the plaza. They attempted to paint these women as socially subversive and moral deviants as mothers to crush the growth of this movement. The leader, Mrs. Azucena de Vicenti, eventually disappeared, never to be seen again along with two French nuns that had been at the forefront of the marched and protest.[37]

As the military government continued denying such activities to the larger world now being apprised of these abductions, the junta launched a press campaign in an attempt to "clear" their name. In December 1977, the Argentine government issued a statement, blaming the disappearances on the mothers' subversive and "nihilistic" protests.[38] In response, the mothers took a courageous and daring step in holding their own press conference with both Argentinian and foreign press in the Plazo de Mayo, blaming the kidnappings on the government. Only four foreign journalists attended this press conference. The mothers were horribly outnumbered by the police and other political officials associated with the junta. While the police were restrained due to the presence of foreign journalists, the menacing posture of the military and policemen remained palpable.[39]

Eventually some of the founders of the *Madres* were abducted never to be seen again. This was a profound loss and affected the protest movement into 1978. While a cadre of these mothers was able to keep the weekly marches going, the harassment intensified. By the beginning of 1979, they found it difficult to continue their marches in the plaza. The violence of the police was becoming so unbearable that they decided to meet in churches instead. Because the junta had made churches illegal sites for these women to hold meetings, this was equally hard as the mothers had to depend on the few sympathetic priests who were willing to put themselves at risk for this cause. Some priests only allowed the women to meet if they met with the lights off and prayed, passing messages on paper notes about the "next steps" in order to avoid being detected.[40] This was one of the lowest points the mothers experienced as a protest group.

Although the authorities thought they had permanently weakened the mothers, the mothers gathered strength and momentum, performing a major act of defiance by May 1979. They first held elections in order to formalize their organization Association of the Mothers of the Plazo de Mayo, which would provide greater stability for the protest activity. Three months later, they legally registered their association, which enabled them to obtain financial support from groups and individuals abroad who sympathized with their cause. They were able to get a bank account and even contribute to the health of children who were orphaned due to their parents' disappearance. By 1980, this movement had evolved into an international organization with funding.[41]

Yet, the most important decision they made was the decision to go back to the Plazo de Mayo to march. They vowed to never acquiesce to the military and give up this space as their context to protest. On January 3, 1980, Thursday, they returned to the plaza, surrounding the monument in the center of the plaza and wearing their flat shoes and white headscarves. The police thought the organization had been smashed back in 1979 but they were thrown into shock when they saw the mothers return to the plaza. The tide had turned. This was certainly their act of ultimate defiance. Fear had not won the day.[42]

Mothers of the Disappeared: Hope as Practice of Motherhood

Many of these mothers and grandmothers who protested their abducted and disappeared children were Catholic. However, the Catholic Church was deeply divided as these crimes occurred. Sectors of the Church in Argentina were largely silent. While Roman Catholicism was not Argentina's state religion, the church did play a prominent role in politics and military affairs. There was a powerful alliance between the church, elite landowners, and the military that had been present for years. In addition, it was understood by most of society that the President had to be Catholic, and most national agencies such as the ministry of education were directed by Catholic citizens. The military also committed itself to the defense of Christianity, even integrating it into its rhetoric of an orderly society. This made it extremely difficult for the church to renounce the state and its violent tactics, as the line between the two were often blurred.[43]

The Catholic Church was also ambivalent about decrying the military regime because while it sympathized with the military's aims, it did not agree with the military's methods. As discussed earlier, the military wrested control over Argentina's government in the midst of fighting among political factions over economic and social resources deeply exacerbated by neoliberal policies. The country was moving into chaos and people needed order. Although most priests knew the human rights abuses occurring underneath the junta and perhaps disagreed with such violence, they remained silent and were complicit due to their inaction. Even among the priests, fear was so palpable that some priests refused to say Mass for those who had been murdered by the military, scared that they would be seen as offering support to subversive activities. Very few priests took up the cause of those who disappeared. In fact, some priests, such as Cardinal Juan Carlos Aramburu, had the federal police clear out his cathedral when the mothers took refuge in his church one afternoon.[44]

However, there were priests in the church who were martyred because of their support of the mothers. In the Buenos Aires suburb of Belgrano, military officials ruthlessly executed three priests and two seminarians. Without their knowledge, these priests and seminarians had been under surveillance by political officials at their parish. A boy from the parish discovered their bodies one morning. Their hands were tied behind their backs. It looked as if the priests had been beaten with machine guns and then shot.[45] The police commander blamed the deaths on subversives and terrorists but everyone knew the truth. After the funeral of the five murdered priests and seminarians, the Archbishop of Santa Fe sent a letter to President Videla, asking for a federal investigation into the deaths of these five church leaders. The letter was sent in private and the military government responded in private to the Archbishop. Of course, church officials felt more secure expressing their grievances in private, as public challenge could bring serious trouble. Consequently, the military regime was always able to "brush aside" and ignore the complaints of human rights abuses being performed. [46]

While some priests stood up for social justice during the Dirty War, the Mothers of the Plazo de Mayo still maintain that they had very little help from the church as they persistently searched for their missing children. In fact, it is documented that some Archbishops even visited places where the police carried out executions and tortures. Archbishop Monsignor Antonio Jose Plaza actually refused to condemn a friend of his, General Ramon Camps (a commanding officer of the Buenos Aires police), who admitted to giving orders to execute several thousand people.[47] This Archbishop simply described General Camps as a man who carried out his duty. The bishop refused to assess whether the General was right or wrong. This overt complicity of church officials with the military regime impeded the mothers activism in calling the government to account for the radical injustices that were being committed against their children. What is ironic about this story is that Archbishop Jose Plaza was seen as the "Prince of the church," as he was known for charity to the poor. Yet, his sermons focused on the need for law and order and therefore, describe the mothers as subversives and threats to the stability of the country.

The Madres movement was a spiritual movement but not in the strict religious sense. They knew that the patriarchal theological limitations of Catholicism problematized their religious and political performance of motherhood. While the religious view of the church tended to privilege law and order, the mothers knew the theological force of defiance. Defiance of religious and secular authorities was often viewed as sinful and even heretical in many church circles. Yet, these women embraced their right to defy both the government and the religious authority of the church, appealing to a higher truth of love and justice in order to defend the vulnerable. Their spiritual activism then was not merely religious participation in the church structure although many of these women were devout Catholics. Instead, these women's Christian activism became countercultural to the religious institution, directly challenging Catholic orthodoxies through their embodiment of a defiant spirituality that refused to be silenced.

Their practice of defiance can be primarily seen through the madres' performance of motherhood. The women's subversive everyday practice of motherhood defied the military narrative of motherhood. The madres' performance of motherhood in the plaza was at odds with essentialized notions of motherhood within the social and religious institutions of Argentinian society. These women "shifted the site of enactment of motherhood from the private sphere to the public, where it became a bid for political recognition."[48] They not only acted out the acceptable forms of motherhood as an individual identity but also acted out more unacceptable forms of motherhood as collective political performance "that allowed women to protest and access a kind of public political power to confront a criminal state."[49] In other words, when these women decided to consciously politicize motherhood, they rebelled against the social and religious norms of womanhood in Argentina. They became public women.

Interestingly, "public" women in Latin America were considered prostitutes or madwomen.[50] They were seen as anti-mothers or unrecognized as "proper mothers" even if they had children. For the Church and the military junta, good mothers were invisible. They did not gather in groups but stayed home with their children. Through their actions on an almost subconscious level, mothers of the disappeared initially tried to overcome these ideological barriers as they made plans to march in protest to the junta by modeling their motherhood after the Virign Mary. For these women, the Virgin Mary was the ultimate mother who transcended the public-private distinction by carrying her private experience into public. This virginal role that these women embodied allowed them "to perform traditionally acceptable 'feminine' qualities such as self-sacrifice, suffering, and irrationality in service to subversive and trangressive public/political activities."[51] These women attempted to reframe the Virgin Mary's role through showing that her self-sacrificial, suffering, and praying character was not about passivity and submission but about engagement with the world itself. The women sought to interpret Mary in a more subversive way.

This more subversive interpretation of Mary involved these women's performance as mourning mothers. They literally marched around the plaza crying and screaming as real expressions of their grief. The junta claimed that it was defending the Christian values that grounded the Argentinian family through punishing "subversives." The junta maintained that law and order were crucial Christian values that held the fabric of Argentinian society together. Without law and order, Argentina would not only decline into a state of public disorder but also would end in destruction due to its rejection of an essentially Christian national character. Through the mother's public mourning and chants, they attempted to expose the contradictions inherent in the junta's rationale on upholding Christian values: the killing and torturing of their children were undermining the very familial foundation and Christian ideals that the government promised to uphold. The junta did not allow these mothers to perform their duties as mothers, being to defend and care for their children.

Within Christian traditions, Jesus' mother Mary mourned over his death at the foot of the cross, a death justified by an imperial order. Likewise, these mothers were mourning the executions and disappearances of their innocent children at the hands of an unjust government. Some mothers who later participated in a documentary stated, "The Virgin Mary had her son in her arms after he died. We don't even have their [our children's] bones."[52] By comparing the disappearances to the death of Jesus, the Madres were sending a clear message to the dictatorship, which publicly prided itself on promoting Christian and family values: kidnapping and torturing the young people of Argentina was as big an atrocity as killing the son of God. Hence, these women's public mourning of their children had deep spiritual meaning and significance as they equated their children with a religious innocence and purity (innocence of Jesus). The performance of public mourning discloses how these women's moral protest was empowered by their spirituality. As one can see, the role of Mary was central to many Madres' sense of spiritual activism.

One might creatively argue that much of the Madres' spiritual activism was undergirded by this subversive reinterpretation of Mary. As Mary, many of these women were attempting to religiously legitimize their moral protest against the government and the institutional Church. As Mary, many of the madres were poor and or/working class women who certainly experienced economic deprivation and gender injustice underneath the junta. Many of these women felt the "double bind" in that they were seen as subjugated to men in respect to the State and the Church. Because these women were alienated and discriminated against within their country and religious traditions, their forms of defiant spirituality gave them the courage to confront the State and Church over their children's disappearances. This defiant spirituality was grounded in their politicization of motherhood through this alternate interpretation of Mary.

However, this reinterpretation of the role of the Virginal Mary collided with the politics of the junta (and the Church). They were not only ostracized from their family and friends but also marginalized by much of the Church. Interpreting the Virgin Mary in a more radical way did not resonate with the church, because while pain was permissible for women, *anger was not allowed*. Silently suffering was allowed for women in the church, but *not vocal and public protest*.[53] For the church and state, the Virgin Mary represents purity, emotion, and heavenly goodness that must remain untainted by a corrupt politics of the world. Once a woman is perceived as "political," she becomes soiled and tainted, even sexually aggressive and active. She becomes akin to a whore.[54] Even the beloved national leader Eva ("Evita") Peron who made it possible for her husband Juan Peron to be elected as President of Argentina, promoted that Peron was "the figure and she was the shadow."[55] Because mothers of the disappeared were "public" women, they were punished through sexual brutality, physical beatings, and death. Because these women were driven by an erotic energy to protest the fear and apathy generated by the junta, they were labeled "enemies of the state." Many leaders and members of the Catholic Church were complicit in contributing to the marginalization and ostracizing of these hurting mothers who simply wanted to find their children.

The state *and* the Church sought to pigeonhole these women into passive roles as mothers. However, these women were furious at the prospect of suffering in silence, not knowing where their children were. While the state and Church sought to regulate and control the voices and bodies of these women, these women used their bodies "to show the presence/absence of all those who had disappeared without a trace, without leaving a body."[56] Through using their bodies to march and protest, the women and their disappeared children "appeared" back into the national public dialogue on justice. The mothers of the disappeared certainly used their bodies in order to protest the disappearance of their children's bodies. Their moral protest was a form of political protest but also spiritual activism as these women unconsciously were challenging religious notions of

motherhood through their performance as mothers. They were theologically legitimating countercultural notions of motherhood that
took seriously the ways in which women could passionately express
hope, love, and justice in the public sphere (and not merely in the
private sphere). These women knew that the private was profoundly
public. In order for justice to be actualized, these mothers used moral
protest to form communities of hope and love that would demand
truth telling from a genocidal state.

These women's Christian activism deeply informed their politics of
resistance. As previously noted, these women were not initially motivated by political ideology but by the sheer weight of their horrendous circumstances. They refused to forget the injustices perpetrated
against their children, becoming "self-proclaimed custodians of a history of terror and oppression."[57] While the mothers were attempting
to incriminate the Argentina junta and bring their children's torturers
to trial, they did not see themselves as being political in the traditional
sense. For instance, the mothers clearly practiced a politics of resistance against the junta and against traditional Catholic notions of
motherhood. Yet, they also maintained what some might label "patriarchal stances" as they said their efforts were not for the "liberation of women" but for their children. In fact, some of these women
rejected "feminism" as such, if this term meant a certain Western
liberal notion of women. Certainly, this movement was full of contradictions in terms of what the movement meant. However, one fact
stands: they simply wanted their children back. They also wanted to
destroy the credibility of the junta in order to expose the truth concerning human rights abuses.

For them, a politics of hope was about engaging the past. It was
about being attentive to the injustice of the present world in order
remake it through their social and religious practices. These women
insisted on engaging the past so that the repressed stories of the disappeared could be heard. Engaging the past for them was to make
visible real injustices under the military regime that had been veiled
and covered. Through their religious reinterpretations of motherhood, these women were fashioning a different kind of revolution
that sought to rediscover the lost vocabulary of dissidence in order
to challenge injustice and anti-democratic practices. These women
worked to revitalize the dying political dialogue in Argentina, which
had been co-opted by neoliberal structures and practices of market
greed and violence. They wanted to keep the memory of trauma alive
so that loss and injustice were not systematized but challenged.[58] The

new could be born from the old. Future democratic possibilities were contingent on remedying the cries of justice rooted in the past. This revolution was to make the disappeared "reappear" through truth telling and sacred remembrance. The revolution was about the democratic soul of their country in which the past needed to be redeemed in order to understand the present in a way that made their longings for a democratic future possible.

This sacred remembrance was rooted in their interpretation of the past as catastrophic, a past that was built on the shedding of innocent blood. These women's spirituality would not allow them to see the future as redeemable without returning to and rectifying the past. Hope was about social practice for these women—rehearsing and resurrecting the memories of those who had died. But such redemption involved political honesty of what had happened. Engaging the past was about the role of memory in relation to democratic vitalities.

The mothers knew that the promise of democracy that the Argentine Constitution expressed was not possible without remembrance of the country's horrific past. History must be told from the perspective of the disappeared. In fact, the disappeared must "reappear" for Argentina to have a democratic future.[59] Therefore, the use of sacred remembrance was central to the mothers in redeeming the promises of democracy associated with the Argentinian constitution. Sacred remembrance enables dissent and dialogue as well as the ability to tell the repressed stories of the oppressed, which are the conditions under which a democratic future is possible.

In an effort to disclose the disappearances the junta attempted to erase from national memory, the mothers "marched in weekly processions, wearing white masks and white handkerchiefs to represent the silenced conscience of the disappeared."[60] They demonstrated in the streets with young activists and international human rights advocates, demanding the return of their precious children. They even engaged the international community through writing and publishing their own newspaper, *Madres de Plazo de Mayo*, and appealed to the United Nations.[61] The mothers created an alternative space for the practice of truth telling, sacred remembrance, and solidarity through their radical resistance and spiritual protest as mothers.

Their practice of sacred remembrance attempted to communicate that the Argentine military regime was the product of a past catastrophe.[62] The mothers were certain that even their dead children will not be safe from despotism if they are not mourned and through mourning and truth telling, re-awakened. The mothers did not see democracy as something we progress toward as the junta thought, which allowed them to legitimate violence in the name of neoliberal progress. The mother's focus on the past indicates that they saw the past as a catalyst for the future. They believed that the "old" needed to be distilled into the new. The "past histories of loss and defeat are the lifeblood of the political" and its democratic future.[63] The mothers' performance of the political focused on repeating the truth about past injustices against their children in order to pull into the present possibilities toward the remedying of such brutal atrocities. From marching in the streets to speaking in Geneva, these women strived to re-awaken the memory of the dead in order to create dialogue surrounding justice, love, and hope. In other words, for these mothers, "radicalizing democracy is about a return in time and in memory – a transgression against the grain of existing political structures in Argentina."[64]

These women foreground the past because they know that such injustices not only cry out for redemption but also signal the repetition of further atrocities if not corrected. The mothers knew that human injustices left unaddressed are the breeding ground for further human violations. We are unable to move forward. Instead, we are stuck, trapped within our own barbarity that we claim as progress. The mothers rejected the "civilizing" discourse the junta articulated as their message of "law and order" by exposing what lurked behind the message of order: neoliberal ideologies and totalitarian practices that sought to crush dissent at any cost. There was no possibility for Argentina to cultivate communities of care and trust if it could not remember the past rightly. The women demanded that the past be remembered rightly, which included truth telling and movements toward justice.

The mothers wanted the junta to come clean on the real story that was drenched in blood, horror, and tears. The blood of their loved ones cried out from the ground. They knew that this national wound would not heal without the actualization of truth for those who were mourning their disappeared relatives. These women were witnesses to truth. The terrible truth of the calculated murders of their children needed to be released. The past needed to be reclaimed. This is why the mothers marched. And their grief and loss became political. Their movement became deeply spiritual, a movement to confront the junta's veiling of the truth. This movement sought to render audible the voices of their children in hopes of a different future, a future that could make their children "reappear" in memory even if their bodies were never recovered.

Hope within Neoliberal Societies

The Madres movement offers up a different kind of human subjectivity than the neoliberal subjectivity offered within global market contexts. These women were dangerously offering *another mode of being built on radical relationality* through their subversive protests centered on motherhood. In fact, motherhood for them was a vocation of love and this vocation of love reflected a rich interplay between agapeic and erotic love. As discussed in chapter 3, the erotic is not the pornographic but is a life source and unifying power that creates intense, passionate connections between the world and us. As black feminists and womanists (such as Lorde and Baker-Fletcher) remind us, it is through eros that agape can be fully actualized, as love is manifested through the flesh (through bodies in motion). These mothers fought the numbness and apathy that the junta attempted to generate by infusing erotic power into their spiritual activism. They not only struggled for justice in relation to their murdered children but also sought to emotionally re-awaken Argentinian citizenry to the passionate, intense pursuit of democratic dialogue in order to transform their society.

Moreover, the Madres demonstrated that erotic energy is needed to change unjust systems as well as social relationships based on fear and apathy. Neoliberal regimes annex the erotic in order for oppressive systems to regulate and control citizens. Consequently, people are unable to be vulnerable and "love big" within their social contexts, as radical distrust and disconnection frame the wider world. When people are forced to "love small" within the context of social relationships, potential sources of energy (such as erotic energy to connect with one's neighbor and transform society) are reduced and weakened.

The calculating, self-interested individual of neoliberal ideology is directly challenged by these mothers' embodiment of love and cooperation. Neoliberal logic does not privilege the idea that human beings are called into communities of care, connection, and sharing without the *quid quo pro*. Instead, such logic interprets the individual as nothing more than a subject who maximizes her or his interests (so love, for instance, is interpreted according to the unit of market value as discussed in chapter 2). Consequently, market structures often do not see notions of the common good as possible or achievable. These women's way of being through cooperation demands that we re-think this central economic assumption about individuals' basic moral orientation. Human beings are called to live in community with and for other individuals. They are called to experience love as a vocation. Privileging more cooperative notions about the individual is important to living well together within the context of both cultural and economic arrangements.

Human beings do not self-actualize in a vacuum. Instead, we experience self-actualization and our full humanity within social bonds, which means that these social bonds must be taken into account within market arrangements. In short, human beings never experience fulfillment through money or economic wealth alone. Human fulfillment is achieved as individuals find meaning within the communal contexts they inhabit. This cooperative way of being then holds promise in influencing social, political, and economic systems. For the Madres, their lives were not their own but were partly defined in relation to their children's lives. This radical relationality impacts how love and even hope are understood: love and hope are interpreted as actual possibilities rooted already in the social practices of life among those who are defiantly resisting. These women's social practices surrounding motherhood offer an ethical agenda that can have implications on how we economically structure our lives together.

In relation to the economic cronyism that undergirded much of the political actions of the junta, these women's actions also held promise in critiquing the ethical orientations of neoliberal global market structures they resided in. As discussed earlier, global economic logic (austerity measures, the dismantling of Welfare State, and increasing foreign investment), in part, was responsible for the economic devastation and subsequent political dictatorship that took root in Argentina during the 1970s. Global capitalist processes and the growing disparities between the rich and poor played a role in why political tyranny emerged, complicating the experience of freedom among citizens in Argentina. Moreover, the abduction of children was due to the ways in which particular families politically dissented and critiqued the inequitable economic conditions and oppressive political decisions of the ruling military government. The complete lack of cooperative virtues such as social trust and care among the ruling Argentinian officials led to one of the greatest global human catastrophes. The competition among ruling factions was deeply influenced by the desire to control the political and economic resources of the country. The increasing privatization and deregulation of the Argentinian economy through IMF structural adjustment programs exacerbated values of rabid individualism and "winner-take-all" market approaches. Such market values began to inform political leadership. The Madres sought to expose how market-driven values lead to the disintegration of community and relations of care. They wanted their children back but their actions were simultaneously attempting to inaugurate another mode of being that saw cooperation as a necessary moral end for Argentine society.

The mothers exposed the radical social distrust that existed in Argentina, which had grave consequences. This sense of social distrust was not only fueled by political corruption but also driven by neoliberal market decisions that accelerated the march toward totalitarian control and human rights abuses in Argentina. These women's spiritual activism sought to foreground the necessity of caring, trusting relations in any democratic society. Through their subversive ideas of motherhood, they identified caring relations within all structures of society as a necessary part of God's design toward the actualization of humanity.

Even today, mothers of the Disappeared continue to march to honor the memories of their children. They march for their disappeared children and grandchildren who were dissidents that advocated for social and economic justice. While the mothers were simply looking for the return of their children, the movement grew to demand the "reappearance" of the democratic vitalities their children fought for in efforts to actualize a more free and equal Argentina. As the mothers' organization grew, they realized that the whereabouts of their children mattered as well as their child's message for a more vibrant democracy, which included greater socio-economic parity. The junta knew that they were attempting to "disappear" the fight toward social and economic justice among young subversives. They were attempting to crush any social revolution that challenged the totalitarian government.

Mothers of the Disappeared have split into a few organizations over the last several decades but continue to unite in calling the government to account for these crimes. In 1986, President Raul Alfonsin came to power and offered pardons and amnesty in varying degrees to members of the military. His justification for such pardons was to promote "healing" in Argentina and unite the country by moving past the fractious memory of the Dirty War. The decision met with outrage among some mothers and they declared Alfonsin's administration an extension of Dirty War politics. Other mothers disagreed with this assessment and felt this perspective perhaps impeded their ability to appeal to Alfonsin to punish war criminals. Some mothers wanted to support the new democratic republic under Alfonsin, hoping for greater measures of truth telling. Other mothers simply saw Alfonsin as complicit with the junta's politics of covering up and rejecting any measures toward reconciliation without truth telling. These post-junta conditions and difference in perspective among the mothers resulted in an internal rift that could not be reconciled. In 1986, twelve mothers felt that the Founding Line (Madres de Plazo de Mayo) was not acting in the best interests of the country and jeopardizing democracy so they left the organization. Many followed. There were two thousand members in each group when the split was finalized.

The Dirty War might have ended a little over 30 years ago but the trials of military officials accused of these horrendous crimes continue. And many of these men who have been accused are part of the Catholic Church. As of March 13, 2013, a young woman who had been tortured and raped in one of the concentration camps pointed out a number of her torturers, including one who liked to burn breasts with cigarettes and another who tied her to a cot and raped her. What her torturers had in common was that they were "wearing a curious badge: white and yellow ribbons, the colors of the Vatican, to honor the Argentine Cardinal Jorge Mario Bergoglio who had been named Pope Francis I the night before."[65] This incrimination of the church during the Dirty War remains a heartbreaking aspect within the national memory of Argentina. Moreover, many grandmothers are still looking for the babies that were given up for adoption to childless couples who were loyalists of the military regime. This fight is far from over as these women continue to demand answers and accountability for the crimes the junta committed.

This case study demonstrates that hope and moral imagination emerge at the site of *ordinary and everyday lived experience for these women who were deeply affected by neoliberal economic and cultural processes.* The Madres did not articulate their vision of social transformation in supersessionist terms. Rather, these women embodied a moral imagination about future possibilities that were grounded in the social worlds they already inhabited. Their longings and yearnings for a just, compassionate, caring, and democratic society compelled them to fashion subversive social practices of hope in efforts to inaugurate a more egalitarian future(s). Any pragmatic politics of hope must take seriously how new worlds are conceptualized and birthed: through the richly textured world of social practices.

Conclusion

Radicalizing Hope: Toward Beloved Communities

We can be different individuals by rejecting the subjectivities that neoliberal market cultures offer us. The Madres movement's social practices demonstrate that the transformation of neoliberal subjectivity is necessary and possible. Their social practices demonstrate that justice, love, and care are not merely regulative ideals but concrete actions that foster redemption and renewal of *this* world toward a more just, compassionate society. They "radicalize" hope. The possibility of loving and trusting communities not only is a future horizon but also needs to be prefigured in the here and now. They demonstrate that the cynicism and apathy associated with neoliberal capitalism do not have the last words. The present and future can change, as we are not trapped in the "sameness" of the present. Radical hope offers the conditions that give rise to alternative social worlds out of which beloved communities can emerge and flourish.

This chapter suggests that religious social movements (such as Madres de Plazo de Mayo) point to the critical importance of building beloved communities, which contribute to the question of hope today within neoliberal capitalism. The Madres movement's form of religious protest radicalizes hope and leads to a pragmatic politics of love out of which new communities oriented toward cooperation, care, and solidarity can flourish. This politics of love is not merely benevolent and/or empathetic feelings but concrete acts of solidarity with and for each other. Radicalizing hope and love leads to a new collective community out of which new alternatives are "enfleshed," opening up possibilities beyond neoliberal forms of rationality and governance. Radicalizing hope leads to beloved communities.

Radical Hope

One might ask what kind of revolution a politics of hope envisions in response to neoliberal culture and its acquiring, hyper-competitive, individualistic modes of being. Moreover, what is the outcome of revolution grounded in a politics of hope? A politics of hope aims toward the building of beloved communities. However, before discussing the fashioning of beloved communities as an act of radicalizing hope, I further elaborate on what I mean by "radicalizing" hope.

To speak of "radicalizing" hope is to acknowledge that hope moves *beyond feelings of mere optimism*. In fact, radical hope is *not* optimism. To understand the character of hope is to acknowledge its precondition: despair and darkness. As Marxist philosopher Terry Eagleton asserts, "Hope and history travel in different directions, as the former is thrown into relief by the bleakness of the latter."[1] As discussed in chapter 1, history is not a linear progression toward happiness and civility. To the contrary, history has disclosed profound atrocities and catastrophes that belie any benign narrative of democratization, progress, and equality. I advanced a tragic understanding of history, a history that turns in upon us with horror. We are met with shock and tragedy as we face down various forms of inhumanity as history unfolds. Even if greater freedoms are experienced among some of the living, this observation is tamed by the fact that our ancestors were "hauled through hell" to achieve liberties we take for granted. Tragedy is connected to hope so that "hope is held in fear and trembling, with a horror-stricken countenance."[2] Hope includes existential anxiety and a recognition of real, radical loss. It involves the presence of death in some ways, this "death" being a darkness that is incomprehensible and impenetrable (whether social death, existential death, psychological death, physical death, etc.). Hope enters into human history at "ground zero."

Despite death and darkness, hope is an audacious conviction that genuine newness in history is possible. But this hope or genuine conviction in another future is not based on the hegemonic grid of meaning within the present social order. These possible other futures are based on the radical social practices and defiant liberative projects of those who are marginalized, as these groups articulate new visions and meanings of love, freedom, and justice. When one speaks of optimism in the future, one is speaking of faith in a future that might be varied but within a "vector of coordinates already in place in the present."[3] Optimism is within the dominant grid of meaning available to us within present neoliberal structures of domination. Optimism attempts to reform within the hegemony of the visible. To the contrary, radical hope is not something that is calculable from within current hegemonic structures of meaning, as it is associated with a "newness of circumstances, a future that is not more of the same but qualitatively different."[4] Hope invokes a future that is not merely a reformulation of the present. Consequently, hope is more of an existential stance imbued with new meaning, along with more just structural-social practices, than wishful thinking or calculable guesses that mark optimistic thinking.

The distinction between hope and optimism is also related to the means and conditions under which moral and social transformation is possible. While optimism turns to the means and conditions of transformation *within* dominant configurations of politics, hope conveys the idea that *the means or conditions for creating a more just, loving society can be mined from the radical social practices among the vulnerable and disenfranchised, practices that remain outside of the hegemony of the visible.* So then, radicalizing hope within neoliberal capitalism means that the conditions under which communities of love, cooperation, and solidarity take shape remain hidden or concealed within current political configurations. We must turn to marginalized communities and their social movements and practices for freedom and human flourishing in order to render visible their re-envisioning of different futures. These populations' social practices offer conditions under which different, more emancipatory futures are possible. As a result, radical hope within neoliberalism hinges on making visible "the invisible," that is the invisible practices of vulnerable, suffering populations who point toward new futures of love and care based on their social practices. Reclaiming or redeeming social practices of hope is a defiant act as it confronts the hegemony of the visible.

Recognizing the *suppression and concealment of conditions* toward hope within neoliberalism allows one to question current conservative and liberal proposals for resisting structural inequities (poverty, inadequate healthcare, etc.) and social pathologies (lack of care, compassion, social trust, etc.). For instance, contemporary critical social theorists often assume that a different kind of future (or way of being) in contrast to inequality and inequity begins with procedural justice in which peaceful, democratic dialogue is employed to reach an informed consensus. This is an assumption of conservatives and liberals alike within nation-states that espouse democratic forms of governance. As critical theorist and philosopher Jurgen Habermas argues, addressing our deep moral, social, and political divisions involves the "giving and taking of reasons" within the context of our public and political institutions.[5] If procedural rules of discourse are established within our political decision-making processes, social change and transformation can be possibilities. When following Habermas' argument, one might infer that society can be optimistic when participating in procedural democratic institutions within the public sphere.

I would argue however that this procedural, dialogic view of justice does not acknowledge that such procedural institutions are always and already fashioned and legitimated on the hegemony of the visible. While democratic institutions are necessary and essential, such procedural institutions toward democratic dialogue do not admit that persons are always and already conditioned within systems of hierarchal power and difference. For example, poor women of color around the world are often locked out of the dominant public/political sphere where institutional policymaking occurs. As a result, such dialogic structures reflect the presence of authority, power, and domination, which complicate democratic dialogue. Institutional dialogue or discourse is structured in deep patterns of hegemony, which points to the contradictions of institutional "democratic" discourses. Hence, a radical hope in relation to contemporary political discourse does not merely seek to "renegotiate the coordinates of this order but exchange them for others."[6] The Madres movement I discussed in the previous chapter did not simply propose reform within their nation's political sphere. They didn't express mere optimism. They created their own public spheres through protests, marches, chants, and prayers in order to perform and articulate new conditions under which different futures were possible within Argentinian politics. They challenged the dominant institutional political space by crafting alternative counter-publics out of which they articulated possible futures of love, care, and democratic living. Madres offered conditions toward radical hope.

Even within democratic institutions in the United States, many vulnerable groups (poor blacks, Mexican immigrants, etc.) are excluded from the procedural structures that formulate and implement policies. Consequently, these groups fashion counter-publics out of which they articulate different, more democratic futures of care and love. The presence of procedural institutions does not guarantee social justice nor indicate that the hegemony of the visible is absent. To the contrary, procedural structures can be built upon hegemonic relations within the public sphere and dominant political space within society. Neoliberalism, in fact, colludes with the state, which is often formally governed by such procedural "democratic" rules. Optimism encourages people to believe that socio-economic revolution and moral transformation come from within these procedural institutions. But, as one might see, this is not self-evident. Contrasted to optimism, radical hope interrogates such claims that promote the inherently democratic nature of procedural institutions. Without deconstructing and resisting the hegemonic practices of power that tend to undergird procedural institutions, transformation remains unrealizable.

Another reason why hope must be distinguished from optimism is because radical hope aims for a more radical human subjectivity. Radical hope demands a different kind of human subjectivity that does not allow neoliberal rationality to set the terms of discourse. The Madres movement demanded that their society take seriously more humane existential ways of being (alongside true democratic governance for and by the people). In fact, these women's embodiment of cooperation, social trust, and erotic love are foreign and even irrational to present neoliberal thinking and practices. Their courageous acts do not compute on the social calculus of meaning under neoliberal rationality, as neoliberal rationality aligns with the market demands and instrumental interests of the state. These women knew they could not render their grid of meaning intelligible within neoliberal logic and structures, so their protest sought to overturn this neoliberal grid altogether in order to assert more radical subjectivities. This new grid of meaning (in contrast to neoliberal rationality) involved the articulation of a new subjectivity not defined by market values of rabid individualism, acquiring modes of being, hypercompetition, totalitarianism and so forth. This new grid of meaning that radical hope offers is unfiltered through the neoliberal gaze, as it demonstrates that care, trust, and compassion are real political possibilities.

The Madres refused to play the neoliberal political game as others played it. They wanted to not only disrupt neoliberal rationality and governance but also rupture these systems. They were dreaming dangerously through their social practices of radical togetherness, love, care, and justice, which called into question an entire way of life in Argentina built on a rationality and subjectivity sponsored by neoliberalism. As seen through these women, radical hope emphasizes a wakefulness in relation to the catastrophe of present social structures and the social pathologies that are reproduced.

To be clear, this radical hope is not redemption from this world but redemption *of* this present world. As discussed in chapter 1, there is a certain liminality or "in-betweeness" that radical hope possesses as it is neither in radical discontinuity or continuity with the present. Radical hope demands a different future but this future is an unrealized potentiality from the past. Yet, this future nevertheless is qualitatively different from anything in the present. It is not a complete rupture from the past but is a genuine new future, which critiques the inhumanities of the present. This liminal character of the future associated with radical hope reveals hope not as apocalyptic in the sense of seeking the complete eradication of the present but hope as something genuinely new, which remains located in the present (through the invisible social practices of marginalized communities who are resisting neoliberal modes of helplessness and despair).

I have so far discussed what it means to radicalize hope. Yet, what is this hope *for*? To what ends does radical hope direct itself? I maintain that hope directs itself toward a particular kind of revolution, being the creation of beloved communities. If the creation of beloved communities is a primary end goal, this revolution then also is a confrontation with who we really are as humans: a humanity that is disfigured within our current neoliberal cultures. Revolution is not about repressing this darkness or disfiguration but acknowledging this darkness as our *own* and not someone else's.[7] Within our neoliberal society, exploitation, greed, and excessive profit are articulated as "unintended consequences" of global markets. Naming these deleterious effects as unintended consequences deflect the blame and responsibility away from human beings and toward impersonal, abstract market mechanisms. These effects are not named as cultural productions of evil and injustice created and exacerbated by *human beings* with power and authority. The kind of revolution that radical hope births is a revolution that names such darkness as something we have done wrong toward our own selves and our neighbors. It calls on us to be accountable to the fear that lurks behind crass consumerism and rabid individualism associated with neoliberal ways of being. This revolution seeks to create another type of human subjectivity that moves away from fear and disconnection toward connection and neighborly love. In fact, neighbor love or an affective politics of love is the revolution, as discussed in the previous chapters.

This kind of revolution is not necessarily antithetical to the argument for reform of market institutions and governance. However, revolution is *not* mere reform. Radical hope does not stop with reform. I acknowledge that there are reforms around the world that have been deeply revolutionary to the neoliberal status quo. The Civil Rights Movement in 1960s and the Feminist Movement of the 1970s disclose the ways in which peaceful revolutions also function as reforms to social structures and sets of relations within society. Revolution does not have to be understood as a complete break with the past or a total upheaval of sorts.[8] Reform might then be extremely revolutionary in the sense of "getting the ground ready" for broader shifts in economy and culture. However, there is a point where reform might be inadequate as it may not address the affective dimensions of who we are and how we live into togetherness, love, and care.

One additional critical aspect of radical hope is the recognition that radical hope is a *collective, cooperative* endeavor, not merely an individual act. Within neoliberal logic, politics tends to be framed in hyper-individualistic terms. The individual sits at the center of all economic, social, and political activity. The Madres understood their embodiment of love and care as a collective effort, not simply the individual. And their collective endeavors are acts of radical hope because they remain committed to practicing more egalitarian and ethical ways of being in order to resist the violence and projective disgust that marked the Argentinian regime. The Madres did not know fully how their new community would transform their society. Yet, they were courageous enough to imaginatively envision and practice conditions of trust and care under which social transformation might occur. I think that these women exemplify that radical hope is profoundly communal and a radical act of faith.

Visions of Beloved Communities

Radical hope is directed toward an affective politics of love, which can lead to the creation of beloved communities. It is in beloved community that love can ground a different subjectivity and collectivity. The "Beloved Community" is a term that originated with the American philosopher-theologian Josiah Royce, who lived from 1855 to 1916. He made original contributions in ethics, philosophy of community, philosophy of religion, and logic. His major works include *The Religious Aspect of Philosophy, The World and the Individual, The Philosophy of Loyalty,* and *The Problem of Christianity.* His last work consists of a series of lectures given at Manchester College, Oxford in 1913 in which he briefly talks about the idea of beloved community.

In Royce's 1913 lectures at Oxford, he speaks about the term beloved community as a collectivity grounded in shared loyalty, memory, and hope. Beloved community is cultivated as individual selves begin to identify with the life of the community. Next, when individual selves become mutually aware of this identification and the love they share for their common life in the midst of differences, the beloved community becomes fully awake. Finally, the love that so completes the consciousness of the community calls on the members to wholeheartedly extend themselves in furtherance of the ideal life of the community. For Royce, beloved community, in part, cultivates in two stages: the community of memory and the community of hope. Royce's beloved community is grounded in an ideal of loyalty, love, memory, and hope that enables humans to experience a transformation in individual subjectivity from rabidly individualistic to communally oriented, giving way to a "universal community."[9]

Forty years after Royce's death, the idea of the beloved community was re-interpreted and popularized by Dr. Martin Luther King, Jr. While some assert that King deepens Royce's notion of the beloved community, others argue that King's vision of the beloved community completely diverges from Royce's articulation of this term.[10] I agree that King's notion of the beloved community is radically different from Royce's idea. For King, the beloved community is not simply a lofty ideal that promotes loyalty and shared goals within community (as Royce describes). Rather, beloved community is a community shaped by an affective politics of love, which requires this community to dedicate itself to non-violent methods in response to projective disgust and its forms of hegemony.

For King, the beloved community cannot be understood without acknowledging the violent social world that it prophetically rejects and critiques. The beloved community is not just a shared community of memory and hope that seeks to actualize some idyllic harmony (lion lying with the lamb). This community seeks to confront and dismantle the hegemony of the visible (dominant norms that disenfranchise and oppress) through non-violence. Beloved community is about the embodiment of prophetic utterance, revealing the "gaps" between norms and practices, which inevitably vitiate our ability to actualize our own humanity with and for each other. One can see that King's vision of beloved community is about radical hope. While

Royce certainly helps one begin to think about beloved community in terms of loyalty and shared experience, King re-conceptualizes the project of beloved community altogether by asserting that it is a community called to disrupt oppressive structures through love. Love then becomes deeply defiant and subversive as a religious, political, and social force.

Moreover, King saw creative conflict as an important condition under which beloved community could be actualized. For King, the beloved community must embrace conflict as a key ingredient toward its process of self-actualization. King recognized that conflict was endemic to the human experience and that conflict was not necessarily destructive. Conflict can be *creative* in generating understanding and ultimately reconciliation in ways that open us up to our neighbors who might radically differ from ourselves. Cooperation was central to King's philosophy and methods of non-violence. Cooperation would be essential to beloved community. But King was not referring to surface, uncritical types of cooperation. Real cooperation must wrestle with conflict that is always present in the midst of differences. Therefore, for King, conflict does not negate the possibility of beloved communities. Conflict can be creative, making possible the conditions under which cooperation is truly realizable. Beloved communities demonstrate that creative conflict can be a social good that fosters cooperation.

King also saw agape at the core of beloved communities. For King, agape was not merely friendly affection or sappy sentimentalism experienced between two individuals who identified with each other. Agape more deeply encompassed love for the sake of the other person, whether friend or enemy. In fact, agape does not distinguish between friends and enemies. Agape directs love toward both groups in fashioning beloved community. King's notion of beloved community held agape as a political possibility.

In an article published by the *Christian Century Magazine* on July 13, 1966, King notes that agape as a political possibility challenges capitalist societies' exercise of political power. For capitalist societies, political power is treated as an end. Economic power is also engaged as the final goal. As a result, violent capitalist ideologies and practices can be justified insofar as they are directed toward end goals of economic and political power. However, interpreted in light of agape, political power is redefined. Political and economic power are not end goals but means used to secure objective and subjective goods we seek in life such as food, shelter, clothing, cultural respect, and social dignity. Political and economic power can be used in creative ways toward more just and compassionate communities. This *creative* employment of power is a socio-political possibility of agape.

For King, justice was also an expression of agape, which affirms agape as a political possibility. Justice is about ensuring all persons, especially the oppressed and marginalized, can flourish and thrive. Justice as such is rooted in and directs itself toward love as it performs the task of actualizing beloved communities. Dissimilar to Royce who didn't substantively address themes of justice in relation to beloved community, King's beloved community was deeply committed to justice as an expression of love. King's beloved community is where all people can share in the wealth of the earth. Poverty, hunger, and homelessness will not be tolerated within beloved community because international standards of human decency will not allow it. Within beloved community, a spirit of togetherness and cooperation replaces racism, classism, heterosexism, and all other forms of bigotry. In the beloved community, international disagreements will be negotiated and resolved by peaceful conflict-resolution and reconciliation of opponents, instead of military power. Love and trust will triumph over cycles of fear and hatred. King's beloved community was a religious and political question about how we should live together in order to dismantle racist, hetero-patriarchal capitalist societies.

I want to note that King's privileging of agape does not grapple with how the erotic actualizes love within beloved communities. Because the erotic is about the movement of bodies toward each other in radical connection, desire, and deep-shared feelings instead of a pushing away from each other through fear and disconnection, the erotic enables agape to be "enfleshed." Agape can be *incarnated* through erotic sets of practices such as joy, empathy, freedom, and pleasure (for friendships and romantic relationships). The erotic dimensions of life empower agape to be a socio-political possibility. Moreover, erotic power is a deep part of the religious quest and seeks to articulate a "power in right relation," which is a central characteristic of agape. Neoliberal societies employ a "power over" model, which inevitably leads to abuse and domination within national and global communities. However, eros is the urge and movement toward mutuality and right relationships with our neighbors. Eros enables us to develop the capacity out of which to exercise agape, to avoid loving in selfish and abusive ways. The erotic moves beloved communities toward the sharing of power in ways that call forth each person to wholeness, to become more fully human. In other words, the erotic answers the question on *how* we lovingly live together in the worlds we inhabit, through an intense desire and passion to be with and for each other. Consequently, agapeic and erotic loves can be seen as mutually inter-twined in articulating love as a concrete socio-political possibility, what I previously refer to as an affective politics. Erotic and agapeic loves empower us to transform our social worlds, resisting apathy in order to embrace passion for social justice and radical togetherness. I think that black feminist ideas of the erotic offer a corrective to King's notion of beloved community, which is overly defined by the agape motif.

One can also see that King's beloved community reflects a real-ized eschatology. As discussed in chapter 1, a realized eschatology does not necessarily see redemption as being contingent on some final act that comes outside of history (Jesus' second coming, Messiah's return, etc.). Rather, realized eschatology points to the possibilities for rebirth, renewal, and "becoming" in the present. Within libera-tionist, womanist, and postcolonial theologies, Jesus' ministry is seen as paradigmatic of how hope can be actualized in the present. We do not need to wait until some final culminating act outside of history to experience redemptive hope. This realized eschatology provides rich, fertile ways of re-thinking moral imagination in the present in relation to market societies and its neoliberal cultural forms. King's beloved community asserted that hopeful transformation can occur within human history, which compels one to consider what kind of moral imagination and action is required in the present to concretize love and hope.

I want to return to my discussion of hope as a social practice in which my major contention was that new social worlds *are already being born*. We must turn to the ordinary, quotidian experiences of marginalized women of color (and other marginalized groups) who resist social and economic pathologies associated with neolib-eral markets. We do not need to solely look to an outside Divine or otherworldly force that can remedy our social ills. Hope does not need to be described according to supersessionist vocabulary. Unlike some religious theologies that emphasize an apocalyptic eschatology, King's idea of beloved community emphasizes hope as a social prac-tice in which such a community orients itself toward the realization of love, peace, joy, care, and more in the present order. King's vision of beloved community then radically provides the communal con-text out of which hope can be practiced and realized. Radicalizing hope is the task of beloved communities. Within beloved communities, love, care, and justice become socio-political and even economic possibilities.

We saw in chapter 5 that Madres de Plazo de Mayo practiced hope through their embodiment of motherhood. They resisted the violent Argentinian government through a non-violent orientation, which reflects the commitment of beloved community. The Madres do not advocate for violent resistance but employ non-violent methods to resist the hegemony of the visible. The Madres also possess a realized eschatology in which love, care, and justice are seen as concrete revolutionary practices in the present. Madres de Plazo de Mayo exemplifies a belief in erotic and agapeic love and hope as political possibilities through their marches, chants, and protests on behalf of their children. Yet, they also march on behalf of the disappearance of democratic dialogue that made violence the norm within Argentina. They were attempting to actualize beloved communities out of which new social worlds could be born. These women believed that new worlds characterized by love and radical solidarity are not just ideals but concrete possibilities that demand our faithful response through the fashioning of beloved communities. For the Madres, this spirit of love and justice can transform opposers into friends. It is this type of radical hope that can transform the deep gloom of the old age into the exuberant gladness of the new age. It is this love, which will bring about miracles in the hearts of women and men.

Beloved communities, then, are essential to radicalizing hope. While such communities offer an audacious vision of social transformation, these communities also provide a pragmatic politics out of which love and justice are realizable. I now turn to how a pragmatic politics of beloved communities holds promise in transgressing neoliberal forms of fragmentation and despair.

A Pragmatic Politics of Beloved Communities: Transgressing Neoliberalism

Love can play a critical role in transforming human subjectivities within this neoliberal moment. As black queer theorist and activist Darnell Moore says, "Love is a movement. Actually love is *the* movement. It is that which moves each of us towards one another."[11] This love is not just a regulative ideal but also a pragmatic politics that makes room for transformed subjectivities grounded in cooperation, compassion, trust, and care. Transgressing and dismantling neoliberalism involves more than asking for greater federal regulations over markets or requesting more federal social service assistance to vulnerable populations. While these efforts are important, these actions do not disrupt and rupture the neoliberal character of the state itself that shapes policy responses according to market values and economic utility, further contributing to the deprivation and disenfranchisement of marginalized groups such as poor black and brown women. A pragmatic politics is necessary. I want to suggest that beloved communities move us toward a pragmatic politics that resists neoliberal forms associated with global capitalism.

For certain, the Madres movement teaches us something about resisting and transgressing neoliberalism. First, these women instruct us on the kind of pragmatic politics we need to envision another story about how we might live together. Neoliberalism does not have the last word on what is possible within human communities. It does not possess the power to reify market relations as the only way of being in our world. Second, for these women, the language of liberation is not reducible to structural transformation, although they hope for and demand systemic change. The language of liberation and flourishing is also about the transformation of our subjectivities, social relationships, and moral orientations toward our neighbors. This language is about decrying practices of neoliberal violence and tragedy that impoverish what it means for us to be human. Resisting neoliberalism involves a radical change of heart. Certain liberationist discourses might benefit from this intentional focus on the conditions under which we might actualize neighbor love and care. Finally, they teach us that moral courage is critically important when resisting neoliberalism. They remind us that love and hope are politically efficacious despite current neoliberal logic that scorns such actions as idealistic at best.

There are three modes of resistance I commend in the final pages of this chapter that reflect a pragmatic politics of beloved communities. These three modes do not exhaust what a pragmatic politics oriented toward resisting neoliberalism might include. Rather, these three modes begin the conversation on the ways in which beloved communities are politically efficacious. Beloved communities offer political possibilities through their embodiment of love and hope. These three modes of resistance are potent and even make possible the sustainability of structural change.

For beloved communities, the first mode of resistance to neoliberalism is remembering the dead as both sacred and *political* phenomena. Early in the book, I spoke about the importance of reclaiming and redeeming past unrealized hopes for flourishing as sacred phenomenon or sacred remembrance. Sacred remembrance is about reclaiming a radical hope that resides in the past, dreams and hopes often murdered with the bearers of such hopes and dreams. Remembering and repeating past hopes, having faith in their realization, point to the possibility of them being actualized within the present. We must gaze backward and return to the egalitarian visions of love and justice lodged in the hearts and minds of those who have come before us. Sacred remembrance is about resurrecting hopeful possibilities in order to be a witness to truth.

Yet, remembering the dead can also be interpreted as *political phenomena*. Isn't the physical and social death of marginalized, oppressed populations within American democracy a political phenomenon? The memory of the suffering is often depoliticized in efforts to conceal the violence associated with neoliberal markets. The depoliticization of this memory does not recognize suffering as political trauma, a trauma to both oppressed communities and our professed democratic commitments. The suffering of marginalized communities under neoliberal hegemony is political phenomena in that such suffering invites a conversation on the unfinished business of American democracy. Politicizing such suffering reveals that American democracy itself possesses a legitimation crisis.

For instance, ealier this year, the Texas State Board of Education approved new history textbooks, which rewrite the history of slavery and racism in America. These textbooks downplay slavery's role in the Civil War."[12] In addition, these new history books omit the historical presence of the Klu Klux Klan and Jim Crow Laws.[13] What is really at stake in the Board's action is to ignore and depoliticize the past of those who have suffered. Acknowledging the memory of the oppressed forces this country to register the memory of the dead in *political* terms. The suffering of the enslaved and the diverse forms of social misery African Americans endured disclose the hypocritical character of "democratic practice" in the United States.

Politicizing the past suffering of oppressed communities doesn't allow the narrative of the victors to reign, a narrative that tries to re-describe America as a land of liberty and opportunity for all. Understanding the dead as political phenomena enables the narratives of the conquered to critique democracy itself, demanding that this country make good on its promise for all to flourish. The Madres movement certainly argues that their disappeared children correlate to the disappearance of democratic rights in their country, Argentina. This movement re-politicizes the historical cries of those who were unable to actualize their dreams of a more just, loving, and compassionate society. Recognizing the dead as political phenomena allows one to challenge neoliberal society and its destruction of democratic rights.

Beginning in 2014, the protests in Ferguson and Baltimore over police brutality reflect the practice of remembering the dead as political phenomena in order to challenge the depoliticization of murdered black bodies at the hands of violent American institutions. This outcry over the thousands of black lives murdered at the hands of rogue police departments led to the Black Lives Matter Movement (BLM). According to BLM website, every 28 hours the police or vigilante murders a black man, woman, or child. This movement challenges the depoliticization of these murders by law enforcement and political authorities who interpret the murdered as criminals or "deviants" who were responsible for their own deaths. Instead, BLM remembers the dead as poitical phenomena in order to expose the hypocrisy of America's democratic ideals such as justice, parity, and freedom.

Remembering the dead also allows communities to participate in "thinking backwards" about future possibilities. As discussed in chapter 1, thinking backwards expresses one truth: any nation's interpretation of history always conceals alternative histories. In thinking backwards, what really happened in the past is perceived against the background of what might have transpired, and this alternative possibility is offered as a potential path to follow today. Thinking backwards to "what-if" histories reclaims the voices of the vanquished, allowing them to shape what the future might become. These past voices offer new pathways on compassionate communities in the present, which informs the future. Thinking backwards does ground a pragmatic politics because it offers new political choices that potentially allow us to finally actualize missed potentials from the past. Hence, remembrance of the dead is critical to a pragmatic politics, giving beloved communities an opportunity to concretize justice and love in sets of practices.

A pragmatic politics of beloved communities interprets sacred remembrance of the dead as a political act. Yet, neoliberal language does not allow one to interpret sacred remembrance as political. Sacred remembrance cannot be calculated on the grid of profit and individual choice. Sacred remembrance is too concerned with social responsibility, compassion, and trust to be rendered intelligible within the context of neoliberal values. It does not offer a *quid pro quo* to those who seek to advocate for the dead (their longings for justice and care) in the present. Moreover, sacred remembrance is deeply subversive to neoliberal rationality and governance as it deconstructs how market values lead to the diminishment of human meaning and worth. This remembrance exposes the unfulfilled promise of democratic freedom because it systematically shows how America's political system has *intentionally* disenfranchised and excluded particular populations who are treated as inferior or substandard. Sacred remembrance identifies the neoliberal character of society as fundamentally violent and terroristic, not progressive and democratic.

The second mode in resisting neoliberalism is wrestling with the violent arm of the state. Throughout this book, especially as seen through the Madres movement, I attempted to reveal the violent neoliberal character of the state. The state cannot be interpreted as a "savior" of sorts, as the state (re)produces and reinforces neoliberal logic and policies. I have already mentioned that politically liberal parties around the world tend to argue that federal involvement through social service programs (welfare, medicare, etc.) will ameliorate and/ or eradicate poverty and other forms of inequity. While federal social services should certainly be seen as necessary in aiding vulnerable populations who are affected by market processes, such social services do not provide a solution to deeper realities in which governments shape social service policies according to neoliberal rationality. Welfare reform in the United States is one example of how welfare policies (such as the 1996 TANF Reform Act) are shaped by market logic. People in the state of Wisconsin reported that women who were required to be off of welfare rolls within five years were given non-living wage jobs that human resource departments had set up with certain corporations for the state's benefit. These women found themselves right back in poverty, even though they were working and no longer on welfare. Welfare reform was unhelpful as it was so deeply fashioned by the market.[14] The US government's employment of neoliberal logic exacerbates the cultural and economic violence and deprivation that marginalized populations endure.

Governments within "developing" countries also disclose such neoliberal violence. In chapter 1, I maintained that sex tourism is not just a shadow, criminal economy in relation to the state. Instead, sex tourism (and even human trafficking) is central to the government's wealth producing structures. For some governments, sex tourism is used as a revenue stream, which belies the state as innocent in relation to the human suffering neoliberalism produces. Wrestling with the neoliberal character of state violence awakens one to the state as destructive and complicit with economic, racial, and gender violence (among other forms of violence).

Another example of neoliberal violence was the abduction and trafficking of Nigerian girls. In May 2014, an Islamist militant group called Boko Haram abducted over 270 Nigerian girls from their school. Some were raped and others were victims of human trafficking. What remains interesting about this horrific situation is that little to no media coverage was present about these girls. In fact, social media campaigns and local rallies emerged to protest the lack of media coverage on these Nigerian girls when they were first abducted. Organizations began to circulate petitions, urging citizens to put pressure on both the US government and Nigerian government to quickly rescue these girls.

However, contradictions on the Nigerian government's actions began to arise. While the government initially articulated their will to rescue these girls, subsequent news coverage disclosed the ambivalence of Nigerian politicians in intervening and bringing Boko Haram to justice. There was a lack of transparency and commitment to fashioning military strategies or interventionist methods among Nigerian political officials. In addition, the first lady of Nigeria (President's wife), Patience Jonathan, publicly stated that she would plan a protest and march directly into the forest areas where Boko Haram has been holding the girls. Yet, it was claimed by Nigerian female activists that they were arrested underneath the orders of Nigeria's first lady because these activists were protesting on behalf of these girls.[15] Questions of Nigerian political corruption swirled around the abduction of these girls. Why did the government not have the names of these girls if they were kidnapped from the school? Why hadn't the principal come forward to help identify these victims? Why did we not hear interviews in a timely manner from several Nigerian girls that escaped from Boko Haram?

One might argue that militant groups like Boko Haram are not the only groups with "dirty hands" in relation to the kidnapping and trafficking of young girls. Governments are known to be complicit in supporting human trafficking as it provides a source of revenue toward economic growth. Countries such as the United States, China, Ghana, and India have certainly reinforced forms of sexualized violence (such as human trafficking), benefiting from the sex slave trade. It is not far fetched to believe that certain Nigerian governmental officials were involved in the kidnapping of these girls. It is not a secret that certain industries within developing nations obtain their slave labor through the underground economy of sex trade. And governments, fully aware of this dynamic, still contract with corporations and groups that use such labor. This type of neoliberal violence is sanctioned by the state, which means that one *cannot simply appeal to the state for justice.*

The prison industrial complex is another example of the neo-liberal character of the state. Within the United States, prisons are being privatized more and more in which profit (not rehabilitation) is the goal of prisons. It has been documented that prisons unethically employ prison labor for pennies on the dollar to produce products.[16] The possibility of profit maximization using prison labor motivates corporations to invest in prisons. When attempting to challenge the privatization of prisons, one cannot simply appeal to the state for justice solutions, as the state is complicit with the prison industrial complex. The exploitation and violence that prisoners experience as cheap labor is supported by the policies of the state. The neoliberal rationality the state employs justifies prison labor as punishment for deviant offenders. However, such deviant offenders are neverthe-less human beings with certain basic rights concerning their labor. Moreover, the criminal justice system reflects the fact that while the majority of the two million imprisoned are black and Latino, the majority of illicit drug consumers are white.[17] Therefore, this neolib-eral rationality is also profoundly racist, disproportionately affecting people of color.

Wrestling with the neoliberal character of the state compels com-munities to recognize the state as productive *and* destructive rather than ethically neutral. Human rights violations emerge from the state as the state is informed and shaped by neoliberal reason. A prag-matic politics of beloved communities invites compassionate, loving, and justice-seeking communities to recognize that the state is a major player that must be critiqued and resisted. The state cannot save us.

A final mode in resisting neoliberalism involves recognizing that building beloved communities must happen from the bottom up rather than building from the top down. Building solidarity and cooperation from the bottom up is the best way to counter unitary or hierarchical forms associated with neoliberal society. While neoliberal societies are hierarchical in terms of power, beloved communities are "shaped by egalitarian sociality that rejects dominance and concentrations of power."[18] A number of black feminist and womanist thinkers reflect on radically democratic models of leadership that enable beloved communities to take root and flourish.

Black feminist Cheryl Higashida speaks about the need to resist hierarchal forms of leadership, which might help one think about the kind of leadership required in this neoliberal moment. For instance, within early nationalist models of black liberation, a black revolutionary identity was often singularly privileged in anti-capitalist and anti-racist politics.[19] Traditional models of political leadership have tended to demand a "politics of celebrity" in which movement-building was created from the top down. However, feminists and queers of color "promote multiply situated, coalitional subjects who adopt historically contingent strategies of resistance."[20] This emphasis on multiple coalitional subjects who shape strategies of resistance is critical to uncovering diverse possibilities toward socio-economic change and transformation. One major leader (celebrity leader) cannot simply issue a vision to be implemented at regional and local levels. Rather, diverse visions of human flourishing are fashioned and cultivated in relationship to the local and regional needs of communities. These needs are deeply contextual, which means that strategies of resistance are evolving, changing, and reflective of local contexts. Building communities grounded in a politics of love involves democratic participation in the process of community building itself.

This kind of non-hierarchal model of leadership has been the genius of the Black Lives Matter Movement. While we continue to witness a concerted national outcry concerning how young blacks are violently treated by law enforcement, BLM's implementation of activist strategies to combat racist police brutality is customized according to local and regional contexts. BLM's activist focus is deployed locally in which multiply situated coalitional subjects employ ever changing strategies of resistance. There is no "celebrity leader" that will guarantee success for BLM. Instead, BLM relies upon each scholar, activist or leader to contribute toward local strategies of resistance in response to this national problem. BLM recognizes that this model of leadership is important in that it makes room for persons who have been previously marganizalized from movement building (such as black women, black gays, lesbians, and transgendered people). Moreover, including previously marginalized subjects expands the vision of black liberation to include black women and same-gender loving people. BLM's vision of leadership promotes radical solidarity out of which beloved communities can flourish.

Building beloved communities in non-hierarchal ways reflects radical solidarity. Radical solidarity cultivates a truly democratic society wherein power is used to actualize justice rather than obstruct justice and care. This radical solidarity demands an active reaching out among individuals, which results in action together. In solidarity, people desire to address alienation within communities. Solidarity is about attempting to heal the fissures, divisions, and separations in society through concerted action.

As a result, solidarity promotes empathy. Empathy is an impossibility within neoliberal orders as individuals are not encouraged to treat another person as an end. Rather, individuals are treated as means to a social or economic end. Empathy attempts to demonstrate that one is listening to the other and attending to someone on her or his *own terms*. Empathy encourages non-alienated action in that the listener must go outside of herself (her own conceptions, views of social life, etc.) in order to understand the plight of the other person, who may be radically different from her. Within solidarity, we are forced to recognize the real differences between ourselves and other individuals/groups, which means we cannot imagine ourselves as them in order to understand their social complaints or problems. Instead, we must journey into the other's life and circumstances through their own ideas, descriptions, longings, and worldviews. Empathy is then extremely demanding but necessary for solidarity if we are to act together despite our real and deep differences.

Building radically egalitarian communities involves encouraging local grassroots organizations to form coalitions around local issues. While persons should certainly protest human trafficking in other parts of the world such as Nigeria, human trafficking transpires in Western nations such as the United States. Atlanta is a major hub of the human trafficking of girls and communities would do well to collaborate in addressing that local issue (which is also of global importance). Beloved communities see the connections between the local and the global, and commit to organizing locally in order to make a difference that can be felt around the world.

A part of grassroots local activism in resisting Western neoliberal hegemonic forms of life can be observed through the arts. The arts (performative, visual, dramatic, photographic, and musical forms) have always served as a vehicle used to resist dominant systems' epistemologies and practices. For instance, US artistic movements like the Harlem Renaissance and the Black Arts Movement of the twentieth century deployed the arts as a way to articulate radical democratic visions of justice and love in response to the failed experiment of democracy in America. These artistic movements critiqued the non-egalitarian projects of projective disgust that structured socio-economic and political realities in the United States. The arts can promote critical conversation and emotional participation in ways that bind people to particular commitments oriented toward mutual understanding and justice within societies. The arts can summon up powerful emotions, inviting people to pose questions about the taken-for granted logic of rabid individualism and social distrust associated with neoliberal societies. Through an encounter with the arts, people may feel compelled to ask what *should* we do to cultivate new, healthy ways of being toward each other.

There are social movements around the world today that are employing the arts in resisting dehumanizing cultural ideas and practices associated with neoliberal global markets. SAVVY Contemporary is one movement that employs the arts in order to reformulate both the questions and answers in relation to Western cultural and economic hegemony. For this movement, the arts can be a site of intellectual and cultural exchange, a catalyst in which "ideas are transformed to forms and forms to ideas"[21] in order to challenge the status quo. Based out of Berlin, SAVVY employs the arts (performance art, painting, film, drama, photography, and more) to "pre-write" histories and new possible futures for and with "subaltern" brown and black folk around this world. A central aim of SAVVY is to destabilize the *episteme* that frames Western art, and by extension, what is then considered "beautiful," "true," "historical," "civilized," and so forth. In order to deconstruct and destabilize this Western rationality in relation to art and philosophical concepts that undergird dominant art, SAVVY invites intellectuals and artists from Africa, Asia, the Carribean, and South America (among other Two-Thirds World artists), as these artists are using their work as epistemic interventions into Western hegemonic thought. SAVVY seeks to use art to articulate "epistemologies from beyond" (concepts that resonate and reflect the lived experiences of subaltern, non-Western people around the world).

Savvy refers to itself as a "laboratory of form-ideas," as it sees art as important in *forming* new visions or ideas of just, loving, compassionate, and cooperative societies, which collides with certain Western ideas of art as an end unto itself. Art does not just reflect reality but can help to form and shape reality. For SAVVY, art offers the seed that "grows" a particular idea. Ideas then make possible different actions in the present. It is these actions that cultivate emerging worldviews and potential movements. Consequently, artistic work is foundational to visions of justice, love, and care. Moreover, art enables people to form *emotional commitments* to resisting and challenging practices and structures of projective disgust that denigrate and dehumanize vulnerable populations. As I discussed earlier, critical reasoned conversation is essential, but people must also form emotional attachments to their intellectual commitments if these commitments are to be sustainable. SAVVY employs the arts to create both intellectual and emotional participation in relation to projects of justice around the world.

This organizational movement also holds exhibitions around the world in order to dream of different futures beyond the neoliberal global market context that merely "re-colonizes" the non-West. In July 2014, I attended a SAVVY exhibition in Berlin entitled "Giving Contours to Shadows." This exhibition focused on "voiceless shadows" of non-Western artists and thinkers and their alternative narrations of "History." The exhibition is driven by Édouard Glissant's poetic allusion to giving forms to historical narratives and to recognizing the sheer elasticity and fluidity of history itself. These non-Western artists and thinkers elucidated their alternative narratives without necessarily uttering words. These artists recounted and reclaimed their past to present narratives through their artistic works, which stood as a voice of the unspoken or the unuttered. For these artists, they do not represent their alternative narrative histories as "historical facts," as they realize that history is certainly a subjective question of interpretation. However, they do allow their alternative historical narratives to interrogate and question the dominant canon (in terms of philosophical questions related to Truth, Beauty, History, Civilization, Taste, and more within the discourse of Western aesthetics).

For instance, Wanuri Kahiu's film *Pumzi* was an artistic work at this exhibition, attempting to give voice to the voiceless being African women. As I discussed in Introduction to this book, *Pumzi* is a film that deeply interrogates neoliberal capitalist culture and offers a vision of flourishing through foregrounding trans-African feminist epistemology. This film envisions how the objectification of human bodies and the earth body leads to a world disaster that destroys most of civilization. This film certainly critiques how neoliberal Western rationality ultimately endangers and destroys the world as we know it. Hyper-individualism and gross commodification leads to World War III that returns the world back to a state of genesis. Clearly, in this film, Western rationality with its markets, culture of individualism, and self-interest has failed the world. Contrasted to Western heroism, this film lifts up the heroic efforts of a young African woman, the Mother of a new civilization, which would be marked by compassion, care, and peace. One might infer that Kahiu is asserting the importance of a trans-African feminist epistemology. Interestingly, women bear the brunt of economic, social, and cultural injustices around the world. Women of color disproportionately endure material and symbolic oppressions that make it difficult for them to survive and thrive. Women are excluded from the very social and economic structures that affect them the most. However, in this film, it is an African woman that restores humanity. An African woman becomes the savior of the world. She offers a new view of what is possible. The salvific presence of the African or "Black" woman is a powerful image or "form" that can give shape to feminist ideas concerning different social and moral worlds in relation to justice, peace, and care. In turn, these ideas can take root to form movements that place women of color at the center of justice efforts. *Pumzi* provides a profound black feminist/womanist metaphor of transformation and change in response to neoliberal danger and violence.

Afro-Caribbean artist and activist Alanna Lockward refers to these artistic interventions as "decolonial aesthetics." Lockward acknowledges that art theory has been a colonized site in which Europe has used art to produce "civilizing missions." In this case, art functions as a dominant epistemology in which whiteness as the ideology has served as *the* interpreter of artistic expression and normative standards of "taste" (good/bad, beautiful/ugly, tasteful/distasteful). Art remains a key epistemic vehicle in which whiteness asserts its view of the world, making European standards of taste and beauty the "measure" against which all other communities are assessed. Decolonial aesthetics dislodges and challenges the "giveness" of European epistemologies that underlie art. It deconstructs such European standards through the artistic expressions of indigenous communities. Through these communities' artistic works, a certain kind of radical subjectivity and future world can be envisioned at the epistemic and practical level among previously colonized subjects. Through indigenous arts, they are attempting to practice the decolonization of aesthetics itself and, by extension, deconstruct epistemological categories (embedded within art) that harm people of the Global South. SAVVY would be a movement that reflects decolonial aesthetics.

In addition, decolonial aesthetics focuses on the impact of mental colonization among indigenous communities. Lockward states, "We call the resistance to the exploitative capitalist European enterprise, the quest for the healing self-empowerment of liberation, decoloniality." For Lockward, decolonial aesthetics is not just a critique of Western colonial hegemony. This aesthetics movement "goes beyond the Fanonian project of addressing the colonizer in her/his lost humanity."[22] This arts movement is an epistemic project that "emphasizes the self-liberation agendas of certain artistic practices."[23] Lockward attempts to highlight how colonial projects not only negatively affect system-structures among the previously colonized but also affect subjectivities among such groups. Consequently, this aesthetics movement among the Global South is about raising the question of healing and self-actualization for previously oppressed subjects. Those participating in decolonial aesthetics employ their indigenous artistic practices as a way to envision possible futures beyond European neoliberal hegemony.

This focus on the healing and empowerment of indigenous communities around the world is essential to decolonial aesthetics. Alternative discourses to Western colonial and neocolonial domination often emphasizes the "decolonization of 'the' gaze as an aftermath [of colonial epistemologies and practices]."[24] Here, colonial power and praxis is epistemologically centered out of which indigenous communities resist, respond, and/or react. As a result, indigenous identities and modes of resistance are merely reactionary and even dependent upon the existence of colonial centers. To the contrary, decolonial aesthetics de-centers the colonial gaze as the "starting point" of thinking about decoloniality as well as issues of self-actualization and empowerment for communities of the South. This aesthetics movement asserts a different departure point in which indigenous artistic practices and their quest for wholeness and healing are employed as the measure or "canon" against which colonial epistemologies and practices are "read" and interpreted. Through indigenous artistic practices, this way of re-canonizing ideas about history, truth, civilization, and so forth moves European epistemic assertions to the side and disallows such assertions to be the starting points of alternative worldviews and possible futures that the previously colonized may envision.

For example, in Ecuador and Colombia, indigenous and communities of the African diaspora reinvent themselves against the colonial matrix of power through using various artistic and cultural traditions.[25] While these communities are interested in re-articulating the colonial encounter between "modern" West and the Global South, they are, more importantly, interested in liberating and healing themselves in response to imperial and colonial psychological wounds in order to re-assess what decolonial options are needed. Often, post-colonial countries end up reinforcing European colonial ideologies and practices, which lead to the continued economic, cultural, and psychological impoverishment of their people. In order to prevent this, indigenous communities must participate in projects of healing and empowerment, which can enable them to discern what projects of decolonality are viable and needed.

Decolonial aesthetics is about epistemic positionality. This arts movement desires to center indigenous epistemologies through various artistic expression in order to more clearly deconstruct and critique European knowledge and practices that engender violence. Clearly, *Pumzi* as a film is participating in decolonial aesthetics by disclosing the impending violence associated with neoliberal global markets and the culture of greed and commodification that is affecting human communities and the earth. It attempts to offer an epistemic intervention into the claim that global markets produce "progress." Its trans-African, feminist-centered epistemology reveals how neoliberal markets disrupt and rupture the world as we know it. *Pumzi* also re-asseses the importance of women of the Global South. The African woman represented is not merely objectified, treated as helpless and poor. She is the savior and the mother of a new global community. The world is saved because of her leadership. This artistic expression confronts European practices as barbaric (rather than the traditions of the Global South).

The arts are deeply transgressive to neoliberal culture. The arts can serve as a pragmatic politics toward cultivating a person's intellectual and emotional commitments to new futures of justice, care, and love. These artistic movements reveal the formation of communities that are attempting to live into alternative ways of being, characterized by compassion and radical care. At the heart of these arts movements is the transformation of subjectivities in this neoliberal moment. For certain, structural transformation remains essential to new futures. However, without transformed subjectivities, resisting neoliberalism remains difficult, if not, impossible.

A pragmatic politics of love is "enfleshed" in and through beloved communities and these communities are dreaming dangerously. Beloved communities offer a way of imagining different futures of love, care, and justice that neoliberalism disallows. Beloved communities offer a pragmatic politics that is rooted in concrete revolutionary practices, which groups are courageously embodying around the world. Beloved communities embody the revolution of love, knowing that love is a concrete practice. As one can see, beloved communities are radical and subversive, without having to assert violence. In fact, they reveal the violence of the neoliberal state as well as the cultural and economic practices that reproduce alienation and deep disconnection within society. Beloved communities are possible. They are already being realized. And they demand that we "radicalize" hope.

Notes

Introduction   Neoliberalism and the Religious Imagination

1. Refer to the work of Christian theologians such as Stephen Long, Douglas Meeks, and Kathryn Tanner who explore at length the relationship between theology and economy. Their analyses not only focus on market capitalism but also emphasize doctrinal considerations (Trinitarian thought, Christology, etc.) in addressing economic inequality. These analyses primarily apply theological ideas to free market concerns without any attention to neoliberalism, race, and gender.
2. Manfred Steger and Ravi Roy, *Neoliberalism: A Very Short Introduction* (Oxford: Oxford University Press, 2010), 5.
3. Ibid.
4. Ibid., 9. Also refer to David Harvey, *A Brief History of Neoliberalism* (Oxford: Oxford University Press, 2007) for further discussion on how adverse conditions associated with globalization precipitated the rise of neoliberal economic paradigms and policies.
5. Manfred Steger and Ravi Roy, *Neoliberalism: A Very Short Introduction*, 19.
6. Elizabeth Bernstein and Janet Jakobson, "Introduction: Gender, Justice, and Neoliberal Transformations," in *The Scholar and Feminist Online*, Barnard Center Research for Women, accessed on September 13, 2013, http://sfonline.barnard.edu/gender-justice-and-neoliberal-transformations/introduction/
7. Ibid.
8. Staurt Hall, "The Neoliberal Revolution," *Soundings*, Volume/Issue 48 (Summer 2011), 2.
9. Ibid.
10. Ibid., 12.
11. Ibid., 10.
12. Ibid., 10.
13. Pierre Dardot and Christian Laval, *The New Way of the World: On Neoliberal Society*, trans. Gregory Elliot (London: Verso Press, 2013), 5.
14. Ibid.
15. Ibid.

16. Ibid. Michael Foucault speaks of the "art of government" in the *History of Sexuality*, in which government is more about an activity (rationalities, techniques, etc.) that seeks to regulate and control citizens.
17. Ibid., 7.
18. Ibid.
19. Kate Bedford, *Developing Partnerships: Gender, Sexuality, and Reformed World Bank* (Minneapolis: University of Minnesota Press, 2009), 35–51.
20. Darnell Moore, "On Love, Empathy, and Pleasure in the Age of Neoliberalism," in *The Feminist Wire*, published July 9, 2013, http://thefeministwire.com/2013/07/on-love-empathy-and-pleasure-in-the-age-of-neoliberalism/

1   The Myth of Progress

1. Walter Benjamin, "Theses on the Philosophy of History," in *Illuminations: Essays and Reflections*, ed. Hannah Ardent (New York: Harcourt Brace Jovanovich, 1968), 258.
2. Ibid.
3. Ibid.
4. Irving Wohlfarth, "The Measure of the Possible, the Weight of the Real, and the Heat of the Moment: Benjamin's Actuality Today," in *The Actuality of Walter Benjamin*, eds. Laura Marcus and Lynda Nead (London: Lawrence and Wishart, 1998), 27.
5. Joseph Schumpeter, *Capitalism, Socialism, and Democracy* (New York: Routledge, 2010), first published in 1934, 65.
6. Schumpeter discusses at length in the chapter, "Can Capitalism Survive?," that the "creative destruction" of capitalism would actually lead to its undoing, as capitalism's technological and economic creativity generates human and cultural loss.
7. Refer to Milton Friedman, *Capitalism and Freedom* (Chicago: University of Chicago Press, 1962) and *Why Government Is the Problem* (Stanford, CA: Hoover Institution Press, 1993). Refer to Friedrich Hayek, *The Road to Serfdom: Texts and Documents* (London: Routledge, 1944). Friedman and Hayek refer to the idea of creative destruction throughout these works, arguing that the market's internal mechanisms to return an economy to equilibrium are generated by the destruction of old economic companies and strategies in favor of more economically efficient companies and strategies.
8. Benjamin, "Theses on the Philosophy of History," 258.
9. Jan Mieszkowski, "Art Forms," in *The Cambridge Companion to Walter Benjamin*, ed. David Ferris (Cambridge: Cambridge University Press, 2004), 40.
10. Ibid.
11. Gershom Scholem, *On Kabbalah and Its Symbolism* (New York: Schocken Books, 1996), 113–115.
12. Benjamin, "Theses on the Philosophy of History," 258–260.

13. Gershom Scholem, *The Messianic Idea in Judaism: And Other Essays on Jewish Spirituality* (New York: Schocken Books, 1995), 43.
14. Walter Benjamin, *Illuminations*, trans. Harry Zohn (New York: Schocken Books, 1977), 254.
15. David Ferris, *The Cambridge Introduction to Walter Benjamin* (Cambridge: Cambridge University Press, 2008),134.
16. Ibid.
17. Ibid.
18. Wohlfarth, "The Measure of the Possible, the Weight of the Real, and the Heat of the Moment," 27.
19. Benjamin, *Illuminations*, 254.
20. Slavoj Zizek, *Living in the End Times* (London: Verso Press, 2011), 84.
21. Ibid.
22. Ibid., 84–85.
23. Ibid., 86.
24. Ibid.
25. Ibid.
26. Ibid., 87.
27. Ibid., 87–88.
28. Ibid., 88.
29. Ibid.
30. Ibid., 89.
31. Zygmunt Bauman, "Walter Benjamin, The Intellectual," in *The Actuality of Walter Benjamin*, eds. Laura Marcus and Lynda Nead (London: Lawrence and Wishart, 1998), 75.
32. William Katerberg, "History, Hope, and the Redemption of Time," in *The Future of Hope: Christian Tradition and Modernity and Postmodernity* (Cambridge: Eerdmans Publishing, 2004), 60.
33. Benjamin, *Illuminations*, 255.
34. Saskia Sassen, "Global Cities and Survival Circuits," in *Global Woman: Nannies, Maids, and Sex Workers in the New Economy* (New York: Henry Holy and Company, 2002), 265.
35. Ibid., 266.
36. Denise Brennan, "Selling Sex for Visas: Sex Tourism as Stepping-Stone to International Migration," in *Global Woman: Nannies, Maids, and Sex Workers in the New Economy* (New York: Henry Holy and Company, 2002), 155.
37. Sassen, "Global Cities and Survival Circuits," 269.
38. Ibid.
39. Brennan, "Selling Sex for Visas," 160.
40. Ibid., 161.
41. Ibid., 159.
42. Ibid., 167.
43. Ibid., 165.
44. Ibid., 273.
45. Ibid.

46. Willoughby Mariano, "Despite Millions Spent, Human Trafficking's Scope is Unknown," in the *Atlanta Journal Constitution*, http://www.ajc.com/news/news/despite-millions-spent-human-traffickings-scope-is/nTjRn/

47. Joy Zarembka, "America's Dirty Work: Migrant Maids and Modern-Day Slavery," in *Global Woman: Nannies, Maids, and Sex Workers in the New Economy* (New York: Henry Holy and Company, 2002), 143.

48. Ibid., 144–145.

49. Barbara Ehrenreich, "Maid to Order," in *Global Woman: Nannies, Maids, and Sex Workers in the New Economy* (New York: Henry Holy and Company, 2002), 94.

50. Delores Williams, *Sisters in the Wilderness: The Challenge of Womanist God-Talk* (Maryknoll: Orbis Books, 1993) is an excellent example of a womanist project that is grounded in a realized eschatology in which the embodiment of Jesus' ministry is understood as the impetus for redemptive transformation within history. For Williams, we do not need to wait until some sudden act from the outside of history to experience hope and redemption. Rather, redemption sits in the present by incarnating Jesus' radical actions of love and liberation.

51. Karen Baker-Fletcher, "Strength of My Life," in *Embracing the Spirit: Womanist Perspectives on Hope, Salvation, and Transformation*, ed. Emilie Townes (Maryknoll, NY: Orbis Books, 1997), 127.

52. Zizek, *Living in the End Times*, 117.

53. Refer to the work of other womanists such as Katie Canon, Monica Coleman, Melanie Harris, Emilie Townes (among other womanists), as they theologically theorize human agency through realized eschatologies.

54. Zizek, *Living in the End Times*, 79.

55. Ibid.

56. Ibid.

57. Ibid., 117.

58. Ibid.

59. Ibid.

2   Resisting the Acquiring Mode

1. Eric Fromm, *To Have or To Be?* (New York: Continuum Publishing, 1997), 63.

2. Ibid.

3. Ibid.

4. Ibid.

5. Ibid.

6. Ibid.

7. Ibid., 74.

8. Ibid.

9. Ibid.

10. Keri Day, *Unfinished Business: Black Women, the Black Church, and the Struggle to Thrive in America* (Maryknoll: Orbis Books, 2012), 109.

11. Ibid.
12. Ibid.
13. Refer to Stacey Floyd-Thomas, *Mining the Motherlode: Methods in Womanist Ethics* (Cleveland: Pilgrim Press, 2006). Floyd-Thomas describes self-love as a central tenet of womanist ethics that enables black women to embody radical subjectivity.
14. David Gouwens, *Kierkegaard as Religious Thinker* (Cambridge: Cambridge University Press, 1996), 210.
15. Ibid.
16. Ibid., 211.
17. Ibid.
18. Ibid., 212.
19. Soren Kierkagaard, *Two Ages: The Age of Revolution and the Present Age*, ed. and trans. Howard Hone and Edna Hong (Princeton: Princeton University Press, 1978), 75.
20. Ibid., 88–89.
21. Ibid., 92.
22. Ibid., 74.
23. Ibid., 81.
24. Ibid.
25. C. Stephen Evans, *Kierkegaard: An Introduction* (Cambridge: Cambridge University Press, 2009), 3.
26. Soren Kierkegaard, *Concluding Unscientific Postscript*, ed. and trans. Howard V. Hong and Edna H. Hong (Princeton: Princeton University Press, 1992), 249.
27. Ibid.
28. Gouwens, *Kierkegaard as Religious Thinker*, 11.
29. Ibid. Gouwens notes that the ethical self is shaped by enduring commitments or virtues, which are worthy and honorable habits that form exemplary character in the individual. Kierkegaard is clear to not characterize enduring commitments of the individual merely as "dispassionate intellectual beliefs nor arbitrary acts of will" (11). The evolving "self" is fashioned and shaped through each choice as every decision one makes is a decision about who one hopes to be.
30. Soren Kierkegaard, *Either/Or*, trans. Howard V. Hong and Edna H. Hong 2 volumes (Princeton: Princeton University Press, 1987), 168.
31. Katie Cannon, *Black Womanist Ethics* (Eugene, OR: Wipf and Stock Publishing, 1988). Refer to Chapters 4 and 5 where Cannon talks about these virtues at length.
32. See Lisa Tessman, *Burdened Virtues: Virtue Ethics for Liberatory Struggles* (Oxford: Oxford University Press, 2005), 23.
33. Melanie Harris, *Gifts of Virtue, Alice Walker, and Womanist Ethics* (New York: Palgrave McMillan, 2010), 57.
34. Refer to Chapter 4 of *Gifts of Virtue* to obtain the complete list of womanist virtues Harris infers from Alice Walker's nonfiction work.
35. Lewis, *Kierkegaard: An Introduction*, 91.
36. Gouwens, *Kierkegaard as Religious Thinker*, 207–212.

37. Ntozake Shange, *For Colored Girls Who Considered Suicide When the Rainbow Is Enuf* (London: Methuen Publishers, 1977), 87.
38. Monica Coleman, *Making a Way Out of No Way: A Womanist Theology* (Minneapolis: Fortress Press, 2008), 16.
39. Ibid., 45.
40. Coleman offers a rich description of the role of African ancestors in a process theological framework of salvation. She also explores spirit possession within African religions and how it enriches soteriological religious concepts.
41. Please refer to a paper given at the 2007 American Academy of Religion conference by Kierkegaardian scholar David Gowens, "Kierkegaard on the Universally Religious and the Specifically Christian as Resources for Interreligious Conversation," in Andrew J. Burgess, ed., *Kierkegaard and Religious Pluralism: Papers of the AAR Kierkegaard, Religion, and Culture Group, and the Soren Kierkegaard Society.* AAR 2007 Annual Meeting, San Diego. Eugene, OR: Wipf and Stock Publishers, 2007, 83–104.
42. Please refer again to Melanie Harrris' *Gifts of Virtue* and Katie Cannon's *Katie's Canon* as both texts emphasize the central importance in including virtue ethics as central to the work of social transformation.
43. Gouwens, *Kierkegaard as Religious Thinker*, 207.
44. Ibid.
45. Soren Kierkegaard, *Works of Love: Some Christian Reflections in the Form of Discourses*, trans. Howard and Edna Hong (New York: Harper and Row, 1962), 237.
46. Gouwens, *Kierkegaard as Religious Thinker*, 212.
47. Ibid.
48. Ibid.
49. A number of womanist texts explore moral imagination in relation to radically critiquing the established oppressive order. Texts such as Delores Williams, *Sisters in the Wilderness: The Challenge of Womanist God-Talk* (Maryknoll, NY: Orbis Books, 1993); Marcia Riggs, *Awake, Arise, and Act: A Womanist Call for Black Liberation* (Cleveland: Pilgrim Press, 1994); and Emilie Townes, *Breaking the Fine Rain of Death: African-American Health Issues and a Womanist Ethic of Care* (New York: Continuum Publishing, 2001); among others.
50. Gouwens, *Kierkegaard as Religious Thinker*, 213.
51. Ibid.
52. Soren Kierkegaard, *Practice in Christianity*, trans. Howard V. Hong and Edna H. Hong (Princeton: Princeton University Press, 1991), 219.
53. Soren Kierkegaard, *Kierkegaard's Attack upon "Christendom" 1854–1855*, trans. Walter Lowrie (Princeton: Princeton University Press, 1944), 282–283.
54. It is important to note that this active opposition cannot be secured through politics for Kierkegaard. Kierkegaardian Scholar David Gowens expounds upon Kierkegaard's reflections on the boundaries between the public and private, between politics and religion. For Kierkegaard, his intention is not to make the claim that the private is unrelated to the public or that religion is

unrelated to the political sphere. Rather, he is wary of the claim that politics achieves human happiness and ultimate claims to justice through the victory of a political party or political leader. Politics is unable to achieve salvation. One's private view in terms of the way one relates to the neighbor is certainly a public matter. However, active opposition is not in service to the promotion of earthly institutions in bringing about salvation. Instead, active opposition is enacted through Christian discipleship, that is, through being a witness in action to "Christ as Pattern" in the world. Christ as pattern is about the character of Christ in embodying faith, hope, and love, which can be a profoundly radical critique of the existing order.

55. Kierkegaard, *Practice in Christianity*, 205.
56. Gouwens, *Kierkegaard as Religious Thinker*, 216.
57. Ibid.

3   Loss of the Erotic

1. Refer to James Evans, *We Have Been Believers: An African American Systematic Theology* (Minneapolis: Fortress Press, 1993) as well as James Cone, *A Black Theology of Liberation* (Maryknoll, NY: Orbis Books, 1986) and *God of the Oppressed* (Maryknoll, NY: Orbis Books, 1997) in order to see how love is discussed. Eros is absent from discourses on love (in favor of agape as the highest expression of Divine and human love).
2. Alexander Irwin, *Eros toward the World: Paul Tillich and the Theology of the Erotic* (Minneapolis: Fortress Press, 1991), 10. Also refer to Werner Jeanrond, *A Theology of Love* (New York: T&T Clark, 2010) for substantive discussions on Tillich's integration of eros with philia and agape.
3. Irwin, *Eros toward the World*, 10.
4. Ibid.
5. Paul Tillich, *Systematic Theology*, Volume 1 (Chicago: University of Chicago Press, 1951), 281.
6. Ibid.
7. Paul Tillich, *Love, Power, and Justice* (New York: Oxford University Press, 1954), 25.
8. Irwin, *Eros Toward the World*, 10.
9. Karen Baker-Fletcher, "The Erotic in Contemporary Black Women's Writings," in *Loving the Body: Black Religious Studies and the Erotic* (New York: Palgrave McMillan, 2006), 201.
10. Ibid.
11. Ibid., 203.
12. Audre Lorde, *Sister Outsider: Essays and Speeches* (Berkeley: The Crossing Press, 1984), 54.
13. Ibid.
14. Ibid., 55.
15. Ibid.
16. Patricia Hill Collins, *Black Feminist Thought: Knowledge, Consciousness, and the Politics of Empowerment* (New York: Routledge, 1990), 150. Also

refer to Collins, *Black Sexual Politics: African Americans, Gender, and the New Racism* (New York: Routledge, 2005).

17. Ibid.
18. Lorde, *Sister Outsider*, 57.
19. Ibid.
20. Ibid., 59.
21. Judith Plaskow, *Standing again at Sinai: Judaism from a Feminist Perspective* (San Francisco: Harper and Row, 1990), 201. Also refer to Plaskow, *The Coming of Lilith: Essays on Feminism, Judaism, and Sexual Ethics 1972– 2003*, ed. Donna Burman (Boston: Beacon Press, 2005).
22. Ibid., 172.
23. Ibid.
24. Ibid., 173.
25. Ibid., 175.
26. Carter Heyward, *Touching Our Strength: The Erotic as Power and the Love of God* (San Francisco: Harper and Row, 1989), 187.
27. Ibid., 190.
28. Ibid., 191.
29. Toni Morrison, *Sula* (New York: Vintage, 1973), 44.
30. Ibid.
31. Ibid., 118.
32. Ibid., 95.
33. Ibid.
34. Ibid., 118.
35. Ibid., 119.
36. Ibid.
37. Ibid., 84.
38. Ibid., 119.
39. Ibid., 122.
40. Ibid.
41. Ibid.
42. Ibid., 121.
43. Ibid., 123.
44. Ibid.
45. Barbara Smith, "Toward a Black Feminist Criticism," *Women's Studies International,* Quarterly 2, No. 2 (1979), 189.
46. Morrison, *Sula*, 174.
47. Ibid.
48. Alice Walker, *By the Light of My Father's Smile* (New York: Ballantine Books, 1998), 108.
49. Ibid.
50. Ibid., 10.
51. Ibid., 132.
52. Ibid., 133.
53. Ibid.
54. Ibid., 132.
55. Ibid., 62.

56. Ibid.
57. Ibid., 81.
58. Ibid.
59. Ibid., 111.
60. Ibid., 162.
61. Lorde, *Sister Outsider*, 56.
62. Ibid., 58.
63. Rosemary Hennessey, *Profit and Pleasure: Sexual Identities in Late Capitalism* (Great Britain: Routledge, 2000), 22. Also refer to Hennessey and Chrys Ingraham (eds.), *Materialist Feminism: A Reader in Class, Difference and Women's Lives* (New York: Routledge, 1997) and Hennessey, *Materialist Feminist and the Politics of Discourse* (New York: Routledge, 1992) for further discussion on how sexual identities are shaped and impeded in and through late capitalist processes.
64. Ibid., 23.
65. Ibid., 5.
66. Ibid., 6.
67. Ibid., 23.
68. Ibid., 25.

4   Love as a Concrete Revolutionary Practice

1. Darnell Moore, "On Love, Empathy, and Pleasure in the Age of Neoliberalism," in *The Feminist Wire*, published July 9, 2013, http://thefeministwire.com/2013/07/on-love-empathy-and-pleasure-in-the-age-of-neoliberalism/
2. Bell hooks, *All about Love: New Visions* (New York: William Morrow and Company, Inc., 2000), 5.
3. Ibid., 4.
4. Ibid., 12.
5. Ibid., 18–22.
6. Abraham Heschel, *The Prophets* (New York: Jewish Publication Society of America, 1962), 113–114.
7. Ibid.
8. Howard Thurman, "Mysticism and the Experience of Love," in *For the Inward Journey*, ed. Anne Spencer Thurman (New York: Harcourt Brace Jovanovich Publishers, 1984), 13. Thurman also substantively expounds on this love ethics and its impact on interpersonal relationships in *Jesus and the Disinherited* (Boston: Beacon Press, 1976), *The Creative Encounter* (New York 1954), and *The Search for Common Ground* (New York: Harper and Row Publishers, 1971).
9. Ibid., 14.
10. Combahee River Collective, in *Home Girls: A Black Feminist Anthology*, ed. Barbara Smith (New York: Kitchen Table Press, 1983), 267.
11. Alice Walker, *In Search of Our Mother's Gardens: Womanist Prose* (Orland, FL: Harcourt Publishers, 1983), xii.

12. Ibid.
13. Ibid.
14. Jennifer Nash, "Practicing Love: Black Feminism, Love Politics, and Post-Intersectionality," *Meridians*, Vol. 11, No. 2 (2011), 3.
15. Martha Nussbaum, *Political Emotions: Why Love Matters for Justice* (Cambridge: Belknap Press, 2013), 2.
16. Ibid.
17. Ibid.
18. Ibid., 6.
19. Ibid., 3.
20. Ramachandra Guha, *Gandhi before India* (New York: Alfred Knopf, 2014), 9.
21. Nussbaum, *Political Emotions*, 4.
22. Ibid., 142.
23. Ibid., 143.
24. Daniel Batson, "Perspective Taking: Imagining How Another Feels versus Imagining How You Would Feel," in *Personality & Social Psychology Bulletin*, Vol. 23, 751–758.
25. Ibid., 756.
26. Nussbaum, *Political Emotions*, 145. Frans De Waal mentions this experiment in his book, *Our Inner Ape: A Leading Primatologist Explains Why We Are Who We Are* (New York: Riverhead Trade, 2006).
27. Slavoj Zizek, "Dialectical Clarity versus the Misty Conceit of Paradox," in *The Monstrosity of Christ: Paradox or Dialectic*, ed. Creston Davis (Cambridge: MIT Press, 2009), 246.
28. Ibid.
29. Ibid.
30. Ibid., 248.
31. Sigurdson, *Theology and Marxism in Eagleton and Zizek*, 156.
32. Nussbaum, *Political Emotions*, 184.
33. Ibid., 187.
34. Ibid., 186.
35. Walker, *In Search of Our Mother's Gardens*, xii
36. Audre Lorde, *Sister Outsider: Essays and Speeches* (Berkeley: The Crossing Press, 1984), 173.
37. June Jordan, *Some of Us Did Not Die* (New York: Basic Books, 2003), 273.
38. Nash, "Practicing Love," 11.
39. Ibid.
40. Ibid.
41. Jasbir Puar, "I Would Rather Be a Cyborg than a Goddess: Intersectionality, Assemblage, and Affective Politics," in *European Institute for Progressive Cultural Policies*, http://eipcp.net/transversal/0811/puar/en, accessed on July 2, 2014.
42. Ibid.
43. Ibid.

44. Ibid. Also refer to Jasbir Puar, *Terrorist Assemblages: Homonationalism in Queer Times* (Durham, NC: Duke University Press, 2007).
45. Puar, "I Would Rather Be a Cyborg than a Goddess."
46. Ann Cvetkovich, *An Archive of Feelings: Trauma, Sexuality, and Lesbian Public Cultures* (Durham: NC: Duke University Press, 2003), 9.
47. Nash, "Practicing Love," 14.
48. Ibid., 15.
49. Ibid., 16.
50. Ibid., 18.

5   Hope as Social Practice

1. Vincent Lloyd, *The Problem with Grace: Reconfiguring Political Theology* (Stanford: Stanford University Press, 2011), 3.
2. Ibid., 9.
3. Ibid.
4. Walter Brueggemann, "Prophetic Imagination toward Social Flourishing," in *Theology and Human Flourishing: Essays in Honor of Timothy Gorringe*, eds. Mike Higton, Jeremy Law, and Christopher Rowland (Eugene, OR: Wipf and Stock Publishing, 2011), 25.
5. Ibid., 25–26. These five characteristics of the "imagined city" are discussed at length on the aforementioned pages.
6. Brueggemann, "Prophetic Imagination toward Social Flourishing," 26.
7. Ibid., 28.
8. Ibid.
9. Lloyd, *The Problem with Grace*, 20.
10. Ibid., 171.
11. Ibid., 25.
12. Ibid., 174.
13. Refer to Charles Marsh, *The Beloved Community: How Faith Shapes Social Justice, from the Civil Rights Movement to Today* (New York: Basic Books, 2006).
14. Tracy Ke, "Memory, Loss, and Revitalizing Democracy: The Mothers of Plazo de Mayo," in *An Ethical Compass: Coming of Age in the 21st Century*, eds. Elie Wiesel and Thomas Friedman (New Haven: Yale University Press, 2010), 106.
15. John Simpson and Jana Bennet, *The Disappeared and Mothers of the Plaza: The Story of the 11,000 Argentinians Who Vanished* (New York: St. Martin's Press, 1985), 59.
16. Ibid.
17. Ibid.
18. Ibid., 60.
19. Ibid., 61.
20. Ke, "Memory, Loss, and Revitalizing Democracy," 111.
21. Simpson and Bennet, *The Disappeared and Mothers of the Plaza*, 39.
22. Ibid., 40.

23. Ibid., 41.
24. Ke, "Memory, Loss, and Revitalizing Democracy: The Mothers of Plazo de Mayo," 111.
25. Ibid., 112.
26. Jean Elshtain, "Mothers of the Disappeared," in *Finding a New Feminism*, ed. Pamela Grande Jensen (Lanham, MD: Rowman and Littlefield Publishers, 1996), 132.
27. Diana Taylor, *Disappearing Acts: Spectacles of Gender and Nationalism in Argentina's "Dirty War"* (Durham, NC: Duke University Press, 1997), 184.
28. Ke, "Memory, Loss, and Revitalizing Democracy," 108.
29. Simpson and Bennet, *The Disappeared and Mothers of the Plaza*, 157.
30. Ke, "Memory, Loss, and Revitalizing Democracy," 110.
31. Taylor, *Disappearing Acts*, 184.
32. Taylor, *Disappearing Acts*, 191.
33. Simpson and Bennet, *The Disappeared and Mothers of the Plaza*, 158.
34. Ibid.
35. Ibid.
36. Ibid.
37. Elshtain, "Mothers of the Disappeared," 137.
38. Ibid., 163.
39. Ibid., 164.
40. Ibid., 167.
41. Ibid., 168.
42. Ibid.
43. Ibid., 175.
44. Ibid., 176.
45. Ibid., 176–177.
46. Ibid., 178.
47. Ibid., 173.
48. Taylor, *Disappearing Acts*, 194.
49. Ibid.
50. Ibid., 195.
51. Ibid., 195–196.
52. Gilda Rodriguez, "The Political Performance of Motherhood: Las Madres de Plazo de Mayo," in *Serendip*, http://serendip.brynmawr.edu/sci_cult/courses/knowbody/f04/web3/grodriguez.html, accessed on September 20, 2013.
53. Taylor, *Disappearing Acts*, 196.
54. Majore Agosin, "Surviving beyond Fear," in *Surviving beyond Fear*, eds. Majorie Agosin and Monica Bruno Galmozzi (Buffalo, NY: White Pine Press, 2008), 55.
55. Taylor, *Disappearing Acts*, 195.
56. Taylor, *Disappearing Acts*, 198.
57. Ke, "Memory, Loss, and Revitalizing Democracy," 109.
58. Ibid., 118.
59. Ibid., 107.

60. Ibid., 108.
61. Ibid.
62. Ibid., 114.
63. Ibid., 114–115.
64. Ibid., 115.
65. Christopher Dickey, "The Pope's Dirty Past," *World News*, Published on March 16, 2013, http://www.thedailybeast.com/articles/2013/03/16/the-pope-s-dirty-past.html, 1.

Conclusion   Radicalizing Hope: Toward Beloved Communities

1. Terry Eagleton, *Sweet Violence: The Idea of the Tragic* (Malden, MA/ Oxford: Blackwell, 2003), 291.
2. Terry Eagleton, *Why Marx Was Right* (New Haven/London: Yale University Press, 2011), 62.
3. Ola Sigurdson, *Theology and Marxism in Eagleton and Zizek: A Conspiracy of Hope* (New York: Palgrave McMillan, 2012), 192.
4. Ibid.
5. Refer to three particular texts by Jurgen Habermas in which he articulates his theory of communicative action and idea of "discourse ethics" (or deliberative democracy). They include *The Structural Transformation of the Public Sphere: An Inquiry into the Category of Bourgeois Society* (Cambridge: MIT Press, 1991); *Between Facts and Norms: Contributions to a Discourse Theory of Law and Democracy* (Cambridge: MIT Press, 1998); and *Moral Consciousness and Communicative Action* (Cambridge: MIT Press, 2001). Habermas argues that justice is largely a question of "procedural ethics," being the institutionalization of discursive democratic procedures that allow the full participation of everyone affected by a particular policy/political decision. Habermas contends that moral consensus along with equality is more achievable through such a discursive model.
6. Sigurdson, *Theology and Marxism in Eagleton and Zizek*, 186.
7. Ibid., 173.
8. Ibid., 174.
9. For more on Josiah Royce's writings about a universal community or beloved community, refer to *The World and the Individual Gifford Lectures*, Classic Reprint (London: Forgotten Books, 2012) and *The Philosophy of Loyalty*, Reprint (Nashville: Vanderbilt University Press, 1995).
10. Refer to Lewis Baldwin, *Toward the Beloved Community: Martin Luther King Jr. and South Africa* (Cleveland: Pilgrim Press, 1995) and *To Make the Wounded Whole: The Cultural Legacy of Martin Luther King Jr.* (Minneapolis: Fortress Press, 1992). In both texts, he affirms that King's idea of the beloved community was expanded and deepened through his discussion of beloved community in relation to human conflict and non-violent methods.

11. Darnell Moore, "On Love, Empathy, and Pleasure in the Age of Neoliberalism," in *The Feminist Wire*, published July 9, 2013, http://thefeministwire.com/2013/07/on-love-empathy-and-pleasure-in-the-age-of-neoliberalism/

12. Laura Moser, "Texas is Debuting Textbooks that Downplay Jim Crow and Frame Slavery as a Side Issue in the Civil War," in *Slate*, published July 7, 2015, http://www.slate.com/blogs/schooled/2015/07/07/texas_textbook_revisionism_new_textbooks_in_the_lone_star_state_downplay.html

13. Ibid.

14. Refer to Dana-ain Davis, *Battered Black Women and Welfare Reform: Between a Rock and a Hard Place* (New York: State University of New York Press, 2006).

15. See an online article by BBC Africa News entitled, "Nigeria Schoolgirl Abductions: Protest Leader Detained," published May 5, 2014. http://www.bbc.com/news/world-africa-27283278

16. Refer to Marie Gattschalk, *The Prisons and the Gallows: The Politics of Mass Incarceration in America* (Cambridge: Cambridge University Press, 2006).

17. Joy James, *Seeking the Beloved Community: A Feminist Race Reader* (New York: State University of New York, 2013), 149.

18. Ibid., 216.

19. Cheryl Higashida, *Black Internationalist Feminism: Women Writers of the Black Left, 1945–1995* (Chicago: University of Illinois Press, 2011), 8.

20. Ibid.

21. SAVVY Contemporary Website, Concept, Accessed July 30, 2014, http://savvy-contemporary.com/index.php/concept/

22. Alanna Lockward, "Decolonizing the (White) Gaze: Who Is Whipping?" in *Spiritual Revolutions and the Scramble for Africa* (Berlin: Art Labour Archives, 2014), 9.

23. Ibid.

24. Ibid.

25. Ibid., 10.

Bibliography

Books

Baldwin, Lewis. *To Make the Wounded Whole: The Cultural Legacy of Martin Luther King Jr.* Minneapolis: Fortress Press, 1992.

Baldwin, Lewis. *Toward the Beloved Community: Martin Luther King Jr. and South Africa.* Cleveland: Pilgrim Press, 1995.

Benjamin, Walter. *Illuminations.* Trans. Harry Zohn. New York: Schocken, 1977.

Cannon, Katie. *Black Womanist Ethics.* Eugene, OR: Wipf and Stock Publishing, 1988.

Coleman, Monica. *Making a Way Out of No Way: A Womanist Theology.* Minneapolis: Fortress Press.

Cone, James. *A Black Theology of Liberation.* Maryknoll, NY: Orbis Books, 1986.

Cone, James. *God of the Oppressed.* Maryknoll, NY: Orbis Books, 1997.

Cvetkovich, Ann. *An Archive of Feelings: Trauma, Sexuality, and Lesbian Public Cultures.* Durham, NC: Duke University Press, 2003.

Davis, Dana-Ain. *Battered Black Women and Welfare Reform: Between a Rock and a Hard Place.* New York: State University of New York Press, 2006.

Day, Keri. *Unfinished Business: Black Women, the Black Church, and the Struggle to Thrive in America.* Maryknoll: Orbis Books, 2012.

Eagleton, Terry. *Sweet Violence: The Idea o f the Tragic.* Malden, MA/Oxford: Blackwells, 2003.

Eagleton, Terry. *Why Marx Was Right.* New Haven/London: Yale University, 2011.

Evans, James. *We Have Been Believers: An African American Systematic Theology.* Minneapolis: Fortress Press, 1993.

Ferris, David. *The Cambridge Introduction to Walter Benjamin.* Cambridge: Cambridge University Press, 2008.

Floyd-Thomas, Stacey. *Mining the Motherlode: Methods in Womanist Ethics.* Cleveland: Pilgrim Press, 2006.

Fromm, Eric. *To Have or to Be?* New York: Continuum Publishing, 1997.

Gattschalk, Marie. *The Prisons and the Gallows: The Politics of Mass Incarceration in America.* Cambridge: Cambridge University Press, 2006.

Gouwens, David. *Kierkegaard as Religious Thinker*. Cambridge: Cambridge University Press, 1996.

Guha, Ramachandra. *Gandhi before India*. New York: Alfred Knopf, 2014.

Habermas, Jurgen. *The Structural Transformation of the Public Sphere: An Inquiry into the Category of Bourgeois Society*. Cambridge: MIT Press, 1991.

Habermas, Jurgen. *Between Facts and Norms: Contributions to a Discourse Theory of Law and Democracy*. Cambridge: MIT Press, 1998.

Habermas, Jurgen. *Moral Consciousness and Communicative Action*. Cambridge: MIT Press, 2001.

Harris, Melanie. *Gifts of Virtue, Alice Walker, and Womanist Ethics*. New York: Palgrave McMillan, 2010.

Hennessey, Rosemary. *Profit and Pleasure: Sexual Identities in Late Capitalism*. Great Britain: Routledge, 2000.

Heschel, Abraham. *The Prophets*. New York: Jewish Publication Society of America, 1962.

Heyward, Carter. *Touching Our Strength: The Erotic as Power and the Love of God*. San Francisco: Harper & Row, 1989.

Higashida, Cheryl. *Black Internationalist Feminism: Women Writers of the Black Left, 1945–1995*. Chicago: University of Illinois Press, 2011.

Hill Collins, Patricia. *Black Feminist Thought: Knowledge, Consciousness, and the Politics of Empowerment*. New York: Routledge, 1990.

hooks, bell. *All about Love: New Visions*. New York: William Morrow and Company, Inc., 2000.

Irwin, Alexander. *Eros toward the World: Paul Tillich and the Theology of the Erotic*. Minneapolis: Fortress Press, 1991.

James, Joy. *Seeking the Beloved Community: A Feminist Race Reader*. New York: State University of New York, 2013.

Jeanrond, Werner. *A Theology of Love*. New York: T&T Clark, 2010.

Jordan, June. *Some of Us Did Not Die*. New York: Basic Books, 2003.

Kierkegaard, Søren. *Kierkegaard's Attack upon "Christendom" 1854–1855*. Trans. Walter Lowrie. Princeton: Princeton University Press, 1944.

Kierkegaard, Søren. *Works of Love: Some Christian Reflections in the Form of Discourses*. Trans. Howard V. Hong and Edna H. Hong. New York: Harper & Row, 1962.

Kierkagaard, Søren. *Two Ages: The Age of Revolution and the Present Age*. Edited and translated by Howard V. Hong and Edna H. Hong. Princeton: Princeton University Press, 1978.

Kierkegaard, Søren. *Either/Or*. Trans. Howard V. Hong and Edna H. Hong, 2 volumes. Princeton: Princeton University Press, 1987.

Kierkegaard, Søren. *Practice in Christianity*. Trans. Howard V. Hong and Edna H. Hong. Princeton: Princeton University Press, 1991.

Kierkegaard, Søren. *Concluding Unscientific Postscript*. Edited and translated by Howard V. Hong and Edna H. Hong. Princeton: Princeton University Press, 1992.

Lewis, C. Stephen. *Kierkegaard: An Introduction*. Cambridge: Cambridge University Press, 2009.

Lloyd, Vincent. *The Problem with Grace: Reconfiguring Political Theology*. Stanford: Stanford University Press, 2011.

Lorde, Audre. *Sister Outsider: Essays and Speeches*. Berkeley: The Crossing Press, 1984.

Marsh, Charles. *The Beloved Community: How Faith Shapes Social Justice, from the Civil Rights Movement to Today*. New York: Basic Books, 2006.

Morrison, Toni. *Sula*. New York: Vintage, 1973.

Nussbaum, Martha. *Political Emotions: Why Love Matters for Justice*. Cambridge: Belknap Press, 2013.

Plaskow, Judith. *Standing again at Sinai: Judaism from a Feminist Perspective*. San Francisco: Harper and Row, 1990.

Riggs, Marcia. *Awake, Arise, and Act: A Womanist Call for Black Liberation*. Cleveland: Pilgrim Press, 1994.

Royce, Josiah. *The Philosophy of Loyalty*. Reprint Edition. Nashville: Vanderbilt University Press, 1995.

Royce, Josiah. *The World and the Individual Gifford Lectures*. Classic Reprint. London: Forgotten Books, 2012.

Scholem, Gershom. *The Messianic Idea in Judaism: And Other Essays on Jewish Spirituality*. New York: Schocken Books, 1995.

Scholem, Gershom. *On Kabbalah and Its Symbolism*. New York: Schocken Books, 1996.

Schumpeter, Joseph. *Capitalism, Socialism, and Democracy*. New York: Routledge, 2010. First published in 1934.

Shange, Ntozake. *For Colored Girls Who Considered Suicide When the Rainbow is Enuf*. London: Methuen Publishers, 1977.

Sigurdson, Ola. *Theology and Marxism in Eagleton and Zizek: A Conspiracy of Hope*. New York: Palgrave McMillan, 2012.

Simpson, John and Jana Bennet. *The Disappeared and Mothers of the Plaza: The Story of the 11,000 Argentinians Who Vanished*. New York: St. Martin's Press, 1985.

Taylor, Diana. *Disappearing Acts: Spectacles of Gender and Nationalism in Argentina's "Dirty War."* Durham, NC: Duke University Press, 1997.

Tessman, Lisa. *Burdened Virtues: Virtue Ethics for Liberatory Struggles*. Oxford: Oxford University Press, 2005.

Thurman, Howard. *The Creative Encounter*. Reprint Edition. New York: Friends United Press, 1972.

Thurman, Howard. *The Search for Common Ground*. Reprint Edition. New York: Friends United Press, 1986.

Thurman, Howard. *Jesus and the Disinherited*. Reprint Edition. Boston: Beacon Press, 1996.

Tillich, Paul. *Systematic Theology*, Volume. 1. Chicago: University of Chicago Press, 1951.

Tillich, Paul. *Love, Power, and Justice*. New York: Oxford University Press, 1954.

Townes, Emilie. *Breaking the Fine Rain of Death: African-American Health Issues and a Womanist Ethic of Care*. New York: Continuum Publishing, 2001.

Waal, Frans De. *Our Inner Ape: A Leading Primatologist Explains Why We Are Who We Are*. New York: Riverhead Trade, 2006.

Walker, Alice. *In Search of Our Mother's Gardens: Womanist Prose*. Orlando, FL: Harcourt Publishers, 1983.

Walker, Alice. *By the Light of My Father's Smile*. New York: Ballantine Books, 1998.

Williams, Delores. *Sisters in the Wilderness: The Challenge of Womanist God-Talk*. Maryknoll: Orbis Books, 1993.

Zizek, Slavoj. *Living in the End Times*. London: Verso Press, 2011.

Articles and Essays

Agosin, Majorie. "Surviving beyond Fear." In *Surviving beyond Fear*, 28–58. Edited by Majorie Agosin and Monica Bruno Galmozzi. Buffalo, NY: White Pine Press, 2008.

Baker-Fletcher, Karen. "Strength of My Life." In *Embracing the Spirit: Womanist Perspectives on Hope, Salvation, and Transformation*, 125–139. Edited by Emilie Townes. Maryknoll, NY: Orbis Books, 1997.

Baker-Fletcher, Karen. "The Erotic in Contemporary Black Women's Writings." In *Loving the Body: Black Religious Studies and the Erotic*, 199–216. New York: Palgrave McMillan, 2006.

Batson, Daniel. "Perspective Taking: Imagining How Another Feels Versus Imagining How You Would Feel." *Personality & Social Psychology Bulletin*, Vol.23, No. 7 (1997): 751–758.

Bauman, Zygmunt. "Walter Benjamin, The Intellectual." In *The Actuality of Walter Benjamin*, 55–84. Edited by Laura Marcus and Lynda Nead. London: Lawrence and Wishart, 1998.

Benjamin, Walter. "Theses on the Philosophy of History." In *Illuminations: Essays and Reflections*, 253–264. Edited by Hannah Arendt. New York: Harcourt Brace Jovanovich, 1968.

Brennan, Denise. "Selling Sex for Visas: Sex Tourism as Stepping-Stone to International Migration." In *Global Woman: Nannies, Maids, and Sex Workers in the New Economy*, 154–168. Edited by Barbara Ehrenreich and Russell Hochschild. New York: Henry Holy and Company, 2002.

Brueggemann, Walter. "Prophetic Imagination toward Social Flourishing." In *Theology and Human Flourishing: Essays in Honor of Timothy Gorringe*, 16–30. Edited by Mike Higton, Jeremy Law, and Christopher Rowland. Eugene, OR: Wipf and Stock Publishing, 2011.

Combahee River Collective. "Combahee River Collective Statement." In *Home Girls: A Black Feminist Anthology*, 264–274. Edited by Barbara Smith. New York: Kitchen Table Press, 1983.

Dickey, Christopher. "The Pope's Dirty Past." *World News*, Published March 16, 2013, http://www.thedailybeast.com/articles/2013/03/16/the-pope-s-dirty-past.html, 1.

Ehrenreich, Barbara. "Maid to Order." In *Global Woman: Nannies, Maids, and Sex Workers in the New Economy*, 85–103. Edited by Barbara Ehrenreich and Russell Hochschild. New York: Henry Holy & Company, 2002.

Elshtain, Jean. "Mothers of the Disappeared: An Encounter with Antigones Daughters." In *Finding a New Feminism: Rethinking the Woman Question for Liberal Democracy*, 129–148. Edited by Pamela Grande Jensen, et al. New York: Rowman and Littlefield Publishers, 1996.

Katerberg, William. "History, Hope, and the Redemption of Time." In *The Future of Hope: Christian Tradition and Modernity and Postmodernity*, 49–76. Edited by Miroslav Volf and William Katerberg. Cambridge: Eerdmans Publishing, 2004.

Ke, Tracy. "Memory, Loss, and Revitalizing Democracy: The Mothers of Plazo de Mayo." In *An Ethical Compass: Coming of Age in the 21st Century*, 89–120. Edited by Elie Wiesel and Thomas Friedman. New Haven: Yale University Press, 2010.

Lockward, Alanna. "Decolonizing the (White) Gaze: Who Is Whipping?" In *Spiritual Revolutions and the Scramble for Africa*, 5–12. Berlin: Art Labour Archives, 2014.

Mariano, Willoughby. "Despite Millions Spent, Human Trafficking's Scope Is Unknown." *Atlanta Journal Constitution*, Published December 31, 2012, http://www.ajc.com/news/news/despite-millions-spent-human-traffickings-scope-is/nTjRn/

Mieszkowski, Jan. "Art Forms." In *The Cambridge Companion to Walter Benjamin*, 35–53. Edited by David Ferris. Cambridge: Cambridge University Press, 2004.

Monroe, Bryan. "How Texas' School Board Tried to Pretend Slavery Never Happened and Why Your Kid's School May Be Next." *Huffington Post: The Blog*, Published May 24, 2010, http://www.huffingtonpost.com/bryan-monroe/how-texas-school-board-tr_b_586633.html

Moore, Darnell. "On Love, Empathy, and Pleasure in the Age of Neoliberalism." *The Feminist Wire*, Published July 9, 2013, http://thefeministwire.com/2013/07/on-love-empathy-and-pleasure-in-the-age-of-neoliberalism/

Nash, Jennifer. "Practicing Love: Black Feminism, Love Politics, and Post-Intersectionality." *Meridians*, 11, No. 2 (2011): 1–24.

Puar, Jasbir. "I Would Rather Be a Cyborg than a Goddess: Intersectionality, Assemblage, and Affective Politics." *European Institute for Progressive Cultural Policies*, Published January 2011. http://eipcp.net/transversal/0811/puar/en, Accessed on July 2, 2014.

Rodriguez, Gilda. "The Political Performance of Motherhood: Las Madres de Plazo de Mayo." *Serendip* (2004), http://serendip.brynmawr.edu/sci_cult/courses/knowbody/f04/web3/grodriguez.html, Accessed on September 20, 2013.

Sassen, Saskia. "Global Cities and Survival Circuits." In *Global Woman: Nannies, Maids, and Sex Workers in the New Economy*, 254–274. Edited by Barbara Ehrenreich and Russell Hochschild. New York: Henry Holy and Company, 2002.

Smith, Barbara. "Toward a Black Feminist Criticism." *Women's Studies International*, 2, No. 2 (1979): 183–194.

Thurman, Howard. "Mysticism and the Experience of Love." In *For the Inward Journey*, 35–36. Edited by Anne Spencer Thurman. New York: Harcourt Brace Jovanovich Publishers, 1984.

Wohlfarth, Irving. "The Measure of the Possible, the Weight of the Real, and the Heat of the Moment: Benjamin's Actuality Today." In *The Actuality of Walter Benjamin*, 25–32. Edited by Laura Marcus and Lynda Nead. London: Lawrence and Wishart, 1998.

Zarembka, Joy. "America's Dirty Work: Migrant Maids and Modern-Day Slavery." In *Global Woman: Nannies, Maids, and Sex Workers in the New Economy*, 142–153. Edited by Barbara Ehrenreich and Russell Hochschild. New York: Henry Holy & Company, 2002.

Zizek, Slavoj. "Dialectical Clarity versus the Misty Conceit of Paradox." In *The Monstrosity of Christ: Paradox or Dialectic*, 234–306. Edited by Creston Davis. Cambridge: MIT Press, 2009.

Index

CPSIA information can be obtained
at www.ICGtesting.com
Printed in the USA
LVHW081623021221
705093LV00002B/353